MARIA EDGEWORTH AND ROMANCE

Maria Edgeworth
and Romance

SHARON MURPHY

FOUR COURTS PRESS

Set in 11.5 on 13.5 point Centaur for
FOUR COURTS PRESS
7 Malpas Street, Dublin 8, Ireland
e-mail: info@four-courts-press.ie
http://www.four-courts-press.ie
and in North America for
FOUR COURTS PRESS
c/o ISBS, 920 N.E. 58th Avenue, Suite 300, Portland, OR 97213.

A catalogue record for this title
is available from the British Library.

ISBN 1—85182—852—4

SPECIAL ACKNOWLEDGMENT

This publication received a grant in aid of publication
from the Arts Council/An Chomhairle Ealaíon.

Printed in Great Britain
by Antony Rowe Ltd, Chippenham, Wilts.

Contents

Acknowledgments

In its original form this book was a PhD thesis at Trinity College, Dublin. My principal thanks are therefore extended to Aileen Douglas of the School of English, who guided this work through its several stages; I owe Aileen much, but primarily the fact that her confidence in my work gave me confidence in myself. Claire Connolly and Darryl Jones gave me invaluable advice regarding publication, and Éilean Ní Chuilleanáin, Nicholas Grene and Stephen Matterson helped me to make the vital connection between research and teaching. Thanks, too, to Bairbre Fleming, Rhonda Wynne, Anthony Roche and Kay Barry for offering me further opportunities to try out my ideas in class, and to my students at Trinity College, University College Dublin and Dublin City University. I would like to acknowledge the generous assistance of Charles Benson and the staff of the Early Printed Books Department in Trinity College, Dublin, especially Shane Mawe and Rose Reddy. Thanks are also due to the staff of the Berkeley, Lecky and Ussher Libraries. The generous assistance of the staff of the National Library of Ireland, Dublin, is similarly acknowledged, especially Tom Desmond. My gratitude is likewise extended to Ian Campbell Ross, Máire Kennedy, Clíona Ó Gallchoir and Sean Moore, and to all those who gave me the opportunity to give conference papers based upon my research. James McGuire was an unflappable source of invaluable advice, and Jacqueline Belanger provided constructive criticism and cheerful support when both were most needed. Thanks, too, to Sinead Morrissey for spending long periods of time on the telephone discussing romance (and servants), and to Kate Declenn-Laurrenns for being such a supportive Edgeworthian friend. I would also like to express my gratitude to all those postgraduate students who shared room 3160 with me in Trinity College, and offered good-humoured advice and support. A special thank you goes to Patricia O'Reilly and Rosanne Roe, for remaining firm friends despite hearing too much about every stage of my research, and to Moira Higgins, without whose timely support this book would never have been written. An especial note of gratitude is extended to Michael Adams, Martin Fanning, Anthony Tierney and all at Four Courts Press, for encouraging me to envisage the prospective 'reader' of this work. Finally, I dedicate this

book to David Murphy, for being a long-suffering source of historical information and brotherly advice, and to Kathleen and Jimmy Murphy, for being
the best of parents.

Introduction

Maria Edgeworth (1768–1849) was a prolific and innovative author whose varied works were directed at many different kinds of readers – children, adults, the barely literate, the elite. Her work has always attracted critical interest, but too little attention has been paid to her recognition of the power of make-believe, of the imagination – forces that she and her contemporaries particularly associated with the romance mode, rather than the more recent development of the realistic novel. Although separated by over one hundred years, both Helen Zimmern and Joep Leerssen define Edgeworth as a 'mostly' realistic writer, and they observe that, unlike many of her contemporaries, she firmly rejected the fabulous and the fantastic. While Leerssen for his part does allow that 'Edgeworth's novels ... contain echoes of a Romantic Gaelic Ireland', he dismisses these as being of 'secondary' importance to the development of her narratives; they are there, he argues, merely to 'add touches of local colour and intercultural tension which would have been unavailable in an English setting', and so 'the register of ... Romance' that they represent is not central to the working out of Edgeworth's plots.[1] For Zimmern, this circumstance would appear to be not only inevitable, but also readily explained: 'there was nothing [in Ireland] to arouse romance in [Edgeworth]', and 'Romance had no place in her nature'.[2] Despite the evolution of literary criticism, Leerssen, like Zimmern and so many other critics before and after him, maintains that Edgeworth's use of romance in her work is incidental; as he would have it, it adds nothing of real significance to her 'novelistic' plots and settings. This study disputes this commonly held view of Edgeworth's writing, and shows that her use of romance conventions is in fact central to her work.

Edgeworth was at first both popular and critically acclaimed as a writer; she enjoyed huge commercial success, and luminaries such as Sir Walter Scott applauded her literary achievements.[3] This fame proved transitory, though, and

1 J. Leerssen, *Remembrance and imagination* (1996), 42.   2 H. Zimmern, *Maria Edgeworth* (1883), 129–30, 16 and 27.   3 As Marilyn Butler observes, 'The public bought [Edgeworth's] novels in large numbers, ensuring that almost all went into at least three editions within a few years of first appearing. Her publishers paid her up to £2,000 for a single work, a remarkable sum before Scott did even better; Murray offered Jane Austen a conditional £450 for

her works were all but forgotten by the early twentieth century; even today, if she is remembered outside of academic circles, it is but dimly and as the author of *Castle Rackrent* (1800), which is effectively (mis)represented to the general reader as the only truly outstanding example of her work. The reasons for the rise and fall of any author's literary reputation are always complicated, of course, but in Edgeworth's case it is fair to say that the decline in her popularity was particularly linked to the style of her writing. As we shall see below, she was writing at a very particular moment in the development of the novel – at a point when the merit of a work increasingly depended upon its moral content. Despite their diversity, her works ultimately share one feature in common, an overt didacticism, and, having been praised initially for the 'spirit', 'delicacy', and 'precision' of her writing, Edgeworth was increasingly criticized for laying on her moral for her readers with too heavy a hand.[4] In his 1817 review of *Harrington, a tale; and Ormond, a tale*, for example, Francis Jeffrey observed: 'the duties of a *Moral Teacher* are always uppermost in [Edgeworth's] thoughts ... It is this which has given to her composition something of too didactic a manner, – and brought the moral of her stories too obtrusively forward'.[5] Such 'obtrusive' morals became less and less popular during the course of the nineteenth century and, eventually, if Edgeworth was read at all, it was for her children's literature, and her earlier reputation was gradually forgotten.

   The peculiar circumstances of Edgeworth's life also contributed to the decline of her popularity and, ironically, to her eventual re-discovery and re-assessment as a writer. Born in Black Bourton, in Oxfordshire, Maria was the eldest daughter of her father's four marriages.[6] She spent most of the early part of her life in England, and did not settle permanently in Ireland until 1782, when her father decided to return to his estates in Co. Longford in the Irish midlands. Richard Lovell Edgeworth was a huge influence upon his daughter, not only employing her to keep accounts and deal with his tenants, but also encouraging her to read widely; later, he also became her most valued literary adviser, and took an immense pride in her literary career. Edgeworth for her part attached a singular importance to her relationship with her father, noting in 'her' volume of his *Memoirs*, for instance, that it was 'for ... many years ... the pride and joy of [her] life'.[7] In fact, she actively encouraged the popular

Emma': M. Butler, *Maria Edgeworth* (1972), 1. Appendix B to this biography provides a useful overview of both Edgeworth's earnings from her writing and her relationships with her publishers (490–3).   4 F. Jeffrey, unsigned review of the 1809 series of *Tales of fashionable life* in *Edinburgh Review*, 14 (1809) 380.   5 Idem. unsigned review of *Harrington, a tale; and Ormond, a tale* in *Edinburgh Review*, 28 (1817) 391–2.   6 For an account of the circumstances leading up to the marriage of Edgeworth's father to Anna Maria Elers in 1763, see R.L. Edgeworth and M. Edgeworth, *Memoirs of Richard Lovell Edgeworth* (1820), 1: 87–103. See also Butler, *Maria Edgeworth*, 21–3.   7 *Memoirs*, 2: 190. Edgeworth wrote the second volume of this work.

belief that her father was the primary inspiration behind her literary endeavours: that he provided the 'bullion' that she 'coined'.[8]

This interpretation of Edgeworth's relationship with her father eventually
passed into critical and popular imagination, and it survived virtually unchal-
lenged until the middle years of the last century.[9] Successive generations of critics consequently accepted as fact the charge that Edgeworth's father had constantly interfered in her writing and, specifically, attributed to him the blame
for the didacticism of her works. This helps to explain why her works were for
so long ignored by feminist critics: on the one hand, they were no longer widely
read and were difficult to obtain; on the other, the degree of influence that her
father had exercised upon them seemed beyond dispute. Only in the past thirty
years, or so, have critics begun to untangle the threads of this complicated literary relationship, and they have concluded that Edgeworth's didacticism is
'peculiarly' her own, and reflects 'her obsessive desire to promote her father's
opinions':

> Decidedly ... it was not he but Maria who really did try to insist from
> first to last that the fiction and the educational books were indivisible.
> As the story of her entire development shows, it was she who felt most
> anxious to maintain the idea of a partnership. The idea that the fiction
> must be seen as part of his work, so that it would contribute to his
> greater glory ... emanated from her.[10]

8 Maria Edgeworth to F. Jeffrey, 18 Dec. 1806, draft, quoted in Butler, *Maria Edgeworth*, 272. Precisely this analysis
of her and her father's literary relationship informs Edgeworth's recollection of the composition of *Practical education* (1798): 'In [this] work ... the principles of education were peculiarly his ... all the general ideas originated
with him, the illustrating and manufacturing them [*sic*], if I may use the expression, was mine' (*Memoirs*, 2: 190).
9 While the origins of this myth lay with Edgeworth, it was compounded by *A memoir of Maria Edgeworth* (1867),
the first-ever work of 'criticism' that appeared on the author. Edited by Edgeworth's third stepmother, Frances,
with her daughters, Harriet and Lucy, this stresses the special nature of the relationship between Edgeworth and
her father, and quotes at length from the letter that he wrote to his 12-year-old-daughter from the deathbed of
his second wife. In this letter, dated 2 May 1780, Edgeworth's father urged her to cultivate the desire she felt 'of
becoming amiable, prudent, and of USE', insisted that she would only be 'happy' if she was 'good', and prayed
that God would 'make [her] ambitious of that valuable praise which the amiable character of [her] dear [late step-
] mother forces from the virtuous and the wise.' The editors of the *Memoir* remark: 'Such a letter, written at such
a time, made the impression it was intended to convey, and the wish to act up to the high opinion her father had
formed of her character, became the exciting and controlling power over the whole of her future life': F. Edgeworth,
A memoir of Maria Edgeworth, 1: 7–8. As Butler points out, the *Memoir* hugely influenced critical opinion of Edgeworth's
relationship with her father; from it, she notes, Augustus Hare derived most of the material for his *The life and letters of Maria Edgeworth* (1894) and subsequent critics and biographers relied heavily upon Hare (*Maria Edgeworth*, 4).
10 Butler, *Maria Edgeworth*, 303 and 287–8. For the argument that Edgeworth's father in fact discouraged 'the didactic tone into which she fell so easily and comfortably', see P. Murray, 'Maria Edgeworth and her father: the literary partnership' (1971), 43. Ann Owens-Weekes for her part links Edgeworth's didacticism to the circumstances
of her early childhood and her desire 'to replace' her first stepmother in her father's affections. The didacticism,
she concludes, 'is the ultimate if indirect result of the neglect and loneliness of Maria's childhood and of the

By effectively freeing her works of the direct interference of her father, critics
have in this way curiously illuminated the complex nature of Edgeworth's didacticism and its central role in her psyche; they have invited the reader's recognition that it represents but one part of her complex response to both her father
and the age in which she was living.

In the first place, for instance, Edgeworth's father was very much an
Enlightenment rationalist and, as such, he took a particular interest in the education of his numerous children. Influenced at first by Rousseau, he initially tried
to repeat the experiments of *Émile* (1762) with his eldest son, Richard, but this
had disastrous results.[11] Over the years, Edgeworth's father shifted his position
and, still using his children as guinea pigs, he gradually transformed education
into an empirical science.[12] The system that he developed prized reason over the
emotions, and aimed to produce an obedient and useful child. Edgeworth faithfully reproduced the fruits of her father's experimentation in her various works,
which effectively sought to impress an Edgeworthian system of education upon
their readers. Thus, in his preface to the 1809 series of *Tales of fashionable life*, her
father could observe: 'It has ... been my daughter's aim to promote, by all her
writings, the progress of education from the cradle to the grave'; it was her intention in *The parent's assistant: or stories for children* (1796), *Moral tales for young people* (1801),
and in *Popular tales* (1804) 'to exemplify the principles contained in *Practical education*'. These and the projected volumes of *Tales of fashionable life* are intended to
illustrate 'some of the ideas that are unfolded in *Essays on professional education*'
(1809),[13] so we can see that, while each text can be read on its own merits, it can
also be read as representative of a far greater work-in-progress.

The desire to educate therefore infuses all of Edgeworth's writing and, while
her most obviously didactic texts are her educational treatises, *Practical education*
and *Essays on professional education*, each of her works in some way concerns itself
with the education of the reader. The major theme of *Letters for literary ladies* (1795),
for example, is the question of the education of women, an issue that also
informs novels like *Belinda* (1801) and *Helen* (1834), as well as many of her lesser-
known tales and novels.[14] Similarly, Edgeworth traces the significance of a young
man's education in *Essays on professional education* and *Patronage* (1814), and rehearses
this theme for her younger readers in works like *Early lessons* (1801–2) and *Frank:*

consequent desire never to risk exile again': A. Owens-Weekes, *Irish women writers* (1990), 36–7. **11** See *Memoirs*, 1:
273–6. **12** For an account of Richard Lovell Edgeworth's disastrous attempts to repeat the experiments of
Rousseau's *Émile* (1762) with his eldest son, Richard, see the *Memoirs*, 1: 273–6. For details of his 22 children, see
Appendix A in Butler, *Maria Edgeworth*, 489. **13** R.L. Edgeworth, preface, *Tales of fashionable life* (1809) in *The novels
and selected works of Maria Edgeworth* (1999–), 1: 159. **14** Tales like 'The bracelets' in *The parent's assistant* (1796) or 'The
good French governess', which is in *Moral tales*, also revolve around the types of heroines that are common to all
of Edgeworth's writing. See M. Edgeworth, *The parent's Assistant* (1845), 2: 1–48, and *Moral tales* (1802), 3: 1–144.

a sequel to Frank in Early lessons (1822).[15] By the same token, although her Irish tales are celebrated for their lively and sympathetic portrayal of Ireland and the Irish at the end of the eighteenth and beginning of the nineteenth century, *Castle Rackrent, Ennui* (1809), *The absentee* (1812) and *Ormond* (1817) also concern themselves with the national and, implicitly, the imperial consequences of the 'defective Education' of the individual.[16] A striking feature of Edgeworth's work, therefore, is the degree to which she develops and reworks her different themes throughout her writing. The 'writer' of the 'Essay on the noble science of self-justification' in *Letters for literary ladies*, for instance, instructs wives in the art of (mis)ruling the marital home,[17] and the heroine of *The modern Griselda* (1804) illustrates the dangers of taking such advice.[18] *Practical education* warns its readers, among other things, of the perils of young men falling 'victims to the yawning demon of Ennui the moment they are left in solitude',[19] and the hero of *Ennui* reveals that this very habit nearly led to his ruination.

As a daughter of an enlightened gentleman, then, Edgeworth 'was brought up to believe that a sound education, not gender, was the ultimate measure of ability', but she rapidly discovered that a 'gap' existed 'between her faith in the Enlightenment promise of progress, and her growing awareness of Enlightenment fear and distrust of women'.[20] This 'fear and distrust' grew throughout the course of the eighteenth century as individuals struggled to come to terms with a changing social order in which gender roles, and, in particular, the role of women took on increased significance. At the end of the seventeenth century, particular emphasis was placed on the need to properly educate young boys so that they could take their place in society; thus, the principal essay in Locke's hugely influential *Some thoughts concerning education* (1693) is specifically addressed to a father educating his son. Rousseau, however, began to reshape the argument when he published *La nouvelle Héloïse* in 1761, a version of the medieval story of Abélard and Héloïse that effectively argues that the stability of society is predicated upon women; the heroine's potentially revo-

15 *Early lessons* is the first of a series of tales for children that Edgeworth produced between 1801 and 1825. Tracing the adventures of Lucy, Rosamond, Harry and Frank as they grow up, these books resonate with didactic implications for Edgeworth's young readers. 'Forester' appears in *Moral tales* and, as Edgeworth's father observes in his preface to the work, details how 'a young man, who scorns the common forms and dependencies of civil society … by improper management, or unlucky circumstances, [might] have become a fanatic and a criminal' (1: viii). 16 H. More, *Strictures on the modern system of female education* (1995), 1: ix. 17 M. Edgeworth, *Letters for literary ladies* (1993), 63–77. 18 Griselda 'insisted upon being *consulted*, that is obeyed, in affairs which did not immediately come under the cognizance of her sex.' Matters come to a head between Griselda and her husband when the latter tries to win back control in their marriage. Griselda decides to leave her husband, telling him: 'Blame yourself, not me, for all this. – When we were first married, you humoured, you spoiled me; no temper could bear it. – Take the consequences of your own weak indulgence. – Farewell': M. Edgeworth, *The modern Griselda* (1805), 35 and 198. 19 M. Edgeworth and R.L. Edgeworth, *Practical education* (1798), 1: 188. 20 Claire Connolly, introduction, *Letters for literary ladies*, xvi.

lutionary energy, it implies, is diffused only once she properly fulfils her obligations as a mother and a wife.[21] Rousseau's *Émile* similarly repeats this process
of containment: while Émile and Sophy are both educated, Sophy's education
is strictly intended to prepare her for the domestic sphere; Rousseau notes, 'To
be pleasing in [man's] sight,[22] to win his respect and love, to train him in childhood, to tend him in manhood, to counsel and console, to make his life pleas-
ant and happy, these are the duties of woman for all time, and this is what she
should be taught while she is young.' The 'sensible' mother will therefore labour
to make her daughter into 'a good woman', who perceives that 'Nature[23] herself
has decreed that woman ... should be at the mercy of man's judgement'.[24]

This emphasis upon the need to educate women to prepare them for their
domestic role in society features repeatedly in the literature of the period and,[25]
in the revolutionary era, it came to be understood that upon the results of female
education depended nothing less than 'the future of the nation itself'.[26] Writing
in the late 1790s, for instance, Hannah More explicitly links a proper female
education to national security in her text: 'In this moment of alarm and peril',
women must be properly educated so that they can 'come forward, and contribute their full and fair proportion towards the saving of their country';[27]
women who have received a 'defective Education' cannot be expected 'to raise
the depressed tone of public morals, and to awaken the drowsy spirit of religious principle' of their nation.[28] Even a radical such as Mary Wollstonecraft
insisted that domestic women had to be educated properly in order to fulfil

---

21 Janet Todd's analysis of the way in which excess emotional energy came to be understood as potentially revolutionary energy in the closing years of the eighteenth century is useful here. 'The fate of sensibility in England
is allied to the political situation,' she writes. Conservative opinion 'worked to bind sensibility to radicalism,' while
radicals 'were just as eager ... to align sensibility with their opponents': J. Todd, *Sensibility* (1986), 130.   22 In her
examination of literature of the Romantic period, Anne K. Mellor suggests, 'To be pleasing to men: this for
Rousseau is the ultimate social role of women ... Together Burke, Rousseau and Byron define the hegemonic
domestic ideology of the Romantic period: the construction of the ideal woman solely as daughter, lover, wife
and mother, one who exists only to serve the interests of male children and adults, and whose value is equated
with her beauty, submissiveness, tenderness and affection': A.K. Mellor, *Romanticism and gender* (1993), 109.   23 The
way in which the argument concerning what was 'natural' for woman is endlessly reworked in the literature of the
late eighteenth century causes Caroline Gonda to assert: 'Ideology works to present a political or socially constructed state of affairs as natural, as not only the way things should be but the way things are, always have been
and always will be. It does so by reiterating "commonsense" pronouncements about what is natural, normal and
right; by rewriting history to conceal the existence of dissident behaviour; through the imagery of popular culture; and through the forces of education': C. Gonda, *Reading daughters' fictions* (1996), 30–1.   24 J.J. Rousseau, *Émile*,
ed. P.D. Jimack, tr. Barbara Foxley (1993), 392–3.   25 In his study of education in the Romantic period, Alan
Richardson remarks, this 'cultural logic – that woman's "natural" condition entails both a subordinate social role
and an unequal responsibility for the legitimacy (as well as care) of offspring, and that female education should
emphasize at once "pleasing" and "modest" behavior – runs throughout eighteenth-century British conduct books
and educational treatises': A. Richardson, *Literature, education, and Romanticism* (1994), 172.   26 V. Colby, *Yesterday's
woman* (1974), 121. For a similar argument, see N. Watson, *Revolution and the form of the British novel* (1994), 11.   27
More, *Strictures*, 1: 4.   28 Ibid. 1: ix and 4.

their obligations to society. Ill-educated women, she observes, are 'weak beings [who] are only fit for a seraglio! ... [W]hilst [women] are only made to acquire personal accomplishments, men will seek for pleasure in variety, and faithless husbands will make faithless wives ... The box of mischief thus opened in society, what is to preserve private virtue, the only security of public freedom and universal happiness?'[29]

This need to educate women properly necessarily affected writers such as Edgeworth, who came under increasing pressure to provide female readers with 'suitable' reading.[30] Increasingly, as we shall see, it came to be understood that 'suitable' texts were those that impressed a definite moral upon the reader;[31] a recognition, Jane Spencer notes, that particularly affected the female writer and the works that she produced. '[W]orking within a patriarchal society that define[d] and judge[d] them according to ... its notions of ... femininity', she observes, women writers struggled to find a female literary voice acceptable to this society and, as such, manifested various '*response[s]*' to these definitions and judgements in their writing. Denoting these responses as 'protest, conformity, and escape', Spencer remarks that these should not be considered 'as mutually exclusive strategies informing three entirely separate traditions', and also points out that they crucially contributed to the evolution of the novel form: 'Conformity gave rise to the most continuously sustained of the women's traditions, the novel of the heroine's education. The desire to escape informs the romance tradition, which has so strong an influence on the developing novel and leads to the fantasies of women's Gothic.' The tradition of protest 'dealt with many aspects of women's lives, including their education, and their position as daughters and wives'.[32]

Although these observations clearly have several implications for Edgeworth's use of romance in her writing, the contention that women writers were frequently 'drawn to the didactic [or conformist] tradition not because they wanted to preach female subordination, but because this tradition could be used for the development of a new and more complex treatment of female character' throws a very particular light upon the didacticism of her works.[33] The common didactic theme that unites all of Edgeworth's works is the stress that they place upon the importance of a sound early education in the cultivation of a ratio-

29 M. Wollstonecraft, *A vindication of the rights of woman*, ed. Miriam Brody (1975), 83 and 88.   30 Colby, *Yesterday's woman*, 121   31 As Butler observes, the novel writers of the last two decades of the eighteenth century 'knew that their heroes and heroines were supposed to offer a moral pattern': M. Butler, *Jane Austen and the war of ideas* (1975), 30. John Wilson Croker puts the matter even more succinctly in his review of the 1812 series of Edgeworth's *Tales of fashionable life*: 'A novel, which is not in some degree a lesson either of morals or conduct, is, we think, a production which the world might be quite as well without': J.W. Croker, unsigned review in *Quarterly Review*, 2nd edn, 7 (1814) 331.   32 J. Spencer, *The rise of the woman novelist* (1986), ix–x and 108–9.   33 Ibid. 143.

nal mind; a point that is of particular importance for the female reader. The
didacticism of Edgeworth's writing declares that women should not be deprived
of the means to cultivate their reason, but it also stresses that the ultimate aim
of their rational education is to prepare them for the domestic sphere.[34] In their
preoccupation with mothers and mothering, Edgeworth's works therefore trace
the crucial role that the domestic woman plays both in ensuring national stability and facilitating the spread of the empire. As such, Edgeworth's didacticism seems explicitly designed to satisfy the didactic concerns of both her father
and society at the time that she was writing. While scholars may have in recent
years effectively demolished the myth of the direct interference of Edgeworth's
father in her work, such a reading thus promotes the notion of his indirect
influence upon her educational treatises and fiction; it suggests that Edgeworth
'internalize[d] ... and reflect[ed]' in her work both her father's ideology and
that of her age.[35] Some feminist critics have responded to this possibility by
suggesting that Edgeworth's writing in this way finally gives expression to a
'new-style patriarchy' that emerged during the course of the eighteenth century;
one that was based on reason, 'co-operation between the sexes and the non-
coercive exercise of authority', and operated 'according to the ... psychologi-
cally compelling themes of guilt and obligation'.[36] Noting that Edgeworth's
works 'repeatedly thematize the family, rehearsing in particular the roles to be
taken on by daughters and mothers in relation to patriarchy', they conclude that
she finally represents a case study '*in complicity*' with the new-style patriarchy of
her age.[37]

   While useful, this approach to Edgeworth's writing takes its didacticism
at face value, and privileges this one feature over everything else in her works.
Edgeworth's works *are* didactic, and this didacticism is clearly shaped towards
facilitating a moral ending that will educate the reader. At the same time, her

---

34 The enlightened Friend in *Letters for literary ladies*, for instance, defends the education of women by declaring
that it will teach them to hold 'domestic duties ... in high respect' (21).   35 Spencer, *The rise of the woman novelist*,
ix.   36 B. Kowaleski-Wallace, 'Home Economics' (1988), 242–3. Some lines written by Edgeworth's father expertly
illustrate the patriarchal issues at stake in this method of education: 'With boys and girls, a baker's dozen, / With
many a friend, and many a cousin: / The happy father sees them all / Attentive to his slightest call; / Their time,
their talents, and their skill, / Are guided by his sovereign will, / And e'en their wishes take their measure / From
what they think the patriarch's pleasure: / 'How does he rule them? – by what arts?' – / He knows the way to
touch their hearts' (*Memoirs*, 2: 492). This composition of Edgeworth's father is important for several reasons, in
the first instance demonstrating how profoundly the thing of Locke and Rousseau influenced his efforts to regulate his family. In *Some thoughts concerning education*, Locke stresses that the father must perceive the necessity of
adjusting his treatment of his children when they grow up, declaring that the father must take steps to 'imprint'
his authority upon his children in their 'infancy' so as to ensure that they will act as his 'obedient subject[s]' and
then as his 'affectionate friend[s]' in later life': J. Locke, *The works of John Locke* (1797), 8: 33–4. Rousseau adopts a
similar approach in *Émile*, where he urges educators of children: 'Use force with children and reasoning with men'
(65).   37 E. Kowaleski-Wallace, *Their fathers' daughters* (1991), x and 12. See also Gonda, *Reading daughters' fictions*, xv
and 30–1.

didacticism is often predicated upon her use of romance conventions, and romance, we remember, frequently denotes a female author's desire to 'escape' from the restrictions imposed by patriarchal authority.[38] Before we can properly appreciate the significance of romance in Edgeworth's work, we must therefore try to understand how Edgeworth herself would have conceived of this narrative form at the time that she was writing. Northrop Frye, in his *The secular scripture: a study of the structure of romance* (1976), claims that 'the conventions of prose romance show little change over the course of centuries.' Mysterious births, foster parents, adventures involving capture by pirates, shipwreck, narrow escapes from death, recognition of the true identity of the hero and his eventual marriage to the heroine, according to Frye, are just some of the conventions that date from the earliest Greek romances.[39] Samuel Johnson seems to agree: in his celebrated *Rambler* No. 4 of 31 March 1750, he writes: 'almost all the fictions of the last age will vanish, if you deprive them of a hermit and a wood, a battle and a shipwreck'.[40] In his *Dictionary* (1755), though, Johnson defines romance as 'A military fable of the middle ages; a tale of wild adventures in war and love … A lie; a fiction'.[41] What is crucial in this definition is that, while the first part deals with the conventions of romance, the second intimates that romance represents more than just a set of conventions; it implies, in other words, that there is a meaning to this narrative form.

What romance may mean, however, is a profoundly complicated issue, and the meaning may change from age to age as well as from text to text. Pointing out in contradistinction to Frye that romance inevitably 'uses and abuses conventional categories of genre', Diane Elam observes, 'each text must in some way redefine what it means by "romance," must in the process of this redefinition create a meaning for the genre of romance to which it addresses itself, at the same time as it loses older, perhaps, more established, meanings'.[42] Precisely this emphasis manifests itself in the preface to *Don Quixote de la Mancha* (1605–15), for example, where Cervantes' evident ambition is to stress the essential originality of his work. Insisting that his text is 'full of various wild imaginations, never thought of before', Cervantes explains that he has decided to accept the assurance of one of his friends that he has no need to cite 'in [his] margins the books and authors from whom [he] collected the sentences and sayings [he has] interspersed in [his] history.' Although admitting that he draws upon romance in *Don Quixote*, Cervantes is emphatic that his work nonetheless represents an entirely new type of literary form; it is, as his 'friend' would

38 Spencer, *The rise of the woman novelist*, 108. 39 N. Frye, *The secular scripture* (1976), 4. 40 S. Johnson, *Rambler*, No. 4, Saturday, 31 Mar. 1750, in W.J. Bate (ed.), *Samuel Johnson* (1968), 10. 41 S. Johnson, *A dictionary of the English language* (1983). 42 D. Elam, *Romancing the postmodern* (1992), 4 and 7.

have it, a sort of book that was previously 'never dreamed[,] … mentioned, nor … heard of'.[43]

This argument occurs again and again in the literary productions of British authors from the late seventeenth century onwards. In his preface to *Incognita* (1692), for instance, William Congreve insists, 'I resolved … to imitate dramatic writing, namely, in the design, contexture and result of the plot. I have not observed it before in a novel.' Although keen to insist that his work is not a romance, Congreve nonetheless draws heavily upon the mode's conventions; his central characters are all highborn, for example, his heroes dress as knights and 'perform … exercises of chivalry', and confused or disguised identity is central to the plot of his work.[44] Similarly, Horace Walpole stresses that he deliberately set out to surpass pre-existing models of fiction when producing *The castle of Otranto* (1764). In writing the work, he 'attempt[ed] to blend the two kinds of romance, the ancient and the modern' and, in so doing, to create 'a new species of romance' that had never been seen before:

> In the [ancient romances] all was imagination and improbability: in the [modern], nature is always intended to be, and sometimes has been, copied with success. Invention has not been wanting; but the great resources of fancy have been dammed up, by a strict adherence to common life. But if in the latter species Nature has cramped imagination, she did but take her revenge, having been totally excluded from old romances. The actions, sentiments, conversations, of the heroes and heroines of ancient days were as unnatural as the machines employed to put them in motion.

Walpole's decision 'to conduct the mortal agents of his drama according to the rules of probability' has a wider generic significance, of course, and we will explore this point in greater detail below. For the moment, though, what I want to emphasize is that, like Cervantes or Congreve before him, Walpole labours to stress his originality as an author; as he would have it, by 'reconcil[ing] the two [pre-existing] kinds' of romance in *The castle of Otranto*, he 'struck out' a decisively 'new route' in fiction 'for men of brighter talents'.[45]

Romance authors are typically keen to downplay the debt that they owe to their literary forebears. In her preface to the second edition of *The old English baron* (1777), for instance, Clara Reeve identifies her work as 'the literary offspring of the Castle of Otranto, written upon the same plan, with a design to

43 Cervantes, *Don Quixote de la Mancha*, ed. E.C. Riley, tr. Charles Jarvis (1998), 15–20. 44 W. Congreve, *Incognita* (2003) 6 and 46. 45 H. Walpole, *The castle of Otranto*, ed. Michael Gamer (2001), 13 and 9–10.

unite the most attractive and interesting circumstances of the ancient Romance and modern novel', yet she insists that, though 'not new', it represents 'a species … [that] is out of the common track (and) assumes a character and manner of its own', and this significantly distinguishes it from the romances and novels that have gone before.[46] In a similar fashion, if we move on to the early nineteenth century, we discover that Sir Walter Scott is less anxious to acknowledge his indebtedness to his literary ancestors than to draw attention to the originality of *Waverley* (1814) as an historical novel. In his first chapter, Scott notes that he consciously chose 'an uncontaminated name' for his hero and, while allowing in his 'postscript, which should have been a preface' that he has been influenced by 'Miss Edgeworth', he is emphatic that he has 'trace[d] the evanescent manners' of Scotland in a way that has never been achieved in any other work.[47] To make this claim, Scott in the first place downplays the literary efforts of writers such as Elizabeth Hamilton (1758–1816) and Mrs Anne Grant of Lagan (1755–1838), and he also ignores the fact that Charlotte Smith (1749–1806) and Jane West (1758–1852) had already made use of the name 'Waverley' in their novels.[48] Even more importantly, he chooses not to acknowledge how closely he draws upon romance in *Waverley*, using the convention of the quest, for instance, in order to transport his hero, and his reader, back to olden times.[49] This inability, or unwillingness, to confront what we might term 'generic indebtedness' to romance is very significant and, we shall see, profoundly affects any reading of Edgeworth's work.

Ian Duncan's *Modern romance and transformations of the novel* (1992) invaluably traces how the meaning of the mode changed during the course of the eighteenth century. For the first half of the century, he points out, 'romance meant any prose fiction in the vernacular tongue, particularly those associated with "the last age", and more particularly those French *romans héroïques* or *romans à longue haleine*, filled with dilemmas of love and honour and adorned with improbable exploits, written to amuse the *salons* of the age of Louis XIV'. Unlike the chivalric romances, these were typically written by and for women, and so they became synonymous with the 'figure of a female reader, and a feminine culture of romance' that took on increasingly negative connotations. Eventually, these romances became the focus for 'cultural anxieties about the role of women and

---

46 C. Reeve, preface to the second edition, *The old English baron*, ed. James Trainer (1977), 3. Originally published as *The champion of virtue. A Gothic story* in 1777, the retitled second edition of Reeve's text was published in 1778. **47** W. Scott, *Waverley*, ed. Andrew Hook (1972), 33 and 493–4. **48** K. Trumpener, *Bardic nationalism* (1997), 139. **49** Frye makes the same point in his reading of *Waverley*. Scott begins his text 'by outlining a number of facile romance formulas that he is *not* going to follow, and then stresses the degree of reality that his story is to have. His hero Waverley is a romantic hero, proud of his good looks and education, but, like a small-scale Don Quixote, his romantic attitude is one that confirms the supremacy of real life' (*Secular scripture*, 40).

about an expanding constituency of readers thus coalesced in the figure of the female Quixote'; romance reading came to be understood as 'pleasure without instruction', and was seen as inherently dangerous for young ladies.[50] In this context, Charlotte Lennox's *The female Quixote* (1752) provided a cautionary tale: Arabella, the heroine, is an avid reader, who is encouraged by her father, the marquis, to make full 'Use of his Library, in which, unfortunately for her, were great Store of Romances, and, what was still more unfortunate, not in the original *French*, but very bad Translations'; these romances had belonged to Arabella's mother, and, from her reading of them, Arabella's 'Ideas, from the Manner of her Life, and the Objects around her, had taken a romantic Turn; and, supposing Romances were real Pictures of Life, from them she drew all her Notions and Expectations'.[51]

Arabella's error, in supposing that 'Romances were real Pictures of Life', sums up what had been identified by the end of the century as the principle danger of reading romance fiction, and it also helps to explain why such reading was seen as particularly dangerous for young women. When we read eighteenth- and nineteenth-century critical reviews of the novel and romance, we can see that the elevation of the novel finally rested not only upon its moral content, but also upon its perceived accurate portrayal of everyday life. In his *Novel and romance, 1700–1800* (1970), for example, Ioan Williams refers to Clara Reeve's 'evidence'[52] that romances were 'eagerly received at reading parties well into the eighteenth century', but observes that, as the century wore on, they were increasingly 'condemned for presenting a ridiculous picture of human life and inculcating standards of behaviour which had no validity outside their own artificial world'.[53] In his preface to *The adventures of Roderick Random* (1748), Tobias Smollett says that this occurred the moment 'the authors of romance ... [lost] sight of probability ... and [applied] to the wonder rather than the judgement of their readers ... [I]nstead of supporting the character of their heroes, by dignity of sentiment and practice, [they] distinguished them by their bodily strength, activity and extravagance of behaviour'.[54]

Notwithstanding the criticism that was levelled at romance, however, the novel form itself continued to be viewed with suspicion until late in the century. Although the publication of *Pamela* and *Joseph Andrews* in the 1740s 'demon-

---

50 I. Duncan, *Modern romance and transformations of the novel* (1992), 10–12.   51 C. Lennox, *The female Quixote*, ed. Margaret Dalziel (1989), 7.   52 Williams' reference is to Clara Reeve's description of such a party in her *The progress of romance* (1785). As she describes it, 'Mother, and a select party of relations and friends, used to meet once a week at each other's houses, to hear these stories; – one used to read, while the rest ply'd their needles': C. Reeve, *The progress of romance*, Facsimile Text Society edn (1930), 1: 69. Reeve's text is hugely important to any discussion of the novel and romance and we will return to it below.   53 I. Williams, introduction, *Novel and romance* (1970), 5.   54 T. Smollett, *The adventures of Roderick Random*, ed. Paul-Gabriel Boucé (1979), xxxiv.

strated that fiction could be popular and yet have artistic and intellectual appeal',
the huge increase of fiction that followed Richardson and Fielding's work simultaneously inculcated 'a widespread belief that this fiction was morally and intel-
lectually dangerous'.[55] In 1778, therefore, Vicesimus Knox could write:

> If it be true, that the present age is more corrupt than the preceding,
> the great multiplication of Novels has probably contributed to its
> degeneracy. Fifty years ago there was scarcely a Novel in the kingdom.
> Romances, indeed, abounded; but they, it is supposed, were rather
> favourable to virtue. Their pictures of human nature were not exact,
> but they were flattering resemblances. By exhibiting patterns of per-
> fection, they stimulated emulation to aim at.[56]

Knox's reasoning is fundamental to any discussion of eighteenth-century
romance: it implies that, as reading inevitably inspires emulation on the part of
the reader, it is far better for him, or her, to read romances that typically depict
virtuous heroes and heroines and noble and heroic acts. Rather than condemning
romances, Knox to all intents and purposes singles them out for (cautious)
praise and, in so doing, highlights the particular anxiety of early reviewers and
readers who argued that the portrayal of entirely realistic characters in fiction
should be discouraged. As Johnson so eloquently puts it in his *Rambler* No. 4:
'It is ... not a sufficient vindication of a character, that it is drawn as it appears
for many characters ought never to be drawn.' The 'purpose' of writing is to
'teach the means of avoiding the snares which are laid by Treachery for
Innocence, without infusing any wish for that superiority with which the betrayer
flatters his vanity; to give the power of counteracting fraud, without the temptation to practice it; to initiate youth by mock encounters in the art of necessary defense, and to increase prudence without impairing virtue.'

Unlike the writers of what he calls 'the romances formerly written', Johnson
maintains that contemporary authors should not only exhibit 'the most perfect
idea of virtue', but also ensure that the virtue they portray is not 'above probability': specifically, that it is something 'humanity can reach'.[57] The same sentiments inform James Beattie's 1783 analysis of *Don Quixote*, which identifies
Cervantes' work as a seminal work: '*Don Quixote* occasioned the death of the

---

55 Williams, introduction, *Novel and romance*, 1 and 13.   56 V. Knox, extract from 'On Novel Reading', 1778, in
Williams, *Novel and romance*, 304.   57 Johnson, *Rambler*, No. 4 in Bate (ed.), *Samuel Johnson*, 11–14. Mary-Elizabeth
Fowkes Tobin remarks that Johnson's argument was entirely representative of those reviewers and readers who
were 'worried that these "mixed characters" would charm readers with their personal beauty and accomplish-
ments, their wit and good-humor, while their lax moral standards would corrupt readers' innocence and virtue':
M.-E. Fowkes Tobin, 'The power of example' (1988), 38.

Old Romance, and gave birth to the New. Fiction henceforth divested herself
of her gigantick size, tremendous aspect, and frantick demeanour; and, descend-
ing to the level of common life, conversed with man as his equal, and as a polite
and chearful companion'.[58] Beattie's further point, though, is that the reader
should not misinterpret his quite lengthy discourse upon romances: the reading of such works is 'a dangerous recreation'; it 'breeds a dislike to history, and
all the substantial parts of knowledge; withdraws the attention from nature,
and truth; and fills the mind with extravagant thoughts, and too often criminal propensities'.[59] 'The fiction of romance', as George Canning put it in 1787,

> is restricted by no fetters of reason, or of truth; but gives a loose to
> lawless imagination, and transgresses at will the bounds of time and
> place, of nature and possibility. The fiction of [the novel], on the con-
> trary, is shackled with a thousand restraints; is checked in her most
> rapid progress by the barriers of reason; and bounded in her most
> excursive flights by the limits of probability.[60]

In this way, although Knox and Canning characterize romance and the novel in
the same manner, Canning evaluates the two genres differently; for him, romance
is ultimately more dangerous than the novel because it encourages the reader
to cultivate his or her irrational mind.

This polarization of the novel and romance is also illustrated by Clara
Reeve's *The progress of romance*, which was published in 1785. The definitions that
The progress of romance offers for both the romance and the novel echo those of
Beattie and Canning, as Reeves declares that what makes the novel distinctive
is its emphasis upon real life:

> The Romance is an heroic fable, which treats of fabulous persons and
> things. – The Novel is a picture of real life and manners, and of the
> times in which it is written. The Romance in lofty and elevated lan-
> guage, describes what never happened nor is likely to happen. The Novel

---

58 Smollett similarly argues, 'Cervantes, by an inimitable piece of ridicule, reformed the taste of mankind, representing chivalry in the right point of view, and converting romance to purposes far more useful and entertaining, by making it assume the sock, and point out the follies of ordinary life' (*Roderick Random*, xxxiv). Hannah More
is more circumspect in her analysis of *Don Quixote*: 'That revolution of manners which the unparalleled wit and
genius of Don Quixote so happily effected, by abolishing extravagancies the most absurd and pernicious, was so
far imperfect, that some virtues which he never meant to expose, fell into disrepute with the absurdities which he
did; and it is become the turn of the present taste to attach in no small degree that which is ridiculous to that
which is serious and heroic' (*Strictures*, 1: 25). 59 J. Beattie, extract from *On fable and romance*, 1783, in Williams, *Novel
and romance*, 320 and 327. 60 G. Canning, *The microcosm*, 26, Monday, 14 May 1787, in Williams, *Novel and romance*,
341.

gives a familiar relation of such things, as pass every day before our eyes, such as may happen to our friend, or to ourselves; and the perfection of it, is to represent every scene, in so easy and natural a manner, and to make them appear so probable, as to deceive us into a persuasion (at least while we are reading) that all is real, until we are affected by the joys or distresses, of the persons in the story, as if they were our own.

According to Reeve, the romance and the novel have been confounded together 'insidiously, by those who endeavour to render all writings of both kinds contemptible'; there are reputable and disreputable examples of each of the genres: if parents properly supervise the reading of their children, these will 'naturally aspire to read the best books of all kinds' when they reach maturity.[61] The reading of young girls is of particular importance, for the perusal of inappropriate novels and romances teach

> young wom[e]n ... to expect adventures and intrigues, – [they expect] to be addressed in the style of these books, with the language of flattery and adulation. – If a plain man addresses her in rational terms and pays her the greatest of compliments, – that of desiring to spend his life with her, – that is not sufficient, her vanity is disappointed, she expects to meet a Hero in Romance ... [or] a fine Gentleman in a Novel.[62]

Reeve's emphasis upon 'the best books' leads us back to *The female Quixote* and to the 'cultural anxieties' that Duncan finds 'coalesced' in Lennox's text. While contemporaries read Arabella's adventures as an attack upon romance fiction, they at the same time illustrate the reasons why she found such fiction so peculiarly attractive. Living in rural isolation in her father's house, and expected by him to follow his orders and marry her cousin, Mr Glanville, Arabella instead (temporarily) empowers herself by insisting upon reading her life according to the romances that she loves. By using the conventions of romance, she therefore resists moving in a straight line from being somebody's daughter to somebody's wife. As Margaret Anne Doody has it, in her introduction to the 1989 edition of the text: 'In acting according to the romances, Arabella ... supplie[s] the lack of an emotional life, create[s] some room for

---

61 Reeve, *The progress of romance*, 1: 111–12; 2: 83. See also Reeve, preface, *The old English baron*, 3–4. 62 Reeve, *The progress of romance*, 2: 78. Reeve's argument here is clearly echoed in Wollstonecraft's observation in *A vindication of the rights of woman* that women who foster 'a romantic unnatural delicacy of feeling, waste their* lives in *imagining* how happy they should have been with a husband who could love them with a fervid increasing affection every day, and all day' (117). Her footnote to her text reads: 'For example, the herd of novelists' (117).

libido, and take[s] upon herself the role of heroic protector of her own chastity'.[63] Put another way, and to paraphrase George Canning, Arabella lets her lawless, 'transfiguring' imagination take 'flight', and she successfully, if momentarily, transcends the boundaries of her patriarchal existence.[64] In so doing, *The female Quixote* thereby reveals the shocking truth that women desire to be more than mere ciphers: a recognition that helps to explain why late-eighteenth-century reviewers heaped such ridicule and condemnation upon romance texts. In a society that was struggling to shore up the patriarchal order in the face of a new age, the 'moral' novel, with its increasing emphasis upon the desirability of the domestic sphere for women, was inevitably perceived as infinitely more suitable reading material for women than the fictions of romance. For, if romances 'tell the truth of female desire', as feminist critics suggest, Arabella's desire to replicate the adventures of which she has read 'declares her determination to create significance. That subversive desire, a threat to the status quo, defines her as more dangerous than a woman driven by obviously erotic yearnings and raises the possibility that this novel embodies a revolutionary "tendency".'[65] Laurie Langbauer puts it this way:

> Arabella is obsessed with the disdainful ladies, the lordly ladies, of romance not simply because she is obsessed with sex, but because even more deeply she yearns for power ... What she most often cites from romance are instances of heroines' power – the preeminence of their every gesture, their absolute authority over their lovers, their mastery over life and death.[66]

What, then, are we to make of the fact that Edgeworth frequently resorts to the conventions of this 'subversive', 'dangerous' and 'revolutionary' genre in her writing? In the first instance, her writing and letters clearly demonstrate that she was a voracious reader, and so it is hardly surprising that she drew upon

---

63 M.A. Doody, introduction, *The female Quixote*, xxxi. 64 In her reading of *Don Quixote*, Gillian Beer suggests that Cervantes' work 'demonstrates that the transfiguring imagination can force the world to imitate its perceptions; imagination need not always mimic external reality': G. Beer, *The critical idiom* (1970), 41. 65 P.M. Spacks, *Desire and truth* (1990), 14. Beer identifies a similar revolutionary dimension in romance, contending that, because the genre is 'absorbed with the ideal, [it] always has an element of prophecy. It remakes the world in the image of desire' (*The critical idiom*, 79). Thus, fears that 'romance would seduce the imagination, as well as mislead, may have been based on a half-acknowledged recognition that women's lives were very circumscribed in their actual possibilities' (53). Fredric Jameson politicizes the argument further when he explores romance 'in the context of the gradual reification of realism in late capitalism.' '[O]nce again', he remarks, the genre 'comes to be felt as the place of narrative heterogenity and of freedom from that reality principle to which a now oppressive realistic representation is the hostage. Romance now again seems to offer the possibility of sensing other historical rhythms, and of demonic or Utopian transformations of a real now unshakeably set in place': F. Jameson, *The political unconscious* (1983), 104. 66 L. Langbauer, 'Romance revised' (1984), 45.

romance, as well as upon history, novels and travel literature to fashion her own narrative form.[67] Further, her correspondence reveals that she particularly appreciated the ability of a text to 'carry' her 'away', and it is in precisely this context that she praises Elizabeth Inchbald's *A simple story* (1791), for example, or Lady Mary Wortley Montagu's *Turkish letters* (1763). Writing of the former to her Aunt Ruxton, she observes,

> I have just been reading, I believe for the 4th time the Simple Story which I intended this time to read as a critic that I might write to Mrs Inchbald about it – but I was so carried away by it that I was totally incapable of thinking of criticism or Mrs Inchbald or of anything but Miss Milner & Doriforth, who appeared to me real persons, whom I saw & heard & who had such power to interest me that I had cried my eyes almost out before I came to the end of their story. I think it the most pathetic & most powerfully interesting tale I ever yet read.[68]

Similarly, commenting upon Montagu's text, she writes, 'My head has been these two day[s] in … [the] turkish letters – & I see nothing wherever I go but visions of beauteous Fatimas and palaces wainscotted with mother of pearl & nails of emeralds'.[69] In responding to books in this fashion, Edgeworth's correspondence also reveals that she was perfectly willing to overlook those moments when a work's (romantic) narrative enabled the limitations of real life to be transcended. Commenting upon Sydney Owenson's *The princess, or, The beguine* (1835) in a letter to her third stepmother, for instance, she remarks that the work is 'exceedingly amusing … both by its merits & its absurdities'; although there are 'various errors' to be 'detected … in [Owenson's] historical remarks & allusions … we must grant a romance writer a few improbabilities – And I would be as charitable as possible whenever [apportioning?] this right of allowance'.[70] Frances Edgeworth also quotes from this letter in her *Memoir* of her stepdaughter, and adds a remark that illustrates that its sentiments were entirely typical of Edgeworth's response to a text: 'Maria was always so much

---

67 Further evidence of Edgeworth's reading habits is provided by the Longford: Saint Mel's college: catalogue of the library of the Edgeworth family, which is held on microfilm in the National Library of Ireland. Apparently compiled by Edgeworth herself, possibly in 1831, this list is both incomplete, and clearly selective. It does reveal, however, that Edgeworth numbered *Don Quixote* and *The female Quixote* among her own books. I am grateful to Dr Máire Kennedy, Divisional Librarian, Dublin City Libraries, for bringing this catalogue to my attention. 68 Maria Edgeworth to Mrs Ruxton, 26 Dec. 1809, letter 722 of MS 10166/7 of *Women, education and literature: the papers of Maria Edgeworth, 1768–1849, part 2* (1994). Unless otherwise stated, references to Edgeworth letters are to part 2 of this microfilm edition. 69 Maria Edgeworth to Mrs Ruxton, 3 Nov. 1803, letter 384. 70 Maria Edgeworth to Mrs Frances Edgeworth, 27 Jan. 1835, letter 33 of MS Eng Lett c701 of *Women, education and literature: the papers of Maria Edgeworth, 1768–1849, part 1* (1994).

interested in a story that she would not stop to reason upon it. I remember when Lady Morgan's "O'Donnel" was being read out in the year 1815, at the scene of McRory's appearance in the billiard room, when Mr. Edgeworth said, "This is quite improbable;" Maria exclaimed, "Never mind the improbability, let us go on with the entertainment".'[71]

Even more significantly, perhaps, Edgeworth's letters demonstrate that this determination to 'go on with the entertainment' frequently swept her away as an author; and this is illustrated by the fact that she steadfastly resisted her father's encouragement to keep a written note of potential material, preferring, instead, to store up possible incidents and characters in her head. In her much-quoted letter upon the art of fiction to her friend, Mrs Stark, she explains, 'I knew that, when I wrote down, I put the thing out of my care, out of my head; and that, though it might be put by very safe, I should not know where to look for it; that the labour of looking over a note-book would never do when I was in the warmth and pleasure of inventing.' She never used a notebook when writing dialogue, emphasizing that she preferred 'imagining [herself] each speaker, and that too fully engrosses the imagination to leave time for consulting notebooks; the whole fairy vision would melt away, and the warmth and the pleasure of invention be gone'.[72] So, as both an author and reader, Edgeworth was not a totally didactic creature; she thoroughly enjoyed reading and producing books that stimulated not only her intellect, but also her imagination and heart.

Secondly, Edgeworth's use of romance might also be interpreted as a concessionary gesture to her readers, through which she attempts to 'sweeten' for them the less appealing didactic connotations of her writing. Henry Stephen posits as much in the *Quarterly Review*, for example, where he delivers his opinion of the 1809 series of *Tales of fashionable life*. 'As a writer of tales and novels', he observes, Edgeworth 'has a very marked peculiarity. It is that of venturing to dispense common sense to her readers, and to bring them within the precincts of real life and natural feeling'; unlike other writers, she delights in portraying the gradual development of character, and this 'is often so exquisitely managed, as to leave the readers of romance no regret for the shining improbabilities to which they have been accustomed ... To our shame, however, we must acknowledge that we always think her most agreeable when she deviates a little from her rigid realities, and concedes to the *corrupted taste* of her readers some petty sprinkling of romantic feeling and extraordinary incident' (ii: 147) (my emphasis).[73] By the time he came to review the 1812 series of *Tales of fashionable life* for

71 F. Edgeworth, *A memoir of Maria Edgeworth*, 3: 166.   72 Maria Edgeworth to Mrs Stark, 14 May 1834, quoted in F. Edgeworth, *A memoir of Maria Edgeworth*, 3: 150–4.   73 H. Stephen, unsigned review of the 1809 series of *Tales of fashionable life* in *Quarterly Review*, 4th edn, 2 (1818) 146–7.

the *Quarterly*, John Wilson Croker had evidently decided that this need to 'sweeten' a work with a 'slight sprinkling of the extraordinary' had vanished. Emphatically declaring that '"*vraisemblable*" is the only legitimate province of the novelist who aims at improving the understanding or touching the heart', he congratulates Edgeworth for moving away from romance in her writing:

> [W]e cannot reconcile ourselves to the violent and unnecessary vicissitudes of fortune and feeling which disfigure, in a greater or less [*sic*] degree, every tale of the first *livraison* of this work ... We are therefore glad to be able to say that in the present volumes we find much less reason for complaint on this point; and we are satisfied that a more genuine and sustained interest is preserved by this attention to probability, than could have been excited by those more amazing incidents and transactions with which Miss Edgeworth has sometimes endeavoured to captivate our attention.[74]

Most obviously, Edgeworth's preoccupation with romance in her writing can be read as yet another manifestation of her ambition to educate her readers: to teach them how to negotiate properly this potentially dangerous narrative form. In all of her works, but particularly in *Practical education* and *Essays on professional education*, she insists that complex gender issues simmer beneath an individual's choice of reading material: responsible parents must properly supervise their children's choice of books. While *Practical education* argues that boys and girls alike must be taught to cultivate their reason, it emphatically declares, 'it may be necessary to remind all who are concerned in *female* education, that particular caution is necessary to manage female sensibility; to make, what is called the heart, a source of permanent pleasure, we must cultivate the reasoning powers at the same time that we repress the enthusiasm of *fine feeling*.' This necessity arises from women's 'situation and duties in society', which call upon them 'rather for the daily exercise of quiet domestic virtues, than for those splendid acts of generosity, or those exaggerated expressions of tenderness, which are the characteristics of heroines in romance.' Clearly echoing Clara Reeve's arguments in *The progress of romance*, *Practical education* insists that young ladies inevitably find themselves dissatisfied with their daily existence once they have fed their imaginations upon inappropriate books. 'Women, who have been much addicted to common novel-reading', it notes, 'are always acting in imitation of some Jemima, or Almeria, who never existed, and they perpetually mistake Plain William and Thomas for "*My Beverly!*"' Such women also labour under

---

74 J.W. Croker, unsigned review of the 1812 series of *Tales of fashionable life* in *Quarterly Review*, 2nd edn, 7 (1814) 329.

'another peculiar misfortune; they require continual great emotions to keep them in tolerable humour with themselves.'

By proposing the means through which women can guard against such dangers, Edgeworth rehearses a strategy that is central to all of her writing: she polarizes science and romance, the rational and the imaginative mind. 'Women, who cultivate their reasoning powers, and who acquire tastes for science and literature', she observes, 'find sufficient variety in life, and do not require the *stimulus* of dissipation, or of romance.' With their sympathy and sensibility 'engrossed by proper objects, and connected with habits of useful exertion: they usually feel the affection which others profess, and actually enjoy the happiness which others describe'.[75] Significantly, this insistence in *Practical education* breaks down the opposition that Edgeworth overtly labours to construct between 'science and literature': specifically, it implies not only that all women yearn for a romantic existence, but also that the best way for them to achieve this is by manifesting resolutely rational behaviour.

The patriarchal anxieties that inform this argument manifest themselves throughout Edgeworth's work, but it is, perhaps, in *Letters for literary ladies* that they receive their most powerful expression. As its name suggests, *Letters for literary ladies* takes the form of an epistolary text, and it has its origins in a series of letters exchanged between Edgeworth's father and his great friend Thomas Day (1748–89). In their correspondence, the two men discussed women's education in general and the possibility of a literary career for Maria Edgeworth in particular. Day was horrified when he discovered that Edgeworth's father was encouraging her to study politics and history, and positively outraged when he learned that she was preparing a translation of Madame de Genlis' *Adèle et Théodore* (1782) with a view to publication. In the event, another translation appeared first, and Edgeworth did not publish her first work until six years after Day's death.[76]

The Friend in *Letters for literary ladies* takes the part of Edgeworth's father in the text and, in the 'Answer to the preceding letter', advances the type of arguments that he put forward in support of her education and literary career. In so doing, he polarizes science and romance, indicating that the reading of romance by women inevitably threatens the stability of the social order:

> [M]any of the errors into which women of literature have fallen, may have arisen from an improper choice of books. Those who read chiefly

75 *Practical education*, 296–8. Edgeworth seems to contradict her argument regarding the power of romance later in the treatise: 'Examples from romance can never have such a powerful effect upon the mind as those which are taken from real life; but in proportion to the just and lively representation of situations, and passions resembling reality, fictions may convey useful moral lessons' (1: 314).   76 See Butler, *Maria Edgeworth*, 149 and 172–3.

> works of imagination, receive from them false ideas of life and of the
> human heart. Many of these productions I should keep as I would
> deadly poison from my child: I should rather endeavour to turn her
> attention to science than to romance, and to give her early that taste
> for truth and utility, which, when once implanted, can scarcely be
> eradicated.

Intriguingly, the Friend's further insistence is that his ambitions in this regard
will be facilitated by the fact that the power of romance has all but vanished.
'The days of chivalry are no more', he observes,

> the knight no longer sallies forth in ponderous armour, mounted upon
> 'a steed as invulnerable as himself.' – The damsel no longer depends
> upon the prowess of his mighty arm to maintain the glory of her
> charms, or the purity of her fame … and from being the champions
> and masters of the fair sex, we are now become their friends and com-
> panions. We have not surely been losers by this change; the fading glo-
> ries of romance have vanished, but the real permanent pleasures of
> domestic life remain in their stead; and what the fair have lost of adu-
> lation they have gained in friendship.[77]

The Friend's arguments here clearly evoke Edmund Burke's treatment of
the passing of the *ancien régime* in his *Reflections on the Revolution in France* (1790). In
his text, Burke famously draws upon chivalric imagery in order to express his
astonishment that 'ten thousand swords' did not leap 'from their scabbards to
avenge even a look that threatened [Marie Antoinette] with insult':

> But the age of chivalry is gone. – That of sophisters, oeconomists, and
> calculators, has succeeded; and the glory of Europe is extinguished for
> ever. Never, never more, shall we behold that generous loyalty to rank
> and sex, that proud submission, that dignified obedience, that subor-
> dination of the heart, which kept alive, even in servitude itself, the spirit
> of an exalted freedom … It is gone, that sensibility of principle, that
> chastity of honour, which felt a stain like a wound, which inspired
> courage whilst it mitigated ferocity, which ennobled whatever it touched,
> and under which vice itself lost half its evil, by losing all its grossness.

---

77 *Letters for literary ladies*, 25–9. See also *Practical Education* for Edgeworth's argument that 'the happiness of domestic life … will be increased by the judicious cultivation of the female understanding, more than by all that modern
gallantry or ancient chivalry could devise in favour of the sex' (2: 550).

'This mixed system of opinion and sentiment had its origin in the antient chivalry', Burke declares,

> But now all is to be changed. All the pleasing illusions, which made power gentle, and obedience liberal, which harmonized the different shades of life, and which, by a bland assimilation, incorporated into politics the sentiments which beautify and soften private society, are to be dissolved by this new conquering empire of light and reason … On this scheme of things, a king is but a man; a queen is but a woman; a woman is but an animal; and an animal not of the highest order. All homage paid to the sex in general as such, and without distinct views, is to be regarded as romance and folly.[78]

Crucially, although he insists that romance and domestic life exist in completely different registers, the Friend in *Letters for literary ladies* seizes upon Burke's imagery in an attempt to promulgate his vision of a new, rational world order. In contradistinction to Burke, though, he evidences a quiet satisfaction at what he perceives as chivalry's 'demise.' Tacitly acknowledging both the power and attraction of romance, the Friend admits that the genre effectively transcends reality, enabling the individual who controls it to impose his or her vision upon the world. While keen to stress that the vanishing of romance has proved advantageous for both sexes, his true recognition is that it has done much to assuage the (patriarchal) anxieties of himself and his friend. Specifically, he perceives that this 'change' has disempowered women, stripping them of the 'homage' that had previously been their due and compelling them to settle for a domestic life. Hannah More draws upon precisely the same type of imagery four years later in her *Strictures on the modern system of female education*, where she writes of not wishing 'to bring back the frantic reign of chivalry, nor to reinstate women in that fantastic empire in which they sat enthroned in the hearts, or rather in the imaginations of men'; at the same time, however, she warns that those who would reform society should be careful that they do not, instead, 'subvert' it: 'We do not correct old systems, but demolish them; fancying that when every thing shall be new it will be perfect'; More fears that the romantic image of womanhood will merely be replaced by one of female 'tyrants', forever seeking their rights.[79]

The fact that the argument of Edgeworth's Friend is perhaps more hopeful than real disturbs the didactic complacency of his 'letter', however, and it informs

---

78 E. Burke, *Reflections on the Revolution in France*, ed. Conor Cruise O'Brien (1968), 170–1. 79 More, *Strictures*, 1: 19–23; 2: 15.

his anxious insistence that woman's education must be carefully managed. '[I]t is absolutely out of our power to drive the fair sex back to their former state of darkness: the art of printing has totally changed their situation; their eyes are opened, – the classic page is unrolled, they *will* read: – all we can do is induce them to read with judgement – to enlarge their minds so that they may take a full view of their interests and ours.' In order to promote this happy patriarchal state of affairs, the Friend is convinced that women must be exposed to 'the unprejudiced testimony of [their] father[s] or … brother[s]; they [must] learn to distinguish the pictures of real life from paintings of imaginary manners and passions which never had, which never can have, any existence.' To put this another way, he is insistent that women must be persuaded to accept men's (rational) view of reality and to give up their romantic (mis)perceptions of real life. Rather than allowing his womenfolk to entertain foolish delusions, the Friend implies, the conscientious male must take every possible opportunity to ensure that his daughter, sister, or wife remakes the world in his patriarchal image.[80]

In the light of such arguments, it is not surprising that Edgeworth's chapter on books in *Practical education* devotes particular attention to the care that must be taken in supervising the reading material of young girls and women. Firstly, the treatise remarks that the role of the mother is crucial; it insists that she must carefully supervise the reading of all of her children. 'We are acquainted with the mother of a family, who has never trusted any book to her children, without having first examined it herself with the most scrupulous attention; her care has been repaid with that success in education, which such care can alone endure'.[81] Such vigilance goes beyond merely marking books with pencil. This mother made herself the ultimate censor of her children's reading material by performing 'some necessary operations [with] her scissors' (1: 322). Even more precautions must be taken, though, when the books in question are destined for young girls:

> With respect to sentimental stories, and books of mere entertainment, we must remark, that they should be sparingly used, especially in the education of girls. This species of reading cultivates what is called the heart prematurely, lowers the tone of the mind, and induces indifference for those common pleasures and occupations which, however trivial in themselves, constitute by far the greatest portion of our daily happiness. (1:332–3)

80 *Letters for literary ladies*, 34. Edgeworth treats this theme to great effect in *The modern Griselda*, where Mr Bolingbroke is nearly unmanned by his wife's desire that he should treat her as a romantic heroine and pay her homage. Belatedly, he 'resolve[s] to assume the guidance of his wife, or at least of himself' (79). 81 *Practical education*, 1: 321–2. Further references to this edition are cited parenthetically in the text.

The negative 'effects which are produced upon the female mind by immoderate novel-reading' cannot be underestimated (1: 333). 'To those who acquire this taste every object becomes disgusting which is not in an attitude for poetic painting' (1: 333). The real threat of this reading, the text reveals, is that it poses a considerable potential danger to the stability of the domestic sphere: 'A tragedy heroine, weeping, swooning, dying, is a moral-picturesque object; but the frantic passions, which have the best effect upon the stage, might, when exhibited in domestic life, appear to be drawn upon too large a scale to please' (1: 333). In order to prevent a young girl from becoming such a 'tragedy heroine', *Practical education* later asserts that 'a mother, or a preceptress' must exercise 'early caution, unremitting, scrupulous caution in the choice of books which are put into the hands of [her female charge]' (2: 550). This is so important that Edgeworth remarks, 'It cannot be necessary to add more than this general idea, that a mother ought to be answerable to her daughter's husband for the books her daughter had read, as well as for the company she had kept' (2: 550).

At the same time as advancing these arguments, Edgeworth asserts that books such as *Robinson Crusoe*, which 'should not early be chosen for boys of an enterprising temper, unless they are intended for a seafaring life, or for the army', are perfectly safe for the female reader (1: 336). This type of reading 'cannot be as dangerous [for girls] as it is to boys; girls must very soon perceive the impossibility of their rambling about the world in quest for adventures; and where there appears an obvious impossibility in gratifying any wish, it is not likely to become, or at least to continue, a torment to the imagination' (1: 336). I think this argument in Edgeworth's treatise is crucial. Firstly, her ostensible contention here is that the reading of romance is always dangerous because it unleashes powerful desires in the reader; these desires, she intimates, are inevitably linked to action: the reader always tries to emulate that of which he or she reads. Unlike Arabella's beloved romances in *The female Quixote*, romances of conquest and adventure like *Robinson Crusoe* (1719) are therefore 'safe' for female readers because they will never physically be in the position to replicate such books.[82] Secondly, while acknowledging the dangers of romance reading, she simultaneously admits its power, even suggesting that it will be to Britain's national and imperial advantage if romance reading is allowed to certain young boys. *Essays on professional*

82 Nancy Armstrong similarly notices the distinction that the Edgeworths make in relation to girls and *Robinson Crusoe*, suggesting: 'There is ... a strong possibility that early educational theorists recommended *Crusoe* over Defoe's other works because they thought women were likely to learn to desire what Crusoe accomplished, a totally self-enclosed and functional domain where money did not really matter. It was no doubt because Crusoe was more female, according to nineteenth century understanding of gender, than either Roxana or Moll that educators found his story more suitable reading for girls than for boys of an impressionable age': N. Armstrong, *Desire and domestic fiction* (1989), 16.

education thus positions *Robinson Crusoe* at the beginning of a long list of rec-ommended reading for the future soldier or sailor; such boys 'should read accounts of shipwrecks and hair-breadth scapes [*sic*], voyages and travels, his-tories of adventurers, beginning with Robinson Crusoe.' Acknowledging that reading inevitably inculcates the reader's desire to emulate what is being read, *Essays on professional education* designates *Robinson Crusoe* as 'the most interesting of all stories, and one which has sent many a youth to sea.' Edgeworth develops this argument in the chapter devoted to the military and naval professions in *Essays on professional education*, declaring that romance reading should not only be exalted, but also positively encouraged in this very particular young male reader:

> The first books that [such a young man] reads should be such as are calculated to rouse in his young mind the notions of honour, and the feelings of emulation. In his education it must be the object to excite enthusiasm, not to subject him at an early age to the nice calculations of *prudence*. Consequently a species of reading, which may be disap-proved of for other pupils, should be recommended to the young sol-dier. His imagination should be exalted by the adventurous and the marvellous. Stories of giants, and genii, and knights and tournaments, and 'pictured tales of vast heroic deeds,' should feed his fancy.

Pointedly, the text observes that the 'grand object' of this boy's education is to 'excite ... in [his] mind, admiration for great actions, and a passionate enthu-siastic desire to imitate' that of which he reads. In this way, Edgeworth's work not only anticipates that the reading of romance texts like *Robinson Crusoe* will inspire young men to travel, but also that it will encourage them to make man-ifest Britain's incontrovertible moral and cultural superiority in their dealings with other races and lands.[83]

Edgeworth's efforts to harness romance therefore demonstrate not only her perception that the genre 'is implicitly instructive as well as escapist',[84] but also the efficacy of Frye's contention that romance is frequently 'kidnapped' into literature in order to support 'the ideology of an ascendant class': 'In every

---

83 R.L. Edgeworth, *Essays on professional education*, 2nd edn (1812), 137 and 142. Although originally published under her father's name alone, it is clear from Edgeworth's correspondence that she was the effective author of this trea-tise. In an 1805 letter to her cousin Sophy Ruxton, for example, she observes, 'father has excited my ambition to write a *useful* essay upon professional education ... I have thrown aside all thoughts of pretty stories; & put myself into a course of solid reading.' Three years later, Edgeworth expresses her anxiety to Sophy at the thought of the treatise's impending publication: 'I cannot help however looking forward to its publication, & fate with an anxi-ety & an apprehension I never felt before in the same degree – for consider my father's credit is entirely at stake!' See Maria Edgeworth to Sophy Ruxton, 26 Feb. 1805, letter 451, and Maria Edgeworth to Sophy Ruxton, 23 [?] Jan. 1808, letter 612. 84 Beer, *The critical idiom*, 9.

period of history', he writes, 'certain ascendant values are accepted by society and are embodied in its serious literature. Usually this process includes some form of kidnapped romance, that is, romance formulas used to reflect certain ascendant religious or social ideas'.[85] This is obviously true of those instances in *Practical education* and *Essays on professional education* where Edgeworth tries to use romance to facilitate directly national and imperial expansion; but it is also true of the way in which she uses the genre's conventions throughout her work in order to cultivate the reason of her other, more general, readers. Through her use of romance conventions, Edgeworth turns this into an ontological issue, and implies that the individual will only be happy if he or she cultivates a rational mind. As what I am suggesting here is particularly informed by my reading of Frye's analysis of romance, it might be useful to briefly state his main contentions at this point.

In his reading of romance, Frye maintains that the genre's heroes and villains primarily exist to symbolize a contrast between two worlds. 'There is, first', he writes,

> a world associated with happiness, security, and peace; the emphasis is often thrown on childhood or on an "innocent" or pre-genital period of youth, and the images are those of spring and summer, flowers and sunshine. I shall call this world the idyllic world. The other is a world of exciting adventures, but adventures which involve separation, loneliness, humiliation, pain, and the threat of more pain. I shall call this world the demonic or night world.

'Even in the most realistic stories there is usually some trace of a plunge downward at the beginning and a bounce upward at the end', and so 'most romances exhibit a cyclical movement of descent into a night world and a return to the idyllic world, or to some symbol of it like a marriage.' The hero or heroine's sense of ontological crisis, or 'alienation', typically compels this 'cyclical movement', with him or her perceiving that he or she no longer occupies an authentic identity, or 'self.' 'Reality for romance' is thus 'an order of existence most readily associated with the word identity. Identity means a good many things, but all its meanings in romance have some connection with a state of existence in which there is nothing to write about.' This state, it may be inferred, typically exists immediately before or after the journey, or quest, which is undertaken by the hero or heroine as a result of his or her sense of ontological insecurity or 'alienation'. Once this journey or quest has been completed, and the

85 Frye, *Secular scripture*, 57 and 29–30.

hero or heroine's identity has been (re)established, the narrative ceases, usually with a profoundly symbolic celebration, such as a marriage, closing the text. Consequently, 'Most romances end happily, with a return to the state of identity, and begin with a departure from it.'[86]

Ennui, *The absentee* and *Ormond* lend themselves most obviously to this model, but, as I see it, Edgeworth draws upon it throughout her writing. In her case, however, her heroes and villains do not exist to symbolize a contrast between two worlds, but, rather, between two ontological conditions, or states. As we shall see, the didactic emphasis of her work is that it is necessary to cultivate one's rational mind in order to be happy and, further, that the individual who fails to do so is inevitably plunged into an underworld life. Overtly, therefore, her writing argues that the pleasures of passion and the emotions always prove to be illusory; the truly contented individual is the one who uses his reason to govern his imagination and heart. While Edgeworth's use of romance conventions in this way appears to immediately facilitate the didactic imperatives that impel her work, the very fact that she relies so heavily upon the genre in the first place introduces some curiously subversive resonances into her writing. Romance is, by definition, a 'prophetic' genre in that it seeks not so much to represent or to interpret reality, as to create an idealized view of the world.[87] As it is always concerned with illustrating the 'potential', the 'possible', or, even more significantly, the 'ideal', there is, inevitably, a strong 'wish-fulfillment element' to romance texts.[88]

Edgeworth goes to great lengths to stress the essential veracity of her work, insisting in her letters and her textual footnotes that many of her fictional 'scenes, sayings and events are ... factually based.' She claims that her father is the primary inspiration behind her work, and intimates time and again that she is merely recording details that have been faithfully drawn from his life. By using romance in order to facilitate 'the transcription of [this] actuality',[89] though, Edgeworth exposes the 'wish-fulfillment element' of her writing, thereby raising the possibility that she is finally unfolding a distinctly Edgeworthian view of reality to her readers. Ironically, this is made particularly apparent by the extraordinary emphasis that her father places upon the realistic nature of her texts. In his preface to *The parent's assistant*, for instance, he assures the reader that the tales that follow are no mere fantasies: they are, he avers, useful lessons that have been drawn from real life. While writing the tales, great care was taken 'to avoid inflaming the imagination, or exciting a restless spirit of adventure, by exhibiting false views of life, and creating hopes which, in the ordinary course

---

86 Ibid. 53–4. 87 My reading here is informed by Beer's observation that the novel 'is more preoccupied with representing and interpreting a known world, the romance with making apparent the hidden dreams of that world' (*The critical idiom*, 12). 88 Frye, *Secular scripture*, 179. 89 É. Ní Chuilleanáin, introduction, *Belinda*, by Maria Edgeworth, ed. Éilean Ní Chuilleanáin (1993), xxiii.

of things, cannot be realized'. What Edgeworth's father effectively asserts in his preface to *The parent's assistant*, therefore, is that the work is incontrovertibly realistic; that it is, in other words, opposed to romance.[90]

This tacit attack upon romance is made explicit when he quotes Johnson's observation that 'Babies do not like to hear stories of babies like themselves … they require to have their imaginations raised by tales of giants and fairies, and castles and enchantments.' His contention is that, even if this is true, 'why … should [babies] be indulged in reading them? It may be said that a little experience in life would soon convince them, that fairies, giants, and enchanters, are not to be met with in the world. But why should the mind be filled with fantastic visions, instead of useful knowledge?[91] Why should so much valuable time be lost?'[92] This same argument features again in the preface to *Moral tales*. The difficulty of writing for youth is repeated once more, and Edgeworth's father indicates that the work is designed for readers who are older than those of *The parent's assistant*. His further assertion is that the tales that follow 'shall neither dissipate the attention, nor inflame the imagination'.[93] By implying that her works are based upon real life, that is, upon lessons learned from the education of his own children, Edgeworth's father does not of course admit that the 'reality' upon which the didacticism of the texts rests is in itself a type of 'romance' in that what he and Edgeworth offer the readers are works based upon a very particular version of their family. While it can be argued that all texts are always slanted to suit the vision of the author, the Edgeworths' didactic vision meant that they had to be the exemplars of the works that they were producing. Put simply, they had to be the living proof of their own lessons on education. It is this recognition that lends a peculiar significance to the letter that Samuel Taylor Coleridge wrote to Sara, his wife, urging her to read *Practical education*:

> I pray you, my love! read Edgeworth's Essay on Education – read it heart & soul – & if you approve of the mode, teach Hartley his Letters … J. Wedgewood informed me that the Edgeworths were most miserable when Children, & yet the Father, *in his book*, is ever vapouring about

---

90 R.L. Edgeworth, preface, *The parent's assistant*, 1: xi. This argument also informs the preface to *Practical education*, which asserts that the treatise adopts only those precepts that have been proven by 'practice and experience' (1: v). The assertion that the text unfolds a model of education that has been tried and tested in real life effectively opposes the treatise to romantic pedagogical theories; it intimates that the reader can trust the work.   91 This emphasis on 'usefulness' features repeatedly in Edgeworth's work, and will have a particular significance for my reading of *Early lessons*.   92 *The parent's assistant*, 1: xi. There is one fairy story, 'Rivuletta', in *Early lessons*, and it asserts that 'even in the wildest flights of the imagination, reason can trace a moral': M. Edgeworth, *Early lessons*, new edn (1815), 2: 92–3. Richardson for his part reads 'Rivuletta' as 'a rational fairy tale', arguing that 'the relation of didactic writers to the fairytale' might best be described as one of 'appropriation' (*Literature, education, and Romanticism*, 115–16).   93 R.L. Edgeworth, preface, *Moral tales*, 1: vi.

> their *Happiness!* — ! — However there are very good things in the work —
> & some nonsense![94]

This comment of Wedgewood's implies that there exists a different 'version' of the Edgeworth family than that which is constructed by Edgeworth and her father in their work, and this recognition obviously has profound implications for their readers. In the first instance, it challenges the didactic efficacy of the works by exposing what I would term their 'aspirational' nature. It intimates that, contrary to the Edgeworths' didactic assertions, the results of their system are not certain, and that there is no guarantee that the outcomes of Edgeworth's works can be extra-textually reproduced. While this recognition clearly impacts upon all of Edgeworth's work, it particularly affects her Irish writing, for, implicitly, each of her Irish tales revolves around the argument that all of Ireland's difficulties will be necessarily resolved once every one of the nation's landlords replicates her father's example. As the *Memoirs* demonstrate, Edgeworth betrays an overwhelming anxiety to stress the familial and domestic connotations of her father's return to Ireland: 'Things and persons are so much improved in Ireland of latter days, that only those, who can remember how they were some thirty or forty years ago, can conceive the variety of domestic grievances, which, in those times, assailed the master of a family, immediately upon his arrival at his Irish home.' Emphasizing that he was a man 'formed to be loved and respected in Ireland', Edgeworth's insistence is that it was obvious her father 'might hope to be eminently useful in improving the habits and condition of the lower classes of the people'; 'My father began, where all improvements should begin, at home.'

By similarly returning 'home' to their Irish estates, Edgeworth avers, Ireland's erstwhile absentee landlords will effectively recover the true lineaments of their Protestant Ascendancy identity and, more than this, they, too, will discover that their reformation will be necessarily recognized and appreciated by their native dependents. In discovering themselves as enlightened landlords and impartial magistrates to their tenants, she asserts, the Protestant Ascendancy will inevitably reap the rewards of their ontological labours; as she would have it in 'her' volume of his *Memoirs*, each, like her father, will be recognized as 'a *real gentleman*' for coming back. 'This phrase, pronounced with well known emphasis, comprises a great deal in the opinion of the lower Irish. They seem to have an instinct for the *real gentleman*, whom they distinguish, if not at first sight, infallibly at first hearing, from every pretender to the character'.[95]

---

94 Quoted in Richardson, *Literature, education, and Romanticism*, 52.   95 *Memoirs*, 2: 2–5 and 37. We shall see in chapter 4 that very particular (colonial) anxieties inform Edgeworth's desire to treat her father's return to Ireland in this manner in her work.

Edgeworth makes extremely complex use of romance imagery and conventions to sustain this argument in her Irish writing, to all intents and purposes (re)presenting her father's 1782 return to Ireland to her readers as an archetypal quest with apocalyptic consequences for national and imperial reform. In so doing, she illustrates a crucial point about romance: namely, that the production of a romance pleasures the author as well as the reader; that the 'desires' of both are fulfilled by the text that is produced.[96] In this context, we shall see, Edgeworth's use of romance peculiarly satisfies her ambition to turn her father's experiences and theories into the 'the structural core' of her fiction; it allows her, that is, to rehearse a 'vision of [her father's] life as a quest' towards the widespread dissemination of reason and knowledge.[97] By constructing her works around her father's 1782 return to Ireland, moreover, Edgeworth simultaneously demonstrates the efficacy of Frye's contention regarding the way in which the manipulation of time contributes to the wish-fulfilment element of romance fiction. 'Time being irreversible', he notes, 'a return to a starting point [in a text] ... can only be a symbol for something else. The past is not returned to; it is recreated', and an author consequently illustrates the 'selective' nature of memory whenever he or she 'brings' something 'back.' Further, by 'recreat[ing] the past and bring[ing] it into the present', the author at the same time 'bring[s] something into the present which is potential or possible, and in that sense belongs to the future'.[98] To put this another way, he or she illustrates what has been identified as the prophetic nature of romance: specifically, the way in which the mode enables the individual who controls it to impose the effects of his or her 'transfiguring imagination' upon the world, and to therefore ignore the limitations of the reality in which he or she is placed.[99]

This point is important, and I want to elaborate more fully upon the issues that it raises by referring once again to *Don Quixote*. In this work, Cervantes' hero evidences a stubborn refusal to accept the reality in which he finds himself and this propensity, critics insist, may or may not be indicative of the fact that he is finally labouring under a deep-seated psychosis.[1] As the canon observes to Don Quixote at one point:

> How is it possible, any human understanding can persuade itself, there ever was in the world ... so many dragons, so many giants, so many

96 I am drawing here upon Beer's observation that 'Romance is always concerned with the fulfilment of desires' (*The critical idiom*, 12). 97 Frye, *Secular scripture*, 15. 98 Ibid. 175 and 179. 99 Beer, *The critical idiom*, 79 and 41. 1 For instance, Frye points out, 'The Quixote who tries to actualize in his life the romances he has been reading is a psychotic, though a psychotic of unusual literary interest.' He further 'suppose[s] psychosis, or certain forms of it at least, could almost be defined as an attempt to identify one's life "literally" with an imaginative projection' (*Secular scripture*, 178).

unheard-of adventures, so many kinds of enchantments, so many battles, so many furious encounters, so much bravery of attire, so many princesses in love, so many squires become earls, so many witty dwarfs, so many billets-doux, so many courtships, so many valiant women ... so many and such absurd accidents, as your books of knight-errantry contain? (485–6)

While men may read such works and even enjoy them, the canon's argument is that any sane man would 'consider what they are' and throw them from him 'against the wall, [or] ... into the fire, ... for being false and inveigling' (486). To counteract the canon's argument, Don Quixote draws upon the ingenious theory of reality that he has earlier constructed for his squire, Sancho Panza. It is the canon, he maintains, who is 'the madman and the enchanted person', having fallen victim of 'the crew of enchanters [that is] always about us, ... alter[ing] and disguis[ing] all our matters, and turn[ing] them according to their own pleasure ... [into] something else' (487, 219). Don Quixote is convinced that his belief in romance actually protects him from these enchanters: 'the order of chivalry', as he calls it, has 'ways of compounding ... everything' and this enables him to pierce through the delusions that blind other men and so see of what reality is truly made (149).[2]

Cervantes' hero persistently denies the reality in which he finds himself to sustain this argument, and the far-reaching consequences of his strategy are most clearly illustrated for the reader when he and Sancho Panza discuss Dulcinea del Toboso, his beloved. Don Quixote asserts that Dulcinea is 'beautiful and chaste', but Sancho rebuts this, observing that the girl in question is in fact a 'jade', Aldonza Lorenzo, who 'will pitch the bar with the lustiest swain in the parish' (226, 224). To contradict the squire's argument, Don Quixote invokes what has been termed 'the aestheticizing language of "as if"',[3] which enables him not only to impose his 'imaginings' upon Dulcinea del Toboso (and others), but also to 'look upon' his fantastic, as-yet unperformed deeds 'as already done' (289). 'I imagine that everything is exactly as I say, without addition or diminution', he tells Sancho, 'and I represent [Dulcinea] to my thoughts just as I wish her to be both in beauty and quality. Helen is not comparable to her, nor is she excelled by Lucretia, or any other of the famous women of antiquity, whether Grecian, Latin, or Barbarian' (226). By acting *as if* Aldonza Lorenzo is beautiful and chaste, in other words, Don Quixote *makes* her become so; the

2 I am drawing here upon Michael McKeon's argument that Don Quixote adopts 'a quite radical method of "conciliation"' to 'accommodate his readings [of romance] to the minimal demands of real life.' This method is the theory of enchantments, a sophisticated exegetical technique whose great achievement is to close the gap between the a priori pronouncements of romance and the phenomenal appearances of daily life by arguing that things "are" what they appear to be only by virtue of having been transformed from their true, romance state by an enchanter': M. McKeon, *The origins of the English novel* (1987), 280.   3 Ibid. 281.

fact that he 'believe[s]' her to possess these qualities is in itself 'sufficient' to turn her into 'the greatest princess in the world' (226).

We will explore the more complex connotations of this 'aestheticizing' strategy in more detail below, but what must be emphasized here is that it peculiarly illustrates the way in which 'kidnapped romance' frequently 'act[s]' as a narrative veil that hides "the language of ideology".[4] By acting at all times as if what he envisions is real, Don Quixote anticipates making what he envisions become real, but, crucially, this involves persuading others to accept his interpretation of himself and of knightly behaviour. When he and Sancho Panza happen upon some windmills, for example, Don Quixote insists upon casting them as 'monstrous giants' (65). In so doing, though, he observes not only that he 'intend[s]' to fight [them], and take away all their lives', but also that this will 'begin to enrich' both himself and his squire (65). Significantly, Don Quixote immediately insists to Sancho Panza that such actions are entirely warranted: 'it is lawful war, and doing God good service to take away so wicked a generation from off the face of the earth' (65). Similarly, Cervantes' hero advances a very particular reading of chivalric romances in order to justify both his own colonial desires and those of Sancho Panza: 'You must know … that it was a custom much in use among the knights-errant of old, to make their squires governors of the islands or kingdoms they conquered; and I am determined that so laudable a custom shall not be lost for me: on the contrary, I resolve to outdo them in it' (64). As Frye would have it, here and throughout the text, Don Quixote uses the rituals of his beloved chivalric romances to '[express] the ascendancy of [the] horse-riding aristocracy' to which he aspires. That is, he draws upon them in order to 'express … [his] dreams of [his] own social function, and the idealized acts of protection and responsibility that [he] invokes to justify that function.' 'This is the process of … "kidnapping" romance', and it demonstrates that, skilfully used, the genre is an extremely powerful ideological weapon.[5]

Edgeworth, we will see, uses romance with a singular talent. On the one hand, her work (overtly) unfolds a vision of reality that is based upon a distinctly rational ideology, and it implies that, in order to be useful and happy, the individual must cultivate his/her reason and reject the delusions of romance in favour of rational knowledge. On the other, it draws heavily upon romance conventions to facilitate this argument in the first place, thereby (covertly) admitting not only the power and pleasure, but also the crucial necessity of the imaginative life. To put this another way, Edgeworth's work simultaneously reveals her perception that reason alone is not sufficient to (re)negotiate existence, and that the passions and imagination are not only necessary, but also have value. This theme is

4 Elam, *Romancing the postmodern*, 20.   5 Frye, *Secular scripture*, 57. The fact that Don Quixote is not a 'don' at all is more widely significant, of course, and we will treat this issue in greater detail in chapter 4.

present throughout all of Edgeworth's writing, but it is, perhaps, in *Helen* (1834) that it receives its most powerful expression. Published some thirty odd years after *Belinda* (1801), Edgeworth's first-ever novel of manners, *Helen* traces what happens when its young heroine is taken into somebody else's marital home and, as such, has much in common with the earlier work. Like Belinda, Helen discovers that women must make considerable sacrifices in the service of motherhood and marriage and, again like Belinda, comes to realize that women inevitably suffer if they read romances. What makes *Helen* different from *Belinda*, or from any of Edgeworth's other works, however, is the fact that the novel nonetheless offers an explicit, spirited defence of romance, with both the youthful Beauclerc and the mature Lady Davenant eulogizing the attractions and the integrity of the imaginative life. In his passionate defence of romance reading, Beauclerc defends romance texts by not only emphazising their transformative powers, but also by insisting that such works essentially protect the very psyche of the reader. 'It is the curse of age to be ... miserably disenchanted', he observes, 'to outlive all our illusions, all our hopes. That may be my doom in age, but, in youth, the high spring-time of existence, I will not be cursed with such a premature ossification of the heart.' The reading of romance keeps the individual emotionally and imaginatively alive; it protects him or her from the enervating effects of a purely rational life. When she admires Beauclerc's 'power ... of being rapt into future times or past, completely at his author's bidding, to be transported how and where he pleased', Lady Davenant echoes Beauclerc's line of reasoning, lamenting the fact that she is no longer able to sustain such flights of fancy. 'As we advance in life', she remarks,

> it becomes more and more difficult to find any book the sort of enchanting, entrancing interest which we enjoyed when life, and books, and we ourselves were new ... the fact is, that [not] only does the imagination cool and weaken as we grow older, but we become, as we live on in this world, too much engrossed by the real business and cares of life, to have feeling or time for factitious, imaginary interests. But why do I say factitious? while they last, the imaginative interests are as real as any others.[6]

Helen represents Edgeworth's last substantial piece of adult fiction, so it is tempting to suggest that her treatment of this theme here is merely representative of the greater maturity that she herself had inevitably achieved by the time she produced the novel.[7] As we shall see, though, Edgeworth's advancement of this argument in this novel merely gives a particularly explicit expres-

---

6 *Novels and selected works*, 9: 104 and 126.   7 For such an argument, see M. Butler, 'The uniqueness of Cynthia Kirkpatrick' (1972), 289.

sion to a contention that variously informs all of her writing: namely, that the
cultivation of one's reason frequently involves tremendous mental, emotional
and, sometimes, physical suffering. This issue, among others, is peculiarly revealed
in Edgeworth's tales for children and adolescents, where she demonstrates her
acute sense of the pain that the child suffers when his/her imaginative excesses
are (re)directed. In this context, it is evident that readers must beware of reading these works as purely didactic set-pieces; they are, in fact, profoundly subversive, and use romance both to rehearse and interrogate (idealized) patterns
of adulthood as well as childhood and adolescence.

In rehearsing and interrogating these patterns, moreover, Edgeworth not only
devotes considerable attention to the education of the young individual, but also
emphasizes that it must always be remembered that such education has wider,
national and imperial consequences. To this end, she qualifies her arguments
about romance in relation to the young male reader, insisting that, for the good
of Britain and her empire, certain young boys should read particular texts.
Peculiarly conscious that romance reading always unleashes desire in the reader,
Edgeworth's point is that such works must be used to produce those desires that
impel Britain's mercantile and colonial expansion and, further, to regulate those
desires *after* they are produced. This argument of Edgeworth's is very revealing,
for it demonstrates that at least one of her intentions in her work is to use
romance as a veil to hide or disguise the less appealing aspects of that ideology
upon which colonial and imperial expansion are based. Rather than addressing
Britain's involvement in slavery and the slave trade directly, she consequently uses
romance to facilitate the construction of a 'paternalistic' vision of reality; as she
would have it, Britons are necessarily honourable and virtuous and so it is to
everyone's benefit that Britain should spread its influence across the face of the
earth. The terms of this colonizing romance are manifestly informed by
Edgeworth's analysis of the social and political situation in late-eighteenth- and
early-nineteenth-century Ireland and, in particular, by her acute consciousness
of her membership of a colonizing class. Faced with the difficulty of negotiating Ireland's colonial situation in her work, she tries to deny or to disguise it,
constructing a vision of Ireland in her writing that both justifies and facilitates
the continuing presence of the colonizing class that she herself represents. In so
doing, of course, Edgeworth concomitantly betrays her perception that the vision
of Ireland that she is producing in her writing is *literally* a fiction, and we shall
see that this recognition is incredibly important to our understanding of how
romance operates in not only her Irish tales, but also all of her work.

CHAPTER ONE

Romancing childhood and adolescence

Letters for literary ladies and *Practical education* stress the importance of a proper early education for children, one that is preferably conducted at home under the eye of a benevolent mother. They insist that only through such an education can a young person be properly prepared to take his or her place in society; girls must receive a different education to that of boys, but both sexes must be persuaded to use their reason to govern their actions and thoughts. In this context, Edgeworth places a singular emphasis upon reading, and the didactic message of her writing is that care should be taken so that women in particular are only exposed to appropriate books; unlike romances, such works will have an entirely beneficial effect upon woman: they will convince her that her own best interests are 'naturally' served by embracing domestic life. In this way, Edgeworth attempts to diffuse and contain cultural anxieties surrounding the issue of women's education; the rational literary lady, she insists, will necessarily contribute to the stability of the existing (patriarchal) social order.

Once we begin to read Edgeworth's works closely, it becomes apparent that each contributes to a greater didactic enterprise and, as such, that no text should be read in isolation from the others. This can even be seen from the publication details of her works. *The parent's assistant: or stories for children* was published in 1796, *Moral tales for young people* in 1801, *Early lessons* between 1801 and 1802, and *Popular tales* in 1804;[1] within the same period, she published *Practical education* in 1798, *Castle Rackrent* in 1800, *Belinda* in 1801, and *Essay on Irish bulls* and *The modern Griselda* in 1802; so it is not surprising that the themes in Edgeworth's works persistently overlap, especially given the often-lengthy intervals that existed between the composition of a text and its eventual date of publication. 'Lame Jervas', for example, was published in *Popular tales* in 1804, although Edgeworth completed the tale itself in 1799.[2] A central theme of

---

1 The composition and publication details of Edgeworth's works are complicated. 'The bracelets', for example, was written in the 1780s, but was not published until 1796 in *The parent's assistant*. 'The purple jar', one of the most celebrated of Edgeworth's tales, was first published in *The parent's assistant* in 1796, and thereafter appeared with the 'Rosamond' tales in *Early lessons* (1801–2). See Butler, *Maria Edgeworth*, 155–65. 2 M. Edgeworth, *Popular tales* (1804) 1: 1–132.

this tale is its celebration of the English way of life and, by implication, of the forces that impel imperial expansion. Between 1799 and the publication of *Popular tales*, England, and its empire, were subjects that hugely preoccupied Edgeworth, as she witnessed the profound effects which the Act of Union had upon Irish politics and society. In this sense, the spirited defence of the English system that lies at the heart of 'Lame Jervas' has implications for the issues of national identity that are raised by *Castle Rackrent*. Each work in its own way attempts to diffuse explosive issues of class and racial identity by envisaging a future in which different societies, and social orders, reach accommodation through mutual respect.[3]

The realization that Edgeworth's tales for children and adolescents are ultimately implicated in national stability and imperial expansion is extremely important. The eighteenth century 'was a turning point in the recognition of childhood as a period with its own distinctive requirements.' Newly invented toys for children made their appearance in newly rational toyshops, but what was even more significant was the huge outpouring of children's literature that took place by the end of the century: 'Between 1750 and 1814 some twenty professional writers of children's books produced some 2,400 different titles'.[4] Crucially, this new literature did much more than entertain its readers: it also sought to contribute directly to their education. These books played a significant role in constructing the notion of childhood that was emerging at the end of the eighteenth and beginning of the nineteenth century; they were 'designed to attract adults, to project an image of those virtues which parents wished to inculcate in their offspring, as well as to beguile the child'.[5] Illustrating the argument that texts for children in general function as 'key agents of socialization[,] diagram[ing] what cultures want of their young and expect of those who tend them,'[6] we can therefore see that

> The construction of childhood in an age of revolution and reform is
> neither a politically disinterested nor an ideologically neutral matter.
> In order to grasp the historical significance of the rise of a child-cen-
> tred British culture, it is necessary to explore links between education,
> ideology, and power within a society that underwent a profound shift

3 My arguments here are also illustrated by Edgeworth's decision to include 'The little merchants' in *The parent's assistant* from the 1800 edition. This tale is set in Naples, and an important point of the narrative is that Arthur, its English hero, refuses to entertain a prejudicial opinion of Neapolitan society.   4 L. Stone, *The family, sex and marriage in England* (1979), 258. J.H. Plumb similarly remarks, 'there can be no doubt that the children's world of the eighteenth century – at least for those born higher up the social scale than the labouring poor – changed dramatically': J.H. Plumb, 'The new world of children in eighteenth-century England' (1975), 65.   5 Plumb, 'The new world of children in eighteenth-century England', 81.   6 M. Myers, 'Impeccable governesses, rational dames, and moral mothers' (1986), 33.

from traditional hierarchical structures of domination to more con-
sensual forms of managing political and social relations.[7]

In other words, this new literature played its part in underpinning the social order
by cultivating very particular attitudes to gender, class and race in its readers. The
final aim of this literature was overtly didactic: its ambition was to 'manage' the
child *and* the parent both inside and outside of the text that was produced.[8]

Not surprisingly, perhaps, readers and critics for a long time responded
purely to the didactic level of such works, failing to appreciate how female writers in particular 'smuggle[d] … their own symptomatic fantasies' into their
writing. '[H]owever tirelessly didactic and ostensibly down to earth' such works
may appear, after all,

> [the] paradigms of benign and powerful maternal governance and good
> girlhood [that they depict] reflect both female fantasies and real cul-
> tural change. On the one hand they read nurture as power, showing a
> decided preference for maturity over the childishness male preceptors
> recommend to women and perhaps also evincing a longing to have been
> nurtured themselves, for a surprisingly large number of the [Georgian]
> period's women writers record unhelpful or absent mothers.[9]

In her pioneering readings of Edgeworth's literature for children and adolescents, Mitzi Myers has suggested how Edgeworth uses her tales both to rewrite
her own childhood and negotiate 'the paternal *and* maternal narratives and languages made available to her by her culture.' By 'Romancing the moral tale', as
she would have it, Edgeworth transforms her stories into 'the site of maternal
longing and magical thinking as much as reason and "useful knowledge", of
feelings as well as the "facts" that the preface lauds'.[10] My analysis of
Edgeworth's tales for children and adolescents has much in common with that
of Myers; like her, for instance, I believe that Edgeworth uses her tales to
romanticize and rewrite her early life. In doing this, though, Edgeworth clearly
labours under what we have already identified as her overriding compulsion in
her work: namely, her desire to rehearse and celebrate her father's achievements
and theories. While 'narrativiz[ing] female fantasy', Edgeworth thus simultaneously endeavours to celebrate her father's didactic vision, and we are going

7 Richardson, *Literature, education, and Romanticism,* 24–5. 8 I am drawing here upon Richardson's argument: 'In the
children's literature which developed during the final decades of the eighteenth century … the child inside the
text was to be as manageable as the child outside the text' (*Literature, education, and Romanticism,* 145). 9 Myers,
'Impeccable governesses, rational dames, and moral mothers', 34 and 54–5. 10 M. Myers, 'Romancing the moral
tale' (1991), 100–1.

to explore how she attempts to use romance conventions to facilitate both of these ends.

In the interests of 'managing' the textual and extra-textual child and parent, Edgeworth's works in the first instance plainly keep an eye on their adult as well as their child audience. In two of the tales in *The parent's assistant*, for example, Edgeworth contrasts two little boys and the types of education that they receive from their fathers. The hero of 'Lazy Lawrence' is the good-natured and hard-working Jem, while Francisco is the exemplary little boy in 'The little merchants.' One aim of each of these tales is to persuade their young readers to emulate these hard-working and honest little boys, but another is to impress upon their paternal readers that they will be punished like the fathers of Lawrence and Piedro if they similarly neglect the education of their children. 'Lazy Lawrence' pointedly observes that Lawrence's father 'was an alehouse-keeper, and being generally drunk, could take no care of his son; so that Lazy Lawrence grew every day worse and worse.' At the end of the tale, this father is publicly shamed when he discovers that it is his son who is being led away as a thief: '"I *will* – I tell you, I *will* see the thief!" cried the drunken man, pushing up the boy's hat. It was his own son. "Lawrence!" exclaimed the wretched father. The shock sobered him at once, and he hid his face in his hands'.[11] In the same way, Piedro's father in 'The little merchants' discovers that it is foolish to believe that nothing much matters when a child is '*but a child*.' Piedro is led away to prison at the end of the tale, with his father likewise having learned that 'it was scarcely reasonable to expect, that a boy who had been educated to think that he might cheat every customer he could in the way of trade, should be afterwards scrupulously honest in his conduct towards the father whose proverbs encouraged his childhood in cunning'.[12]

Similarly, 'The good French governess', which appears in *Moral tales*, traces how the exemplary Madame de Rosier re-educates both the Harcourt children and their mother. This lady 'had good abilities, but, as she lived in a constant round of dissipation, she had not time to cultivate her understanding, or to attend to the education of her family'; by the end of the tale, Mrs Harcourt has undergone a dramatic transformation: she has seen through the artificial pleasures of the social whirl and consequently abandoned them for the more permanent attractions of domestic life. Crucially, Edgeworth's tale emphasizes that this is neither a sudden nor a painless transformation on Mrs Harcourt's part, and the fact that it at first involves some very real difficulties for the mother is central to the story. Mrs Harcourt is engaged in an ontological struggle: she is trying, that is, to cast out the demons that have prompted her to inappropriate

11 Edgeworth, *The parent's assistant*, 1: 8 and 43. 12 Ibid. 2: 53 and 67.

behaviour. Thus, Edgeworth observes, Mrs Harcourt was not immediately 'quite so happy, as she had expected' when she first decided to stay at home: 'They, who have only seen children in picturesque situations, are not aware, how much the duration of this domestic happiness depends upon those, who have the care of them. People who ... are unexperienced in education, should not be surprised or mortified, if their first attempts be not attended with success.' By the time the tale closes, Mrs Harcourt's transformation has been successfully completed and, faced with Madame de Rosier's imminent departure, she fears greatly for the future of her children. These fears, however, were 'the best omens for her future success; a sensible mother, in whom the desire to educate her family has once been excited, ... may trust securely to her own preserving cares. Whatever a mother learns, for the sake of her children, she never forgets'.[13]

It is clear from each of these examples that the representation of the child *or* the parent is also a reconstitution of the child *or* the parent, and that, as such, a powerful wish-fulfilment element invariably informs the writing of all children's texts. Whether they function as 'a locus for personal longing', or as a site for 'reformist fantasy',[14] such works do not merely represent the world, they seek to (re)create it: specifically, they try to persuade the reader to extra-textually replicate the (idealized) vision of reality that the author has produced. If this recognition clearly has several important consequences for Edgeworth's tales for children and adolescents, it in the first place calls attention to Richard Lovell Edgeworth's singular emphasis that his daughter's readers will find neither fantasy nor illusion in her books. As we have already seen, Edgeworth's father insists in his prefaces to these works that they are the direct result of careful observation of (his) children; they contain, he avers, useful lessons faithfully drawn from real life.

To underpin this argument, Edgeworth's father calls attention to the compositional details of *The parent's assistant*, emphasizing, for instance, that the work is the immediate result of a real-life mother's educational experiments. While it 'seems ... a very easy task to write for children', only those

> who have been interested in the education of a family, who have
> patiently followed children through the first processes of reasoning,

---

13 Edgeworth, *Moral tales*, 3: 2, 75 and 144. The fact that Mrs Harcourt is engaged in an ontological struggle is expertly illustrated at one particular moment in the narrative. When her children send her an invitation to stay at home one evening in order to sample radishes that her son, Herbert, has grown, Mrs Harcourt sends her card with the reply that 'if she had a hundred other invitations, she would accept of his' (3: 58). Mrs Grace, her maid, is subsequently amazed when she discovers the feathers with which she has previously dressed the hair of her mistress abandoned on a table. The symbolism of this is unmistakable: Mrs Harcourt is literally changing her feathers. 14 M. Myers, 'Socialising Rosamond' (1989), 52.

who have daily watched over their thoughts and feelings; those only
who know with what ease and rapidity the early associations of ideas
are formed on which the future taste, character, and happiness, depend,
can feel the dangers and difficulties of such an undertaking.

Effectively, Edgeworth's father claims that she is only able to write the work
that follows because of the prior efforts of the second Mrs Edgeworth. From
1776, he tells the reader, a 'register' was kept in which were noted observations
regarding the education of the Edgeworth children, and '[t]hese notes have been
of great advantage to the writer of the following stories'.[15] In this sense, then,
the preface to *The parent's assistant* anticipates the argument in the preface to
Practical education, where Edgeworth's father similarly attributes the original 'design'
of that work to his second wife. Having carefully explained the contributions
made by himself, Lovell Edgeworth[16] and Dr Thomas Beddoes,[17] he insists that
his daughter was guided by the example of her late stepmother, Honora, in
writing 'the rest' of the work:

> She was encouraged and enabled to write upon this important subject,
> by having for many years before her eyes the conduct of a judicious
> mother in the education of a large family. The chapter on Obedience
> was written from Mrs Edgeworth's notes,[18] and was exemplified by her
> successful practice in the management of her children; the whole man-
> uscript was submitted to her judgement, and she revised parts of it in
> the last stage of a fatal disease.[19]

In this way, Honora Edgeworth is revealed to be the major influence behind
both *Practical education* and *The parent's assistant*; she, according to her husband,
effectively 'mothered' both works.

Edgeworth assists this argument of her father's by taking great pains to
link the didactic lessons of her works to the experiences of real-life (Edgeworth)
children; she repeatedly uses footnotes in her stories, and the cumulative effect
of this is that the factual reality of the fiction she is creating is effectively underlined. When the heroine of 'Simple Susan' tries to bake bread just like her

---

15 R.L. Edgeworth, preface, *The parent's assistant*, 1: vi–viii.   16 Lovell Edgeworth (1775–1842) was Richard Lovell
Edgeworth's son by his second wife, Honora Sneyd.   17 For an account of Beddoes' courtship of Anna, Edgeworth's
sister, see Butler, *Maria Edgeworth*, 109–11.   18 In the appendix to *Practical education*, Edgeworth describes the inestimable contribution of Honora: 'Several years ago a mother, who had a large family to educate, and who had
turned her attention with much solicitude to the subject of education, resolved to write notes from day to day
of all the trifling things which mark the progress of the mind in childhood. She was of opinion, that the art of
education should be considered as an experimental science, and that many authors of great abilities had mistaken
their road by following theory instead of practice' (2: 733–4).   19 R.L. Edgeworth, preface, *Practical education*, 1: x.

mother, for example, a footnote to the tale observes, 'This circumstance is founded on fact.'[20] When Charles Howard remarks in 'The good aunt' that diamonds should be used to weigh diamonds so 'then the changes in the weight of the air would not signify one way or the other', a footnote tells us this observation was likewise 'literally made by a boy of ten years old'.[21] Similarly, when the fictional Frank in *Early lessons* spends an hour and a half putting a jigsaw together, the reader is told that he is merely emulating a real-life 'boy of four years old, [who] spent, voluntarily, above an hour and a half, in attempts to put together a joining map'.[22] By giving instances such as these, Edgeworth underlines the credibility of her fiction and, by implication, her own credibility as a writer of educational texts. Moreover, these footnotes also help her to impress the efficacy of the didactic theories that she is unfolding upon her readers; they suggest that what the reader is reading has already been proven in the Edgeworth household, so that he or she can have perfect confidence that what he or she is reading *can* be reproduced.

This strategy has a further consequence for Edgeworth's writing, of course, in that it helps to break down the division that exists between the tale and the reader. In 'Frank', for example, a footnote is appended to the story of how Henry lends his brother his 'box full of little bricks'; these 'little bricks', it says, 'were made of plaster of Paris', and it details their physical dimensions: the bricks become peculiarly real for the reader: the footnote implies that they truly exist somewhere outside of the fictional sphere and that readers can similarly reproduce them in their own homes.[23] Edgeworth takes this blurring of fiction and reality a step further in 'Eton montem', a three-act play in *The parent's assistant*. At one point, Louisa and Violetta are engaged in activities related to the reading of Edgeworth's 'The little merchants'; Violetta is reading the story and Louisa tries 'to draw the pictures of the little merchants' at her request.[24] By enclosing one piece of fiction in another, Edgeworth helps to break down the distance between the fictional characters and the children who read, or act out, the tale, thereby illustrating the efficacy of Alan Richardson's contention that the ultimate aim of such fiction was to 'manage' the child both within and outside the text. As he puts it,

> By drawing the child reader into a fictional world, and then inscribing it (and teaching it to inscribe itself) with a series of moral narratives geared to developmental stages, the children's book was designed to have a material effect on the middle-class child it typically portrayed;

---

20 *The parent's assistant*, 1: 171. 21 *Moral tales*, 3: 21. 22 Edgeworth, *Early lessons*, 1: 186. 23 *Early Lessons*, 1: 191–2. 24 *The parent's assistant*, 3: 292.

it simultaneously represented and attempted to embody in its readers, the bourgeois vision of the child as innocent and manageable. The goal this genre set itself was one of reforming the child in every sense – capitalizing on the alleged textual quality of the child's mind to make word become flesh and flesh become word.[25]

In Edgeworth's writing, this making of word into flesh and flesh into word has a strangely cyclical nature: the Edgeworth children have already become words in texts, and the aim of these texts is to make flesh of these words once more.

As I noted in my introduction, the recognition of this compulsion in Edgeworth's work for children and adolescents raises some intriguing points for the reader. Firstly, by implying in his prefaces that these tales are based upon real life, Edgeworth's father does not admit that this 'reality' is in itself a type of fiction, or romance, in that is explicitly designed to convince the reader of the happy effects of his educational experiments upon his family. The Edgeworths thus assert in *Practical education*, for example: 'Amongst a large family of children, who have never been tormented with artificial trials of temper, and who have been made as happy as it was in the power of their parents to make them, there is not one ill-tempered child. We have examples everyday before us of different ages from three years old to fifteen'.[26] However, we saw earlier that at least one acquaintance of the Edgeworth family insisted that 'the Edgeworths were most miserable when Children',[27] and Edgeworth family correspondence, indeed, hints at the essential loneliness and pain of Edgeworth's early life.[28] Similarly, Richard Lovell Edgeworth's 'vapouring about [his children's] *Happiness*', as Coleridge so eloquently puts it, makes no mention of any pedagogical failures. Most obviously, it carefully excludes any mention of the disastrous effects of his educational experiments with Richard, his eldest child (1764–96). Clearly, the version of Edgeworthian childhood that Edgeworth unfolds in her works is aspirational as well as selective; its primary ambition is to persuade the reader that her father's paradigm of education really works and that it must be reproduced. The didactic level of these works therefore revolves around one central (romanticized) message: that the reader who faithfully replicates the theories unfolded in the tales will inevitably (re)produce an ideal (adult or) child.

25 Richardson, *Literature, education, and Romanticism*, 141. 26 *Practical education*, 1: 171. 27 See pages 36–7 above. 28 Marilyn Butler quotes in her biography from a letter written by one of Edgeworth's half-sisters in 1838, wherein she recalls Edgeworth's painful recollection of her early life. Writing to Michael Pakenham Edgeworth, Harriet Butler observes, '[Maria] remembered in Dublin getting out of a garret window on the window stool when she was about 6 yr old and some passenger running in and telling the maid of the child's danger and when the maid said as she took her in, "Do you know you might have fallen down and broken your neck and been killed" and Maria answered "I wish I had – I'm very unhappy" – so piteous the idea of so little a child being so very wretched' (*Maria Edgeworth*, 46–7).

Still, Edgeworth's tales for children and adolescents are not simply didactic set pieces, and they do much more than merely rehearse the pedagogical achievements and theories of her father. Their ambition, yes, is to turn words into flesh, but they nonetheless intimate Edgeworth's perception that this process will have profoundly detrimental effects upon the passions and imaginative life of the child or adolescent. What all of the children in Edgeworth's tales in the first instance discover, therefore, is that they can never be entirely sure of the affection and approval of their parents. This affection and approval, the tales intimate, is not an unconditional gift by a parent to its offspring: it is, instead, something that the child or adolescent has to earn. As we shall see, all of Edgeworth's writing for children and adolescents directly equates the child's or adolescent's efforts towards self-improvement with the securing of parental affection, and it requires no great leap of imagination to trace the origins of this equation back to the childhood experiences of their author. In a letter to her Aunt Charlotte Sneyd in 1780, for example, Edgeworth writes, 'I have lately received so much pleasure, from the approbation my friends have bestowed on my conduct, that I hope it will determine me to use every effort, to improve myself, to oblige them, by assiduously attending to whatever they recommend to me'.[29] Edgeworth here demonstrates the extent to which she has internalized her father's maxim that, in order to be happy, she must first of all be good and useful, and it is, finally, precisely this ideological formation that informs all of her works for children and adolescents.

Nor is it difficult to argue that the responses of Edgeworth's fictional children and adolescents to their rational mothers have their origins in her responses to the second Mrs Edgeworth, the implied 'mother' of these works. Upon marrying, Honora Sneyd effectively 'inherited' Edgeworth, along with the three other surviving children of her husband's first marriage. While this cannot have been an easy task, Honora's letters make clear that she was a strict disciplinarian, with very firm views as to how children should be raised. Writing to one of her husband's sisters, Mrs Margaret Ruxton, for instance, she declared,

> It is my opinion that almost everything that education can give, is to be given before the age of 5 or 6 – therefore I think great attention & strictness should be shewn before that age; particularly, if there is anything refractory or rebellious in the disposition, that is the time to repress it, & to substitute good habits, obedience, attention, & respect towards superiors.[30]

29 Maria Edgeworth to Aunt Charlotte Sneyd, 19 Oct. 1780, letter 34. 30 Mrs Honora Edgeworth to Mrs Ruxton, no date [? 1776], letter 10 A.

As the editors of *A memoir of Maria Edgeworth* would have it, Edgeworth was from her very earliest days conscious of the superiority of both her father and her first stepmother. They insist that she 'recollected all her life the minutest advice which Mrs Honora Edgeworth gave to her. She felt great awe of her at the time, but she was long afterwards sensible of her justice, and of the habits of exactness and order in which she trained her.'[31] This analysis of her relationship with her first stepmother is carefully worded, though, and it is tempting to suggest that she herself provided a much more faithful (re)appraisal of this relationship in her writing. As Marilyn Butler notes, for example, when she produced *Helen*, her last substantial piece of adult fiction, Edgeworth revealed that she drew a very particular moral from this novel:

> talented mothers should take care not to make their children afraid of them so as to prevent them from telling the truth & trusting them with their faults & secrets at the time when youth most wants anothers counsel & assistance. In short the moral of Lady Davenant's character is that talents should make themselves objects of Love not fear.[32]

Coolly rational mothers, much like Honora Edgeworth, feature throughout Edgeworth's writing, and she overwhelmingly associates them with childhood suffering in her texts. Such mothers inevitably subject their children to very real mental and sometimes physical pain in the interests of cultivating their rational minds. It would be far better, Edgeworth seems to imply, if such mothers concentrated first of all upon loving their children, thereby making allowances for the power and the pleasure of the child's imaginative life. To illustrate what I am suggesting here, I am first of all going to refer to the 'Rosamond' series of tales, which contains, perhaps, the most (in)famous of all of Edgeworth's mothers. This lady tries to persuade her 'impetuous, fallible' daughter that she should be governed by her reason,[33] insisting that Rosamond will suffer greatly in the future if she does not learn to regulate her actions and thoughts. What the 'Rosamond' series reveals, however, is that she suffers greatly *as a child* as a consequence of her mother's efforts, and the recognition that this may in the end prove counter-productive is central to Edgeworth's writing.

In the most celebrated of all these stories, 'The purple jar', when Rosamond and her mother take a walk together through the streets of London, Rosamond's eyes light upon first one object and then another as they pass by a succession of shop windows and, being a typical child, she wants to buy everything that

31 F. Edgeworth, *A memoir of Maria Edgeworth*, 1: 3. 32 Maria Edgeworth to Lucy Edgeworth, 6 Jan. 1836, quoted in Butler, *Maria Edgeworth*, 476. 33 Butler, *Maria Edgeworth*, 160.

she sees. Exasperated by her mother's insistence that nothing that she desires is useful, Rosamond finally pleads with her mother to let her buy a purple jar that she has seen in a chemist's window. Rosamond's mother responds that her daughter cannot be sure she 'should like the purple vase *exceedingly*, till [Rosamond has] examined it more attentively'.[34] In other words, she tries to use reason to control Rosamond's imagination and thereby introduces a distinctly utilitarian view of reality into the story. Significantly, Rosamond tries to justify the purchase of the jar by reshaping her desire so that it more nearly resembles that of her mother. Pointing out that she will be able to use the emptied out jar as a flower pot, she counters her mother's elevation of utility over beauty by insisting that something that is beautiful can also be of use.

This elevation of utility over beauty, or of reason over the imagination, is replicated throughout the 'Rosamond' series, and the didactic implication of the tales is that important gender issues always simmer beneath the heroine's choices. Every such choice faces Rosamond with a crucial decision: specifically, whether to become more like her mother or to cling, instead, to the inappropriate delusions of the imaginative life. In light of this, the choice that Rosamond makes in 'The two plums' is of particular importance, for, faced with choosing between a 'housewife' in which she can keep her needles and a stone which has been painted to resemble a plum, she symbolically chooses the housewife. This, she insists, will be 'most *useful*' to her, as it will help her to 'cure' herself of her 'little faults'.[35] If Rosamond's choice on the one hand illustrates that she is learning that she must suppress her imaginative desire, it on the other clearly signals that she is beginning to perceive why her mother is encouraging her to use her reason to govern her actions and thoughts. As a future wife and mother, Rosamond is starting to appreciate that she must make choices that will suit her for her future role in society; she must learn, that is, to accommodate her 'self' to the limitations of domestic life.

Although Edgeworth's writing intimates that both parents must carefully supervise their daughter's rite of passage towards responsible womanhood, the pointed emphasis of the 'Rosamond' series is that this duty in the first instance devolves upon the mother. The tales examine in particular how Rosamond's mother rationally instructs her daughter, preparing her to replicate *her* rational self. In 'Rosamond's day of misfortunes', for instance, Rosamond's mother warns her that she 'will not gain any thing by ill-humour.' She thereby rehearses the Friend's argument in *Letters for literary ladies* and effectively equates a woman's

---

34 *Early lessons*, 2: 7. As I noted earlier, 'The purple jar' was originally published in the 1796 edition of *The parent's assistant* and, from 1801, was included in *Early lessons*. My references are to the 1815 edition of the latter text. 35 *Early lessons*, 2: 29–30.

command of her temper to future profit or loss.[36] Rosamond's tardiness in getting out of bed precipitates a succession of misfortunes and, realizing that she
will be late for breakfast, she grows increasingly out of sorts. When she finally
makes a belated appearance in the breakfast room, however, Rosamond remembers her mother's advice, summons up all of her powers of self-control, and is
consequently praised by her father for her ability to 'command' her temper.
When Rosamond later discusses the day's events with her mother, this lady
rehearses an argument that clearly illustrates her perception of her particular
duties as a patriarchal agent. Her ambition (and function) as a mother, she
observes, is to help Rosamond 'to manage [herself] so as to make [her] wise,
and good, and happy', but, 'unless [she] knows what passes in [Rosamond's]
little mind', she cannot accomplish this. Significantly, the tale concludes by
revealing what the child gains by voluntarily submitting to this process of rational instruction: Rosamond is praised for having the good sense to free a robin
that she has saved, and her 'mother stroked her daughter's hair upon her fore-
head as she spoke, and then gave her two kisses'.[37]

Overwhelmingly, the 'Rosamond' tales therefore demonstrate and interrogate both sides of the process through which a daughter is educated to become
more like her mother, and the series recognizes that the child will inevitably
suffer mentally, and sometimes physically, before the completion of this transformation. All of the choices that Rosamond makes in the series are in the first
instance predicated upon what she learns in 'The purple jar';[38] that her mother
will allow her to suffer pain in order to cultivate her reason is an essential point
in the story. Having taken the jar home, Rosamond empties it of its contents,
and is amazed to discover that it was but 'a plain white glass jar, which had
appeared to have that beautiful colour, merely from the liquor with which it
had been filled.' Not surprisingly, she bursts into tears when she makes this discovery, but it is important to note that her disappointment arises directly out
of her efforts to please her mother: before the jar was emptied out, it was beautiful, and it was this beauty, and not its utility, that Rosamond craved. Further,
before she purchases the jar for her daughter, Rosamond's mother warns her
that its purchase will mean that she will not be able to have for another month
the new pair of shoes that she badly needs. The tale then observes, 'many were
the difficulties and distresses, into which [Rosamond's] imprudent choice
brought her, before the end of the month. Every day her shoes grew worse and

36 The Friend's argument is that the tempers of young girls must be cultivated so that they learn to be happy in
whatever situations they are eventually placed (*Letters for literary ladies*, 20).   37 *Early lessons*, 2: 52–4, 61 and 76.   38
In 'The two plums', as we have seen, Rosamond chooses the useful housewife over a beautiful painted stone and,
in 'The hyacinths', she wisely decides not to pick her hyacinth flowers but to let them die back completely so she
can enjoy them again next spring (*Early lessons*, 2: 108–15).

worse, till at last she could neither run, dance, jump, or walk in them.' This is in itself bad enough, but the fact that Rosamond suffers in other ways as well is essential to the tale's didactic purpose: she is unable to accompany her mother on walks, and her father refuses to take her with her brother on a trip to a glasshouse because she is 'slip-shod'.[39] As a result of the purple jar, Rosamond eventually perceives that her mother will use pain as a learning device, and her reaction to her mother in 'The thorn' reveals how expertly she learns this lesson. In this tale, her mother wishes to use a needle to remove a thorn that has lodged in her daughter's finger, but Rosamond is afraid, and observes that she would prefer if the thorn were not removed. This causes her brother to laugh at her, but their mother stops him, saying: 'Had not we better reason with Rosamond than laugh at her?' Rosamond's response is particularly significant: '"Yes, mamma, let us reason," said Rosamond; but she still kept her hand behind her'.[40] The mother's argument, of course, would be that she is subjecting her daughter to minor pain now in the interests of preventing her from experiencing much greater suffering later. Either way, the 'Rosamond' tales illustrate the heroine's growing perception of the fact that her mother will allow her to be hurt.

This use of pain as a learning device features repeatedly throughout Edgeworth's writing for children.[41] In 'Frank', for instance, the hero of the tales is explicitly directed by his parents to associate painful sensations with the lesson that he has learned,[42] and the patent intimation of the tale is that physical pain is a useful tool for governing a child's behaviour. Similarly, we have already seen how one point of a story like 'The little merchants' is that the parent who spares the rod and spoils the child inevitably comes to regret his or her actions. This argument patently illuminates a contention that is central to *Practical education*: 'To make punishment intelligible to children, it must be not only *immediately*, but *repeatedly* and *uniformly*, associated with the actions which we wish them to avoid'.[43] If physical pain is detailed in Edgeworth's writing for children, however, so, too, is mental suffering, and the poignant lesson that characters like Rosamond or Frank ultimately learn is that they must negotiate their way into their parents' affections. The tales therefore stress again and again that, in order

---

39 *Early lessons*, 2: 13–16. 40 Ibid. 2: 100. 41 See 'The little dog Trusty', or 'The orange man; or, the honest boy and the thief', for example, both of which are also in *Early lessons*. In both tales, Edgeworth's narrative indicates that suffering in childhood may spare the individual from something much worse in later life. 42 For instance, Frank develops the habit of fidgeting with his buttons whenever he is trying to recollect something and this causes him to fall from a swing. Frank's parents encourage him to associate the pain of the fall with his fidgeting, suggesting this should provide a powerful incentive to help him cure himself of this habit (*Early Lessons*, 1: 122–4). Intriguingly, Frank's habit of fidgeting is obviously based in part upon the childhood tendency of Edgeworth's father to stand 'upon one leg, buckling and unbuckling [his] shoe', while he learned his lessons. Ordered to stand still when repeating his lesson, his 'memory was directly at fault' and all his 'associations were broken.' 'A *good* whipping', he recalls, 'cured [him] of the trick, and of what *appeared to be* obstinacy or stupidity' (*Memoirs*, 1: 47). 43 *Practical education*, 1: 231.

to be sure of the love of his or her parent, a child must first of all be useful; they infer that it is simply not enough to have an affectionate heart.[44]

This emphasis on the child having to earn parental approval and affection leads us back to Edgeworth and to her own childhood once more, and it demonstrates that, 'if educators invent children, children turned educators invent juvenile selves that simultaneously support and subvert parental premises'.[45] Writing from 'the child's place',[46] Edgeworth thus faithfully rehearses the didactic imperatives that underpin the Edgeworthian system of education, but she also reveals that children inevitably suffer emotionally and physically as a result of this model, both inside and outside of the text.[47] Further, Edgeworth's writing for children affords her another particular privilege: it allows her to (re)construct (her) childhood in the image of *her* imagination and heart. In the 'Rosamond' tales, this means that Edgeworth is able to produce a series of stories in which she is both mother and daughter, and where 'the narrative environment' offers her 'a way to mother herself more satisfyingly than [she was in] real life.' As Myers puts it: 'The maternal writer teases and teaches her juvenile self in the interest of more rational girl readers, but writing as daughter she celebrates that self's imaginative energy and effective needs; better than her mothers real or represented inside the text, the author as mother understands and nurtures the author as daughter'.[48]

If the subversive possibilities of such a strategy are clearly enormous,[49] they are in the first instance, perhaps, best illustrated by the way in which Edgeworth represents Rosamond's 'all wise, antisentimental [*sic*] mother' for the reader.[50]

---

44 In 'Frank', for example, the little boy learns from his mother that 'people like those that are useful to them.' 'I like to be liked, mamma, by you, more than by any body', he observes, 'so I will try always to be as useful to you as I can' (*Early lessons*, 1: 135–6). Rosamond echoes these sentiments in 'The two little plums', noting that her mother 'would smile a great deal more, and be a great deal more pleased with [her]' if she could 'quite entirely' cure herself of her faults (*Early lessons*, 2: 28). 45 M. Myers, 'The dilemmas of gender as double-voiced narrative' (1988), 83. 46 Myers, 'Romancing the moral tale', 101. 47 Myers does not focus upon this particular dimension of Edgeworth's writing in her reading of 'The purple jar', but she nonetheless concludes, 'so vivid are Rosamond's eye and voice that Edgeworth's child self and her mature authorial message coexist in a fruitful tension unusual for the Georgian moral tale, so much so that the subplot of the child's perspective balances and partially undoes the surface plot' ('Socializing Rosamond', 56). 48 Myers, 'The dilemmas of gender as double-voiced narrative', 76–9 and 84. 49 This recognition prompts Myers to read one of Edgeworth's most famous tales for children, 'Simple Susan', as 'a pastoral romance of child empowerment ... [where Edgeworth] fantasizes a family romance in which she remothers herself by rescuing her parents, in effect giving birth to the familial status, and the ideal self she desires, while creating a textual *locus amoenus* that embodies maternal values and thus remothers her child readers as well' ('Romancing the moral tale', 98–9). Crucially, Edgeworth presents her readers with a heroine whose character is essentially established, and infers that love was the primary agent in effecting Susan's maturation. Susan thus significantly observes, '[My mother] taught me to knit, she taught me everything that I know ... and, best of all, she taught me to love her, to wish to be like her' (*The parent's assistant*, 1: 165). The moral of Edgeworth's tale, clearly, is that all mothers should learn from Mrs Price's example: they should realise that, if they wish to turn their daughters into women like themselves, they must secure their affections first. 50 Myers, 'The dilemmas of gender as double-voiced narrative', 82.

Firstly, and as many critics have observed, it can manifestly be argued that Honora Edgeworth was 'the prototype' for Rosamond's mother in the series; like the second Mrs Edgeworth, she 'appropriate[s] ... the rational language of the dominant male discourse' in the tales. If this 'appropriation' on the one hand immediately allows Edgeworth to satisfy her desire to 'consolidate her position with her father', it on the other also helps her to find a seemingly innocuous but 'authoritative public voice'.[51] This voice was for a long time spectacularly successful, convincing readers and critics alike that a compliant Edgeworth merely (re)voiced her father's patriarchal demands. At the same time, though, Edgeworth's works also 'narrativize[d] female fantasy', and their 'rational mother-teachers ... helped keep alive enlightened notions of female education in the reactionary period of the French Wars'.[52] Similarly, 'self-regulated' women such as Rosamond's mother did enjoy (limited) 'authority over the field of domestic objects and personnel where [their] supervision constituted a form of value in its own right and was therefore capable of enhancing the value of other people and things.' Without the domestic woman, it was believed that 'the entire domestic framework would collapse'.[53]

The role of the rational mother and, indeed, of the domestic woman in Edgeworth's work is therefore an extremely complicated one, and it represents a very considerable challenge for her reader. The issue at stake is power: do Edgeworth's works agree that the rational, domestic woman has such authority, or is there a subversive message simmering beneath the didactic surface of her writing? We might usefully recall here the letter that Edgeworth's father wrote to her from the deathbed of his second wife, urging her to cultivate her desire to become 'amiable, prudent, and of USE'.[54] It is this (male) creed that ultimately informs all of Edgeworth's writing; for example, it is finally the precise ideological formation that informs *Letters for literary ladies*. In this context, what is most interesting about 'Rosamond' and 'Frank' is that the demands of this male discourse are typically voiced not by the father in the tales, but by the mother, and that the children learn from their mothers that only if they are good will they be happy. A striking exception to this occurs in a tale entitled 'The birth day present', which appears in *The parent's assistant*. In this tale, intriguingly, it is Rosamond's father who teaches her the true meaning of generosity, telling her that 'to make a present of a thing that you know can be of no use, to a person you neither love nor esteem, because it is her birth-day, and because every body gives her something, and because your godmother says she likes that

51 Ibid. 79 and 82–3. 52 Myers, 'Romancing the moral tale', 101, and 'Socialising Rosamond', 54. 53 Armstrong, *Desire and domestic fiction*, 81–3. Mary Poovey traces this power to the emergence of the middle class, which 'simultaneously enhanced women's position and gave female nature a more strict – if idealized – definition': M. Poovey, *The proper lady and the woman writer* (1984), 10. 54 See note 9 on page 11 above.

people should be generous, seems to me ... to be ... rather more like folly than generosity.' Rosamond is brought to understand that Laura, her sister, displays true generosity when she aids a little lace-maker whose weaving pillow and bobbins have been ruined by a malicious footman. Laura's gift of a half guinea, quietly given, restores the child's means of earning her living, and Rosamond remarks to her father at the end of the tale that this is what it means to be '*really generous*'.[55] After this tale, it is from her mother that Rosamond learns her most difficult lessons.

This, of course, may simply be read as yet another example of the way in which Edgeworth highlights the crucial role that the mother must play in the education of her children, particularly her daughters. At the same time, however, Rosamond's mother teaches what the patriarchy desires, and this 'voicing' of the patriarchy's demands by the mother may be read as a process of virtual 'displacement' on Edgeworth's part. This displacement clearly serves a dual purpose in the tales. In the first place, it allows any resentment towards the lessons learned to be directed away from the father, that is, the patriarchal figure, and displaced, or projected, onto the mother figure instead. This recognition manifestly has a particular significance in light of Edgeworth's own family relationships. At the same time, this displacement allows Edgeworth to effectively interrogate the demands of the dominant male discourse without seeming to directly attack the patriarchy itself. In other words, it enables her to critique the patriarchy through its agent.

The indirect attack that Edgeworth launches on the dominant male discourse in these tales is illuminated by the subversive use to which she puts romance in tales such as 'Mademoiselle Panache', which are explicitly designed to educate her older female readers. In the two parts of this tale, Edgeworth considers foolish and sensible mothers, contrasting the disastrous education that Lady Augusta receives from both her French governess and Lady S—, her mother, with Mrs Temple's careful supervision of Emma and Helen, her daughters. This, obviously, constitutes the didactic level of the tale. 'Mademoiselle Panache' also operates on another, subversive level, though, and what is most remarkable for my purposes is the way in which Edgeworth treats romance in the story. On the surface level, the tale attacks romance, revealing how 'improper' reading can adversely affect the formation of the characters of young girls and women. It also illustrates why women who have fed their imaginations upon romance inevitably pose a serious threat to the stability of the social order. At the same time, 'Mademoiselle Panache' demonstrates why women are in the first instance attracted to such reading. Unleashed in the tale is the recognition that

55 *The parent's assistant*, 1: 128 and 143.

romance empowers women, so that they may, perhaps, be able to challenge the very foundations upon which the patriarchal order rests. Thus while apparently attacking romance, Edgeworth's tale simultaneously reveals its power: it acknowledges, in fact, that romance reading may enable women to force the world to imitate their perceptions.

The first part of the tale appears in *The parent's assistant*, and treats of the very early education of Augusta, and of Emma and Helen Temple. In so doing, it reveals the error of Lady S—'s thinking upon education: '"I would work upon a child's sensibility; that's my notion of education," said Lady S*** to Mrs Temple ... "Take care of the heart,[56] at any rate — there I'm sure, at least, I may depend on mademoiselle Panache, for she is the best creature in the world."'[57] Very quickly, the sensibility of this 'best creature in the world' is revealed to be pure affectation. Mademoiselle Panache tramples a spider to death in front of Augusta, and the text dryly observes, 'So much for a lesson on humanity' (2: 249). The most dangerous aspect of the governess' influence over Augusta, however, is represented by her choice of reading material. Augusta tries to get hold of a romance from her mother's shelves, and Mademoiselle Panache tells her: '*de row of Romans she forbid to be touch, on no account, by nobody but herself in the house. — You know dis, mademoiselle Augusta. — So, en conscience*' (2: 251). Augusta ridicules Mademoiselle Panache, telling Helen that the governess 'has had the second volume of that very book under her pillow this fortnight; I caught her reading it one morning, and that was what made me so anxious to see it; or else, ten to one, I never should have thought of the book; so *en conscience!* Mademoiselle' (2: 251). There are two points to be made about this passage in Edgeworth's tale. In the first place, these romances are portrayed in a distinctly negative light. As we shall see from the second part of the tale, Augusta's reading of romance is of immense significance when she reaches womanhood, and it is through this significance that the subversive powers of romance are revealed. The second point that must be made is in relation to Lady S—'s responsibility to her daughter. Although Mademoiselle Panache acts wrongly in reading these 'forbidden' works and is, thus, directly responsible for Augusta's desire to read romance, Edgeworth's tale indicates that Augusta's mother is even more culpable by having such inappropriate reading material on her shelves.

Crucially, Edgeworth's treatment of this issue here and throughout her work illustrates an overwhelming argument of much late-eighteenth- and early-nineteenth-century literature: namely, that generations of women are invariably

---

56 Edgeworth and her father for their part maintain that 'to make, what is called the heart, a source of permanent pleasure, we must cultivate the reasoning powers at the same time' (*Practical education*, 1: 296).   57 *The parent's assistant*, 2: 238. Further references to this part of the tale are cited parenthetically in the text.

affected when a woman reads inappropriate books.[58] Moreover, if Mademoiselle Panache fails her pupil as a governess, Lady S— fails Augusta twice over as a mother: firstly, by reading the wrong kind of books herself and, secondly, by choosing an inappropriate governess for her daughter. It is therefore entirely significant that the young Emma Temple very quickly sees through Mademoiselle Panache and comes to the conclusion that the 'governess' had, in fact, been a 'milliner' in France (2: 243). Romance reading, the tale implies, blunts the individual's powers of perception: a properly educated child is able to see what a mother who has fed herself on romance cannot.

The second part of the tale is in *Moral tales*, and opens by declaring: 'The tendency of any particular mode of education is not always perceived, before it is too late to change the habits or the character of the pupil'.[59] Lady S— has not reformed as a mother, readers discover, and still prefers 'what is called the world' to the real, permanent pleasures of domestic life (3: 148). She 'was fond of company, and fonder of cards; sentimentally anxious to be thought a good mother, but indolently willing to leave her daughter wholly to the care of a French governess, whose character she had never taken the trouble to investigate' (3: 148). While always intending to remove Augusta from the care of Mademoiselle Panache, Lady S— never actually does so and, ultimately, is unable to act as 'part of the money intended for the payment of the governess' salary, had been unfortunately lost by the mother at the card-table' (3: 149). Mademoiselle Panache therefore stays until Augusta is eighteen, 'endeavour[ing], by all the vulgar arts of flattery, to ingratiate herself with her pupil, in hopes, that from a governess she might become *a companion*' (3: 149).

The crux of this part of Edgeworth's tale, though, revolves around Mr Mountague, an admirer of Helen Temple's who becomes temporarily blinded by Lady Augusta's superficial charms. Mr Mountague knows Lady S— from town as 'a silly card-playing woman', but his hope is that 'her daughter is as little like her in her mind as in her person' (3: 162). Revealing that Mr Mountague is on the point of choosing a wife, Edgeworth uses his deliberations to illustrate the superior claims of a domestic rather than a fashionable education for young girls. Mr Mountague is horrified when he discovers that Augusta 'has been educated by a vulgar, silly, conceited French governess', but consoles himself with the thought that, as she is very young, 'a man of sense might make her what he pleased' (3: 176). In clinging to this belief, Edgeworth emphasizes, Mr Mountague is profoundly mistaken; Lady Augusta has not been rationally edu-

---

58 See, for example, Elizabeth Inchbald's *A simple story* (1791), Mary Hays' *Memoirs of Emma Courtney* (1796), or Amelia Opie's *Adeline Mowbray* (1805). 59 *Moral tales*, 3: 147. Further references to this tale are cited parenthetically in the text.

cated and, consequently, lacks 'the happy power of adapting herself to [the] taste' of the man that she would marry (3: 186). In a similar fashion, the deficiencies of Lady Augusta's education mean that she is unable to recognize the crucial difference that exists between her own affectation and Helen Temple's natural charms. This represents her 'moment of danger', according to Edgeworth, for she was 'little aware, that, when a man of sense began to think seriously of her as a wife, he would require very different qualities from those which please in public assemblies' (3: 195).[60]

In opening Mr Mountague's eyes to Augusta's true nature, the second part of the tale reaches back to the lessons learned in the first; a caterpillar falls from a rose which Augusta is wearing and, 'from habitual imitation of her governess, she set her foot upon the harmless caterpillar, and crushed it in a moment' (3: 199). This instant functions as a moment of recognition in Edgeworth's narrative: 'Lady Augusta's whole person seemed metamorphosed to the eyes of her lover … [H]e saw in her gestures disgusting cruelty; and all the graces vanished' (3: 200). Mr Mountague is effectively disenchanted here; he perceives that, if he marries Augusta, he will be taking a woman who has modelled her 'self' upon a foolish French governess as his wife. 'From imitation', as the tale thus pointedly observes, Augusta 'learned her governess' foolish terror of insects; and from example, she was also taught that species of cruelty, by which at eighteen she disgusted a man of humanity, who was in love with her' (3: 200).

With his eyes newly opened, Mr Mountague rediscovers his earlier appreciation of Helen Temple, and traces the origin of her attractions to the home in which she has been raised. Returning to the Temple household, he sees 'Work, books, drawing, writing! he saw every thing had been going forward just as usual in his absence. All the domestic occupations, thought he, which make *home* delightful, are here: I see nothing of these at S— Hall' (3: 204–5). Mr Mountague reiterates this emphasis upon the domestic attractions of Helen, and of her family, later in the tale in a passage that manifestly rehearses arguments put forward in *Letters for literary ladies* and *Practical education*. Recalling that ennui had never been a visitor 'in the many domestic hours he had spent at Mrs Temple's', he ponders the 'advantages' enjoyed by the man 'who can see a woman in the midst of her own family, … who can see her conduct as a daughter and a sister, and in the most important relations of life can form a certain judgement from what she has been, of what she is most likely to be!' (3: 208). The man who sees his future wife 'only at public places' or never 'without all the advantages or disadvantages of *stage decoration*', on the other hand, is bound

60 For Hannah More's argument that, 'when a man of sense comes to marry, it is a companion whom he wants, and not an artist', see *Strictures*, 1: 107.

to commit 'as absurd a blunder as that of the famous nobleman, who, delighted with the wit and humour of Punch at a puppet show, bought Punch, and ordered him to be sent home for his private amusement!' (3: 209). Two significant points must be made about these observations in Edgeworth's narrative. In the first instance, the tale here insinuates that woman only exists in terms of her relationship to others. What is implied, in a sense, is that a woman's character is never truly her own, that it is inevitably judged in relation to those who surround her throughout her life. This recognition informs not only Edgeworth's work, but also much literature of this period, of course, and we shall explore the issues at stake in greater detail below. Secondly, like Fanny Burney's *Evelina* (1778) or any one of Jane Austen's novels, 'Mademoiselle Panache' also intimates that, in the choosing of a marriage partner, it is always the man who 'has the advantage of choice'.[61] As Edgeworth would have it in this tale, and throughout her writing, the rituals of courtship and wooing are finally representative of nothing less than a marriage market, one in which men control all of the transactions.[62]

Once we recognize this, it becomes easier to understand Mr Mountague's reaction when he discovers Augusta in possession of 'one of the very worst books in the French language, a book which never could have been found in the possession of any woman of delicacy, of decency. [He] stood for some minutes in silent amazement, disgust, and we may add, terror' (3: 211).[63] Echoing Hannah More's argument that certain works 'should not be so much as named among' women,[64] Edgeworth's treatment of Augusta's subsequent adventures illustrates her perception of the reasons why men are so terrified when women read such books. Eventually rejected by Mr Mountague, Augusta ultimately elopes with Mr Dashwood, the 'coxcomb' tutor of her brother (3: 151), and leaves a note for Mademoiselle Panache, instructing her: 'Excuse me to my mother, *you* can best plead my excuse' (3: 234). This instruction of Augusta's on the one hand may simply be read as a piece of cruelty on her part, for Mr Dashwood

---

61 In *Northanger Abbey* (1818), Henry Tilney tells Catherine Morland that he considers the 'country-dance as an emblem of marriage', pointing out that, 'in both, man has the advantage of choice, woman only the power of refusal': Jane Austen, *Northanger Abbey* (1972), 95. 62 In *Practical education*, for example, Edgeworth warns that mothers who 'speculate' on their daughters' accomplishments forget that all parents 'have been for some years, speculating in the same line; consequently, the market is likely to be overstocked, and, of course, the value of the commodities must fall ... In a wealthy mercantile nation, there is nothing which can be bought for money, which will long continue to be an envied distinction' (2: 528–30). For her part, Teresa Michals suggests, 'Much of [Edgeworth's] fiction, like her management of her family's estate, is an experiment in the principles of free-market capitalism.' In *Belinda*, for instance, 'Edgeworth rewrites romance [that is, courtship] as a rational investment in the marriage market, and investment as romance': T. Michals, 'Commerce and character in Maria Edgeworth' (1994), 5 and 16. 63 There are echoes of this scene in *Helen*, where the young heroine inadvertently takes up an inappropriate novel and then expresses her gratitude to Beauclerc for 'instantly, gently, but decidely draw[ing] [it] from her hand' (Edgeworth, *Novels and selected works*, 9: 152–3). 64 More, *Strictures*, 1: 45.

had led Mademoiselle Panache to believe that it was she who had captured his affections. On the other, though, Augusta's observation also obliquely recalls the fact that the governess singularly failed to properly regulate either her own reading or that of her charge. Augusta's point, perhaps, is that Mademoiselle Panache will immediately understand her actions because she will instantly recognize that the girl is merely replicating a plot device that is standard to romances. If *Practical education* asserts, as we have seen, that 'Women, who have been much addicted to common novel-reading, are always acting in imitation of some Jemima, or Almeria, who never existed',[65] 'Mademoiselle Panache' reveals the reasons why women are drawn to such reading. By acting in imitation of some Jemima or Almeria, Augusta effectively empowers herself; she turns her 'self', that is, into 'AUGUSTA DASHWOOD', a woman whose new (marital) identity transcends the limitations of her (patriarchal) existence (3: 234). Augusta's marriage to Dashwood thus illustrates the reasons why men view romances with such terror: they inspire women to challenge the family line, to cut across class barriers and, potentially, to undermine the entire social order.

In this context, Lady S—'s reaction when she finally reads her daughter's note is very significant, and her swoon illustrates her perception that she has spectacularly failed in her duties as a patriarchal agent. Rather than supervising Augusta, Lady S— spent her time at

> the card table, playing very judiciously at whist ... Confident that her daughter, after having gone through the usual routine, would meet with some suitable establishment, that the settlements would then be the father's business, the choice of the jewels hers, she left her dear Augusta ... to conduct herself; or, what was ten times worse, to be conducted by Mademoiselle Panache. Thus to the habitual indolence, or temporary convenience of parents, are the peace and reputation of a family secretly sacrificed. (3: 224).

Effectively painting Lady S— here as a type of female Nero, Edgeworth's narrative insinuates that she foolishly played at cards while the reputation of her family went up in flames around her. Mr Mountague's 'terror' at discovering Augusta in possession of a romance is in this way revealed to have been startlingly prophetic: Augusta's reading finally undermines the stability of not only her family line, but also, by extension, that of the entire patriarchal order.

In 'Mademoiselle Panache', Edgeworth therefore clearly echoes Charlotte Lennox's strategy in *The female Quixote*: she derides romance fiction, while simul-

65 *Practical education*, 1: 296.

taneously revealing both the genre's power and the reasons why it is so attractive to women. Edgeworth perhaps even more effectively demonstrates this
power and this attraction in 'Angelina; or, l'amie inconnue', which appears in
her *Moral tales*. Again, the essential (subversive) point of this tale is that its heroine transforms her 'self' through her reading of romances. Insisting in the first
instance that Anne Warwick's susceptibility and lack of commonsense is the
direct result of 'certain mistakes in her education', Edgeworth's tale once more
demonstrates how important it is for young girls to receive proper instruction
in early life.[66] 'She had passed her childhood with a father and mother, who
cultivated her literary taste, but who neglected to cultivate her judgement', it
notes, 'her reading was confined to works of imagination; and the conversation, which she heard, was not calculated to give her any knowledge of realities' (2: 157). Apart from allowing his daughter's imagination to become
'inflamed' by her reading of inappropriate books, Angelina's father also commits a fundamental error of judgement by appointing Lady Diana
Chillingworth as her guardian. Unlike Lady Frances Somerset, her sister, Lady
Diana is 'a lady who placed her whole happiness in living in a certain circle of
high company in London' (2: 157). She purses, in other words, a fashionable
rather than a domestic life. Disgusted by Lady Diana's lifestyle, Anne is rendered peculiarly vulnerable when she one day chances upon 'a new novel, called
"The woman of genius"' at a circulating library (2: 158). Charmed by the character of Araminta, the novel's heroine, Anne is delighted to be 'informed, by
the preface, that the story was founded on facts in the life of the authoress
herself',[67] and Araminta and the newly styled 'Angelina' are soon correspond-
ing (2: 158). Just like Arabella in *The female Quixote*, Angelina's renaming of her
'self' and her subsequent adventures are the direct manifestation of her desire
to create her own significance. As she puts it in the note that she leaves for her
guardian when she runs away to find Araminta in Wales, her actions are
prompted by her '*unalterable determination*, to *act* and *think* upon every occasion for
[herself]' (2: 160).

There are obviously many similarities between *The female Quixote* and
'Angelina; or, l'amie inconnue' and Edgeworth's narrative deliberately draws the
reader's attention to this fact when Angelina discovers a similarity between her
servant girl, Betty Williams, and Sancho Panza. '[H]er own more striking resem-
blance to The female quixote never occurred to our heroine', the tale dryly
observes, 'so blind are we to our own failings' (2: 220). Further, Edgeworth's

---

66 *Moral tales*, 2: 157. Further references to this tale are cited parenthetically in the text.   67 While Edgeworth's tale
tacitly derides this assertion of Araminta's, it is worth remembering that her father makes precisely such emphatic
declarations in his prefaces to her works.

tale mimics Lennox's novel by first piling up and then debunking romance conventions, a strategy later utilised by Austen in *Northanger Abbey*. Upon her journey to Wales, Angelina 'had the misfortune, and it is a great misfortune to a young lady of her way of thinking – to meet with no difficulties or adventures – nothing interesting upon her journey' (2: 161). Instead, she 'arrived, with inglorious safety, at Cardiff' (2: 161). Similarly, Edgeworth observes that Angelina is distressed when the merry playing of a harper at an inn at which she stops on her way breaks 'the illusion' that she is weaving around herself, and feels worse still when she discovers that the gentleman in question is a 'mere modern harper' who is 'not even blind' (2: 162–3). Angelina's most startling and upsetting discovery, of course, is eventually revealed to be the fact that she has all along been hastening towards an entirely romanticized destination, and this is underlined by the fact that she immediately 'hit[s] herself a violent blow' as she enters Araminta's cottage (2: 172). 'As with the low doorway of ... her romanticized destination, reality keeps cracking [this] would-be heroine on the head.'[68] The 'charming pictures' that Angelina has being forming of her relationship with Araminta are thus inexorably revealed to be pure fantasy, and she is ultimately disgusted to discover that there is not a trace of the 'elegant delicacy' she had confidently expected to find in her 'unknown friend!' (2: 170).

While there are obviously clear resemblances between 'Angelina; or l'amie inconnue' and *The female Quixote*, there are at the same time some very striking differences between the two works. Firstly, Angelina is unlike Arabella in that she does not 'simply translate everyday events into romantic incidents.' Instead, 'She seizes the initiative and makes things happen', so that, 'still more' than is the case with Lennox's heroine, she 'structure[s] a self through – and not just despite – her indulgence in popular reading'.[69] Rather than existing in a state of passive misery and disgust in Lady Diana's home, Angelina acts as her own agent: specifically, she sets off in search of Araminta and, she believes, a better world. Similarly, the motive that impels Angelina's adventures is different to that which impels those of Arabella: unlike Lennox's heroine, Angelina 'seeks a mother, not a lover – a nurturing figure who will help her achieve her full maturity rather than sweeping her off her feet'.[70] The fact that Angelina is absolutely correct in her assessment that she needs such a mother figure is made abundantly clear in Edgeworth's narrative, for a primary emphasis of the tale is that Lady Diana miserably fails in her duties to her ward. After Angelina runs away, for example, Lady Diana admits to her sister that her charge used to talk 'some nonsense about her hatred of the forms of the world, and her love of liberty, and I know not what', and also acknowledges that she knew that

68 M. Myers, 'Quixotes, orphans, and subjectivity' (1986), 26. 69 Ibid. 26–8. 70 Ibid. 27.

Angelina had 'some female correspondent, to whom she used to write folio sheets, twice a week' (2: 150). Lady Diana simultaneously reveals that she failed in her duty to inspect these letters: 'Indeed, in town, you know, I could not possibly have leisure for such things' (2: 150). The fact that Lady Diana was constantly 'engaged' in London, the tale intimates, was primarily responsible for Anne Warwick's transformation into Angelina; this circumstance, it avers, was the entirely foreseeable outcome of Lady Diana's failure to regulate and correct the 'oddities' of her ward (2: 150–1). When she finally meets up with Lady Frances, Angelina therefore immediately recognizes in this woman the mother figure for which she has been seeking. '[U]nder the friendly and judicious care of Lady Frances Somerset', the tale observes, 'she acquired that which is more useful to the possessor than genius – Good sense – Instead of rambling over the world in search of an *unknown friend*, she attached herself to those, of whose worth she received proofs more convincing than a letter of three folio sheets stuffed with sentimental nonsense' (2: 255).

This argument immediately appears to complete Edgeworth's attack upon romance, but there are some intriguing, subversive points to be discerned in the narrative. In the first place, it must be reiterated that her reading precipitates Angelina's first steps away from her unsuitable guardian. Inspired by romance texts, she sets out in search of Araminta, hoping to find a mother figure who will not be 'almost always out … or dressing, or at cards' (2: 241). While the romantic illusion that she has constructed about Araminta is eventually dispelled, the fact remains that Angelina's adventures enable her to transform her existence; they lead, specifically, to that moment in the story when the rational Lady Frances takes control of her life. Secondly, Araminta's role in the tale is much more ambivalent that it at first appears, and Edgeworth uses this character to release some extremely subversive voices into her narrative. These not only hint at the limitations that Angelina will necessarily experience by embracing a rational existence, but also intimate that the apparently ridiculous Araminta has in fact empowered herself through her reading of romances. On the surface, Araminta thus appears to be a purely stereotypical figure, one whose significance would have been immediately understood by Edgeworth's readers. She is 'a woman, with a face and figure which seemed to have been intended for a man, with a voice and gesture capable of setting 'even man, "imperial man," at defiance' (2: 222). In this regard, as critics have remarked, she is clearly 'a forerunner' of Harriet Freke, who appears in *Belinda*, Edgeworth's 1801 novel of manners. This character also debates women's rights; more, she wears men's clothes, and would very quickly have been identified as 'dangerous' by Edgeworth's readers: the 'most obvious outward manifestation of the adoption of masculine attributes – and hence probably usurpation of prerogatives and powers – was women's wearing of male dress.'[71] While she does not actually adopt male attire, Araminta's 'masculine attributes' are emphatically stressed in Edgeworth's narrative, and it is also made quite clear that it is her firm intention to wear the trousers in her and Nathaniel Gazabo's marriage. On the didactic level, therefore, Araminta's character manifestly functions as a site wherein Edgeworth peculiarly encodes cultural anxieties regarding women: specifically, the fear that the male prerogative will be weakened in the face of growing calls for women's rights.

In this context, Edgeworth's portrayal of Araminta reveals the dangerous challenge that romance reading poses to the patriarchy by demonstrating how the empowered Araminta skilfully (re)negotiates the terms of her marriage. Before she will marry Nathaniel Gazabo, Araminta insists that her future husband must solemnly promise never to contradict any of her opinions; he must leave her 'entirely at liberty to act, as well as to think, in all things as [her] own independent understanding shall suggest'; agree to be guided by her 'in all things'; and, finally, must promise to 'love and admire' her for all of his life (2: 223). By insisting that Nathaniel must swear to comply with all of these conditions or she 'will never be [his] Araminta', Araminta in fact uses sleight of hand to conceal the fact that she firmly intends to remain her own 'property', even after she becomes a wife (2: 224). It can thus be argued that Araminta's romance-inflamed imagination enables her to obtain exactly the type of power that Angelina desired when she fled from her guardian's home. Angelina, we observed, expressed her '*unalterable determination* to *act* and *think* upon every occasion for [herself].' This is also Araminta's desire, and it is precisely what she secures in her marriage.

Further, Araminta's arguments also powerfully illustrate the reasons why Mr Mountague is so terrified when he discovers Augusta in possession of inappropriate reading material, for they demonstrate that women learn to speak another, non-patriarchal language by reading romance books. When she writes to Angelina to encourage her to leave Lady Diana, Araminta uses the language of sensibility, or of romance, to undermine the patriarchal boundaries that enclose her young friend. She encourages the girl to (re)negotiate the language of law, or of man, by encouraging Angelina to replicate a romance plot. 'The words *ward* and *guardian*, appal my Angelina', she observes, 'but what are legal technical formalities, what are human institutions, to the view of shackle-scorning Reason? – Oppressed, degraded, enslaved –must our unfortunate sex for ever submit to sacrifice their rights, their pleasures, their *will*, at the altar of public opinion' (2: 155). In this way, Araminta reveals why men are so terrified when woman read romance: its language, she demonstrates, refuses to recog-

71 C. and J. Atkinson, 'Maria Edgeworth, *Belinda* and women's rights' (1984), 102–4.

nize the (legal) boundaries with which men try to protect their patriarchal prerogative. Romance, she suggests, is a law unto itself.

Crucially, Araminta's arguments further imply that women to a large part
only observe such 'male' boundaries in the first place because of their fear of
public opinion, and this point is peculiarly illustrated by Angelina's adventures
when she first sets out in search of her female correspondent. Although a gen-
tlewoman born and bred, Angelina rapidly realizes that her identity is not fixed;
who she is, she discovers, depends entirely upon her relationship to others. A
shopkeeper who spies her unprotected state consequently takes her for 'a girl
of the town', asking her, 'in a saucy tone', whether she wants anything else,
'Rouge, perhaps?' (2: 191–2). Similarly, in the home of a cheese-monger, Dinah
Plait, John Barker, a Quaker, mistakes Angelina for a pauper. Upon leaving, he
thus 'drop[s] his purse into her lap' (2: 195), which causes the upset Angelina
to remark to Dinah that there 'has been some strange mistake, – I am not a
beggar' (2: 43). The point Edgeworth is making, of course, is that Angelina *is*
a prostitute, or a beggar, or anything else that others believe her to be precisely
because she appears to be unprotected.[72] As Mrs Porett puts it to the pupils of
her academy for young girls, Angelina's danger is: 'She is too young to know
how quickly, and often how severely, the world judges by appearances' (2: 207).
It is Lady Frances' recognition of this that prompts her to remark near the end
of the tale that it is essential that others are informed that Angelina is now in
her care so as to prevent a possible scandal (2: 242). In this sense, it can be
argued, what finally divides Angelina from Araminta is the fact that the latter
remains true to her determination to create her own significance. Unlike
Angelina, Araminta insists on making herself: she defines how she will live and
who she will be. Angelina, on the other hand, lacks the courage to pursue such
a course, and agrees to accept the rational Lady Frances' direction. In so doing,
she tacitly consents to continue to accommodate her 'self' to the expectations
of others and, thereby, to embrace the limitations of a rational, domestic life.

Despite the fact that the conclusion of 'Angelina; or, l'amie inconnue'
appears to satisfy the didactic imperatives that impel all of Edgeworth's writing, the manner in which she chooses to conclude her tale curiously disturbs
the overt message of the story. '[W]e have now, in the name of Angelina
Warwick', she notes, 'the pleasure to assure all those whom it may concern, that
it is possible for a young lady of sixteen to cure herself of the affectation of
sensibility, and the folly of romance' (2: 255). Firstly, the tale's insistence that

---

72 This 'status anxiety' is a recurring theme in the work of female authors. In *Evelina* (1778), for example, the heroine is separated from her party during a visit to Marybone-gardens and discovers that her evident unprotected
status encourages 'impertinent witticisms, or free gallantry' from male bystanders: F. Burney, *Evelina* (1982), 233.

Angelina 'cure[d] herself of … the folly of romance' covertly challenges the basic didactic premise upon which all of Edgeworth's works are overtly based. Overwhelmingly, Edgeworth's writing implies that education always makes the man, or woman, and that a proper, early education is therefore positively essential if the individual is to enjoy happiness in later life. The ending of 'Angelina' seems to disrupt this smooth assertion, as Angelina successfully remakes herself despite her disastrous early education and her love of inappropriate texts. This emphasis also serves to distinguish Angelina from Arabella in *The female Quixote*, for unlike Lennox's heroine, she does not require 'a clergyman's lecture' in order to reform her life.[73] Further, the fact that Edgeworth refers to her reformed heroine as 'Angelina Warwick' is also significant: it intimates that Angelina's romance-inspired adventures have enabled her to turn herself into a fully rounded individual, one whose reason has not entirely subjugated the powers of her imagination and heart.

As all of this demonstrates, Edgeworth's treatment of romance in her writing for children and adolescents is extraordinarily complex. On the one hand, she overtly derides what she defines as the delusions of romance, insisting that children and young adults must be persuaded to embrace an existence that is predicated upon reason and logic. On the other, she constructs a romanticized version of her own childhood and adolescence in her works in order to support this argument, thereby revealing not only her perception of the limitations of a purely rational existence, but also of the peculiar power and necessity of the imaginative mind. By framing works like *The parent's assistant* and *Early lessons* within a greater Edgeworthian romance, after all, Edgeworth and her father necessarily admit a crucial recognition into her writing: specifically, they acknowledge that romance reading can be efficacious in certain circumstances providing that the reader is carefully supervised. It is in this context, as we noted in the introduction, that Edgeworth and her father carefully qualify their treatment of romance in *Practical education*. Works such as *Robinson Crusoe* are not 'dangerous' for female readers, they observe, because these never will be in the position to indulge their taste for exotic adventures or travel. Boys will, though, and so *Practical education* consequently insists that colonial romances must be withheld from young men destined for careers in the professions. 'The taste for adventure is absolutely incompatible with the sober perseverance necessary to success in … [the] liberal professions', it warns, and will merely distract the individual from his studies and uselessly 'torment' his imagination and heart.[74]

Edgeworth illustrates the issues that are at stake here in *Frank: a sequel to Frank in Early lessons* (1822), where the young hero's father impresses upon him that it

---

73 Myers, 'Quixotes, orphans, and subjectivity', 27.   74 *Practical education*, 1: 336.

is essential he applies himself to the study of Latin as 'a man cannot be of what
are called the liberal professions' without it.[75] Frank allows himself to be dis-
tracted by his cousin, Mary, who is reading 'Verses, supposed to have been written by Alexander Selkirk, during his solitary abode in the island', and the boy
remarks that it is a remarkable coincidence that she should be reading this work,
as he had just been thinking that he would 'play at Robinson Crusoe when [he]
went out' (1: 65). Franks proceeds to spend the day trying to build a Robinson
Crusoe island, complete with parrot, in the garden, and is horrified when he
eventually hears his father returning. As the tale puts it, he 'would have given
up parrot and arbour, and island and all, for five minutes more time' (1: 77).
Unable to properly repeat the lesson that he had been told to learn, Frank is
disgraced in the eyes of both of his parents. Despondent, he and Mary remember that they have left the parrot in the garden and they go out to retrieve her.
'Poll was sitting silent and moping, but the moment she saw Frank, she screamed
out something like "*Robinson! Robinson Crusoe!*"' (1: 85). The narrative underlines
the point that is being made by wryly observing: 'Ah! all in vain now!' (1: 85).[76]

Significantly, the Edgeworths further qualify their interdiction against colonial romances in *Practical education*, insisting that they ought to be read by the
boys and young men who will serve in Britain's army or navy. The specific aim
of the education of such individuals is to encourage emulation because, unlike
girls, these will one day be in the position to replicate what they have read. If
this argument here and throughout Edgeworth's writing in the first instance
merely illustrates the wider pedagogical contention that informs her work,
namely, that girls should receive a different education to that of boys, it also
demonstrates that this gendered distinction is fundamentally designed to facilitate the continuance of the patriarchal prerogative. The desires of such male
readers, after all, are released for a very particular purpose: to enable them to
remake the world in the light of their patriarchal image. The fact that Edgeworth
attempts to harness the power of romance to facilitate this ambition is therefore extraordinarily important, and we will explore this aspect of her work in
the next chapter.

---

75 M. Edgeworth, *Frank* (1822), 1: 52. Further references to this tale are cited parenthetically in the text.   76 Like
Frank, the hero of 'Forester' in *Moral tales* allows himself to be (temporarily) seduced by the story 'of a man, who
had been cast away, some hundred years ago upon a desert island' (1: 30). The emphasis of the narrative is that
this threatens his ability to properly fulfil his duties as a gentleman in later life: 'His love of independence was
carried to such an extreme, that he was inclined to prefer the life of Robinson Crusoe in his desert island, to that
of any individual in cultivated society' (1: 1).

Romance as an inspirational tool

So far, I have been arguing that Edgeworth's work overtly condemns the reading of romances because the reader imbibes a false view of reality from such reading, and is invariably inspired to attempt to replicate this delusion outside of the book. For the good of society as a whole, Edgeworth insists, the reading habits of young girls and boys must be carefully supervised; they must be encouraged to read only those works that contain useful lessons faithfully drawn from real life. Yet, Edgeworth's interdiction against romance is qualified by her insistence that boys who are destined for careers in either the army or navy should read narratives of adventure and colonisation. Inspired by such reading, she intimates, these young men will wander all over the face of the earth, engaging in adventures that will ultimately prove to be to Britain's national and imperial advantage.

In this way, Edgeworth explicitly anticipates that the reading of works like *Robinson Crusoe* will necessarily lead to travel on the part of the reader, but, unlike conservative writers like Hannah More, she imbues this trajectory with a positive value. More's argument in her *Strictures on the modern system of female education* is that, at 'this moment of alarm and peril', young persons 'should be put on their guard against a too implicit belief in the flattering accounts ... of some of the countries newly discovered.' Similarly, she warns, as all '*General Histor[ies]*, *Natural Histor[ies]*, *Travels, Voyages, Lives, Encyclopedias, Criticism*, and *Romance*' may eventually prove to be nothing less than 'vehicles' of ideological invasion, readers should beware of indiscriminately admiring or replicating such texts.[1] The unwitting reader, More fears, may find him or herself beguiled by a work that functions as an account of 'political tourism';[2] one, that is, which ingenuously

---

1 More, *Strictures*, 1: 4, 192 and 31–2. 2 I am drawing here upon Gary Kelly's reading of the works of Helen Maria Williams (1762?–1827). Taken together, Kelly suggests, Williams' texts effectively represent accounts of 'political tourism', which are ultimately framed in terms of romance. Her *Letters written in France, in the summer of 1790, to a friend in England; containing, various anecdotes relative to the French revolution; and memoirs of mons. and madame du F– (1790)* adopts, 'The overall form ... [of] a romance journey from the narrator's "proper" sphere of home, family, and friends to the apparently unfamiliar and public-political domain, concluding with her imminent return home, more aware of the difference between "home" and "not home", between Revolutionary France and unrevolutionized Britain.' Similarly, Williams' 1798 text, *A tour in Switzerland; or, a view of the present state of the government and*

confounds generic (and political) boundaries in the interests of disseminating the 'poison' of revolutionary France.[3] In contradistinction to this, Edgeworth insists that the young men who will be directly engaged in Britain's national and imperial expansion can safely read and replicate accounts of travel and colonising romances. Such readers will be immune to ideological contamination, according to Edgeworth, for all of their adventures will be informed by their perception of the a priori superiority of the British nation and race. In this context, Edgeworth's sentiments clearly have much in common with those expressed by William Godwin in his essay entitled 'Of history and romance', which he produced in 1797 but never published:

> The study of individual men can never fail to be an object of the highest importance. It is only by comparison that we come to know any thing of mind or ourselves. We go forth into the world; we see what man is; we enquire what he was; and when we return home to engage in the solemn act of self-investigation, our most useful employment is to produce the materials we have collected abroad, and, by a sort of magnetism, cause those particulars to start out to view in ourselves, which might otherwise have lain undetected.[4]

Like Godwin, Edgeworth similarly believes that romance-inspired travellers will 'go forth into the world' already anticipating their 'return home'; their journeys, she is convinced, will merely throw into sharper relief aspects of their British selves that 'might otherwise have lain for ever undetected.'

Edgeworth's effort to reshape and regulate the power of romance in this fashion fulfils two crucial purposes in her writing: it facilitates both national and imperial expansion, while proffering the means through which the mercantile and colonial ambitions that fuel this expansion can be disguised and

manners of those cantons: with comparative sketches of the present state of Paris, 'incorporates travel-writing, the most important and widely read form of non-fiction prose at the time, into Williams' project of feminizing politics and the Revolution': G. Kelly, *Women, writing, and revolution* (1993), 35-9 and 69. For a brief overview of Williams' life and works, see 'Helen Maria Williams' in J. Todd (ed.), *Dictionary of British women writers* (1989), 720–2. 3 More persistently figures inappropriate texts as 'poison' throughout *Strictures on the modern system of female education*. 'Rousseau', she observes, 'was the first popular dispenser of [that] concentrated drug, in which the deleterious infusion [is] strong, and the effect proportionably fatal' (1: 32). This anxiety in More's text, of course, is representative of the wider cultural and ideological concerns of this period. For instance, Seamus Deane argues Burke's *Reflections on the Revolution in France* 'claims that, after 6 October 1789, when the modern world appeared, France became the foreign country *par excellence* … filled with a missionary spirit to convert or pervert all Europe to its model': S. Deane, *Strange country* (1997), 7. 4 This previously unpublished essay is appended to the Penguin Classic's edition of *Caleb Williams* (1988). In his introductory remarks to the essay, Maurice Hindle observes that Godwin's 'manuscript note' to the title of the piece indicates that it 'was produced "while the Enquirer (1797) was in the press, under the impression that the favour of the public might have demanded another volume"': W. Godwin, 'Of history and romance' in *Caleb Williams*, ed. M. Hindle (1988), 361 and 359.

controlled. For this reason, Edgeworth's use of romance illustrates the efficacy of Edward Said's argument that 'Neither imperialism nor colonialism is a simple act of accumulation and acquisition. Both are supported and perhaps even impelled by impressive ideological formations that include notions that certain territories and people *require* and beseech domination, as well as forms of knowledge affiliated with domination'.[5] It is in the context of the 'ideological formations', or, as I would have it, the romances, that are at work in Edgeworth's work that the particular attention that she pays to texts like *Robinson Crusoe* is so important because, as numerous critics have noted, Defoe's hero is ultimately a conqueror of other peoples and lands. Consequently, the novel concerns itself with much more than recounting how Robinson Crusoe survives being shipwrecked and castaway on an island: it also details precisely how he makes himself the incontrovertible 'prince and lord' of all that he sees.[6]

Indeed, the force of the colonizing mission, or impulse, that impels Defoe's writing eventually proves to be too powerful to be contained within a single novel, and so it instead spills out and into other works. In this way, *Robinson Crusoe* can clearly be read as the precursor to a long line of (colonizing) children's texts, which reaches its peak in the mid-to-late nineteenth century's preoccupation with 'fictitious romance[s] for boys ... [which complete] the transition into narrative of that conception of the world in which discovering, or seeing, the world is equivalent to controlling, or subduing, it'.[7] This emphasis, of course, confers a privileged position upon the observer: it intimates that his gaze is necessarily representative of a superior way of life.

As the work of Edgeworth's that is perhaps most concerned with this notion of discovering and then subduing the world, *Essays on professional education* positions *Robinson Crusoe* at the beginning of a long list of reading that is recommended to the future soldier or sailor. Significantly, however, the subsequent works that Edgeworth recommends to these readers encode her conviction that, if such readers are eventually to survey other people and lands, careful steps must be taken to inform and regulate their vision. Edgeworth is thus emphatic that these readers should move on to other 'accounts of shipwrecks and hair-breadth scapes, voyages and travels' after Defoe's novel and, further, that they should allow 'Stories of giants, and genii, and knights and tournaments, and "pictured tales of vast heroic deeds," [to] feed [their] fancy'.[8] Having imbibed these works, such readers will discover that '[f]rom what is grand in fiction, it is easy to lead to what is great in history', and they will

5 E. Said, *Culture and imperialism* (1993), 8. 6 D. Defoe, *The life and adventures of Robinson Crusoe*, ed. Angus Ross (1965), 157. 7 J. Rose, *The case of Peter Pan* (1992), 58. 8 R.L. Edgeworth, *Essays on professional education*, 137. As we noted earlier, Edgeworth's father was originally credited as the sole author of this treatise. Further references to this work are cited parenthetically in the text.

move with ease 'from the knights of romance and chivalry, to the heroes of biography and real life' (146).

This 'transition', as she calls it, is crucial to Edgeworth's purpose, for it facilitates her contention that her romance-inspired readers will eventually 'burn' to emulate real-life noble acts (146).[9] Unlike the hero of *Don Quixote de la Mancha*, for instance, who is only at the very last able to perceive the difference between what is real and what is the product of imagination, Edgeworth's point is that her readers will not waste their time chasing chimeras. Instead, they will evolve as readers and positively ache to recreate deeds drawn from Britain's glorious and honourable past. In light of this, the 'heroic actions of … soldiers and seamen, every instance of bravery and virtue in any rank of life, should be held up to the [particular] admiration' of the young men in Britain's naval and military academies (176). 'What can more strongly excite to glory than the admirable life of Nelson! his disdain of money, his perseverance, his enthusiastic love for his friends, his devoted attachment to his country, and his freedom from professional jealousy. Perhaps no character is more truly British, than his and that of Trowbridge [*sic*]' (177).[10]

Similarly, Edgeworth maintains that future soldiers and sailors should be encouraged to 'celebrate great victories, and commemorate, by festivals, those days which our national heroes have rendered glorious to their country' (176). In this way, she effectively tries to transform romance into the primary inspirational force that impels both empire and nation: she intimates that the initial reading of young soldiers and sailors should necessarily move them to 'love' and wish to (honourably) serve the British nation and race. Edgeworth's strategy here has much in common with that of Edmund Burke in his *Reflections on the Revolution in France*. Mourning the passing in France of the 'pleasing illusions, which made power gentle, and obedience liberal', Burke declares,

> Nothing is left which engages the affections on the part of the commonwealth … The precept given by a wise man, as well as a great critic, for the construction of poems, is equally true as to states. *Non satis est pulchra esse poemata, dulcia sunto.* There ought to be a system of manners in every nation which a well-formed mind would be disposed to relish. To make us love our country, our country ought to be lovely.[11]

9 Edgeworth's analysis of the effects of history reading has much in common with that of William Godwin: 'It is in the contemplation of illustrious men, such as we find scattered through the long succession of ages, that kindles into a flame the hidden fire within us … While we admire the poet and the hero, and sympathise with his generous ambition or his ardent exertions, we insensibly imbibe the same spirit, and burn with kindred fires' ('Of history and romance', 362).   10 Sir Thomas Troubridge (1758?–1807) rose to the rank of rear admiral in Britain's navy, and his career was closely linked to that of Nelson. See the entry on Sir Thomas Troubridge in the *DNB*.   11 Burke, *Reflections*, 171–2.

Edgeworth's point is: 'The love of our country is a rational and salutary principle, which may, and in military education ought to be infused early as a prejudice' (141).

   If the inculcation of this 'prejudice' is to be successful, however, it is essential to Edgeworth's purpose that a way is found to disguise and control the
pecuniary realities that impel Britain's national and imperial expansion. To this
end, she attempts to construct the notion of an abstract British 'virtue', or
'honour', which will regulate the less appealing aspects of Britain's colonial and
imperial life. While this ambition of Edgeworth's is everywhere implicit in her
Essays on professional education, it peculiarly manifests itself at one crucial point in
the treatise. In the chapter devoted to the legal profession, she observes, 'There
is perhaps a portion of what men of the world call romance in all public virtue.
But this romance, if it be such, is far preferable to the selfish, cold, narrow-
minded, venal habits, which are contracted by those who believe neither in
public nor in private virtue' (403). This significant moment in the treatise has
profound implications for all of Edgeworth's work, for, overtly, and without
reservation, it admits that she is trying to construct an aspirational notion of
Britain in her writing. Similarly, it further acknowledges that public and private
virtue, or honour and mercantile ambition, are usually diametrically opposed,
but, and this is what is most important, it proffers the power of romance as
the means through which this conflict can be avoided and the demands of both
honour and mercantile ambition can be satisfied and reconciled.

   Edgeworth's overall aim in this regard is clarified by her treatment of the
types of rewards and punishments that should be utilised by military schools.
Whatever is used

> should never be of a pecuniary nature. Honour should be the great
> reward; and disgrace, or the fear of disgrace, the only punishment. In
> a commercial nation like this, it is peculiarly necessary to guard against
> that mercenary spirit, which is incompatible with the generous martial
> character. When every thing is reduced to a monied rate, honorary dis-
> tinctions lose their value and power over the human mind; and, instead
> of noble enthusiasm in the course of virtue and freedom, a calculat-
> ing, selfish temper prevails; the people are debased and enslaved; mer-
> cenary troops fight their battles without the ardour of freemen, and at
> last a nation, incapable of defending even its darling wealth, falls an
> easy prey to the bold invader. To prevent such a catastrophe, a com-
> mercial country should take every possible means of inspiring the youth,
> who are to form their armies and navies, with a love of honour. (175–6)

This is a powerful passage, and it contains sentiments that resonate throughout Edgeworth's writing.[12] Haunted by pecuniary terms, it in the first instance
makes manifest the cultural tensions that are inevitably caused within a commercial economy. It also reveals, though, that Edgeworth's response to this tension is to produce a definition of England, or, a national 'romance', which both
diffuses and contains the potential threat posed by the 'mercenary spirit.' Her
vision, in other words, is of an 'England' and an English 'greatness' in which
national and personal 'honour' are protected from the sordid realities that inform
mercantile and colonial aspiration.

What Edgeworth is aiming at is perfectly exemplified by the character of
Joshua Crumpe, who appears in 'The contrast' in *Popular tales*. In this tale, Joshua
distinguishes himself from his mercenary relations who are all eagerly anticipating the death of Mrs Crumpe, a rich elderly lady. With 'the true spirit of a
British merchant', Joshua declares he is 'as independent in his sentiments as in
his fortune', and, unlike his relatives, he does not plague the dying woman.
Upon Mrs Crumpe's death, it is discovered that she has left everything to Joshua
precisely because of this exemplary behaviour. As the sole heir, Joshua once
more emphasizes his non-mercenary spirit when he announces that he will 'keep
up to the notion [he has] of the character of a true British merchant' by giving
each of his relations a thousand pounds.[13]

There are obviously considerable difficulties attendant upon this desire to
conflate personal or national honour and mercantile and/or colonial ambition;
difficulties which are similarly encoded in *Don Quixote*, where the desire of
Cervantes' hero for fame and fortune is portrayed as being inextricably linked
to the concept of serving 'the public good' and of 'redressing all kind of grievances.' Notwithstanding this emphasis, the work is unable to avoid the fact that
colonial ambition at least partly impels the aspirations of its hero: Don Quixote,
after all, not only wishes to right wrongs and to win the hand of Dulcinea del
Toboso, but also anticipates making himself the ruler of a conquered land. In
the context of what I am suggesting, however, what is most interesting and significant in Cervantes' novel is that this implicit colonial desire on the part of
Don Quixote is made the explicit, ruling passion of Sancho Panza, his servant.
It is therefore emphasized that Don Quixote's primary motivation is to act
always in a manner that is consistent with his idea of honour, while Sancho
Panza's overwhelming ambition is to secure the island that his master promises

12 The same sentiments manifest themselves throughout *Patronage* (1814), for example, as where Lord Oldborough
rewards his secretary, Mr Temple, for a stirring speech that he makes in the House of Commons. Lord Oldborough
insists a man 'of genius … can become a man of business', thereby illustrating Edgeworth's greater contention
that business is compatible with honour and, further, that Britain's professional men must remember this as they
rise in the world (Edgeworth, *Novels and selected works*, 7: 91). 13 Edgeworth, *Popular tales*, 3: 102 and 170.

him 'might be won in the turn of a hand, and he [Sancho Panza] be left governor thereof.' While mercantile and colonial ambition are thus revealed to be
at least partially responsible for the adventures of Don Quixote and his squire,
Cervantes effectively tries to ring fence 'honour' from the less romantic realities of pecuniary aspiration by stressing the superior character of his hero.
Unlike Sancho Panza, Cervantes avers, the romance-inspired Don Quixote is
not primarily concerned with financial reward; instead, his principal ambition
is to lead an honourable life.[14]

This theme of a disinterested ambition is crucial to Edgeworth's use of
romance in her writing, and it is one of the central premises upon which *Essays
on professional education* finally rests. As we have already seen, for example, it is this
that is proposed as the means through which to preserve the moral purity of
the young men who are destined for a life in the army or navy. While this is in
itself significant, Edgeworth's wish to preserve the young men in the naval and
military academies from the taint of mercenary desire represents but one part
of her overall ambition in her writing. The other is symbolized by her evident
anxiety to create a greater, 'national' romance of Britain in her work, one that
will guarantee the incontrovertible moral purity of the entire British nation,
thereby justifying and excusing its colonisation of other peoples and lands. This
strategy in *Essays on professional education* and throughout Edgeworth's work clearly
reflects that of Defoe in *Robinson Crusoe*: as he would have it, Friday is fortunate
that Robinson Crusoe made him his slave.

Edgeworth's determination to construct a 'national' romance of Britain in
her work is important for many reasons, and not least because it peculiarly demonstrates one of the overwhelming concerns of the English during the Revolutionary
era. In the years following the French Revolution, Gary Kelly points out, the perceived need in England for a decisive national identity was paramount, and this
identity was 'defined not so much from within the "nation" but from external,
global and historical, Revolutionary and post-Revolutionary struggles against
France, America, Russia, and other rivals.' Thus, 'The "nation" was constituted
as its "destiny" to rule and civilize alien peoples throughout the world, to "protect" them from themselves and from predatory neighbours. This imperial "mission" was not separate from the "national" identity and interest, or an extension
of them, but essential to inventing and sustaining them.'[15] Suvendrini Perera makes

---

14 Cervantes, *Don Quixote*, 25 and 63. The fact that Sancho Panza's ambitions are those of a would-be colonizer
is made abundantly clear throughout *Don Quixote*, particularly where he emphasizes he will use any means necessary in order to exact the maximum profit from 'his' colonized lands: 'What care I, if my subjects be blacks? what
have I to do, but to ship them off, and bring them over to Spain, where I may sell them for ready money; with
which money I may buy some title or employment, on which I may live at my ease all the days of my life?' (278).
15 Kelly, *Women, writing, and revolution*, 184–5.

a similar observation in her study of how the novel 'prepared for, or made possible a climate for receiving or accommodating, empire ... If location and national identity were formative forces in the various subgenres of the nineteenth-century novel, a major source of this nationalizing imperative was a sense of moral distinctiveness as the colonialism of previous decades developed into a full-blown doctrine of empire based on the cultural – rather than the military – superiority of Britain'.[16]

Essays on professional education patently demonstrates this 'nationalizing imperative', and it expresses, in the clearest possible terms, the sentiments of cultural rather than military superiority that were to become increasingly prevalent by the end of the nineteenth century. As Edgeworth's work would therefore have it, Britain's army and navy exist only because of the presence of the French across the English channel: 'Since England has a military nation, a nation military *en masse* to contend with, she must herself become military, as far as it is necessary for self-preservation and independence' (188). Unlike the French, the English 'fight on the most legitimate and most noble cause, not to subdue other nations, but to defend our own', and Edgeworth's contention is that this fight is more than justified because of England's unassailable superiority: 'Has any people upon Earth any thing more valuable to defend than we have? – Equal laws, secure property, personal liberty, and freedom of opinion ... we may therefore defy our enemies, if we have energy and unanimity among our people' (219–20). This argument, of course, is not peculiar to Edgeworth's writing, for much literature of this period insists that the English are '*by nature*, the most tenacious of liberty among all the civilized nations', having, 'as it were, a characteristic inherited disposition to be free'.[17] Crucially, Edgeworth yet again draws upon the power of romance in order to support this ideological formation in her treatise, insisting that the deliberate cultivation of that fiction that conflates 'honour' with commercial aspirations is positively essential to the continuance of the British way of life. As she puts it,

> So far as hope of prize money, or of sharing the fund at Lloyd's can *imp* the flights of ambition, the nation is safe: but when England shall have shut up all the ships of the world in their respective ports, the hopes of prize money must sink; the funds at Lloyd's will fail; and the British empire may perhaps find too late, that no mercenary rewards can supply the place of military enthusiasm, and the love of glory. (222)

16 S. Perera, *Reaches of empire* (1991), 7 and 37.   17 J. Barrell, *English literature in history* (1983), 119. Writing in the closing years of the eighteenth century, for example, Hannah More stresses that 'the whole world is looking with envy and admiration' at England, 'the seat of true glory and of comparative happiness: a country, in which the exile, driven out of the crimes of his own, finds a home!' (*Strictures*, 1: 103).

The conflation here of nation and empire is repeated throughout *Essays on professional education*, and it is of crucial significance in terms of the greater national and imperial ambitions that inform Edgeworth's work. Chapter V, 'On the education of country gentlemen, or of men intended for private life', for example, points out that the life of such gentlemen 'is assuredly the happiest life in the world' linked, as it is, to 'their independence of mind; and ... their maintaining [of] what is called *independent fortunes'* (278). Edgeworth's insistence upon the necessity of preserving this independence of fortune represents yet another manifestation in the text of her idea of an honour that is separated from the taint of pecuniary ambition and, again, it is gradually revealed to be essential not only to the stability of the nation, but also to the future prosperity of Britain's wider imperial project:

> Every generous heart must wish, that the gentry of the British empire may preserve that independence, which has made them the envy of foreigners, and what is far more desirable, has rendered them honourably and truly happy. What condition can indeed be more desirable than that of a true English country gentleman; a man in the full enjoyment of personal, civil, and intellectual liberty ... (316)

In placing the English country gentleman at the very heart of both nation and empire, Edgeworth's further point is that it is also essential he be acquainted 'with all that passes in the British parliament, with domestic and foreign politics, and some general principles by which he can reason for himself on public affairs' (293).

Edgeworth's preoccupation with the country gentleman in *Essays on professional education* is extremely important; in the first place, it clearly demonstrates the degree to which she is drawing upon, and developing, early-eighteenth-century notions in her treatise. As Barrell points out, commentators at the beginning of the eighteenth century were particularly preoccupied with the concept of the 'comprehensive view' of landed gentlemen; the independent situation of such men, they insisted, rendered them peculiarly disinterested and, thus, astute observers of the state of Britain and British affairs. By the time Edgeworth came to produce *Essays on professional education*, however, writers such as Daniel Defoe, Richard Steele and Bernard Mandeville had worked to detach the definition of 'gentleman' from the concept of property ownership. Landowners, they perceived, necessarily had 'a political interest', and one that was not inevitably 'identical with the permanent interests of the state.' Indeed, for his part, Barrell contends that 'the possibility of a comprehensive understanding [of society] has disappeared' by the end of the eighteenth century; this, he insists, was 'perhaps the crucial issue between Burke and Paine, as Burke argues that no one man is in a position to grasp … the proper order of government and the function of established institutions, and so to demand that they be changed'.[18]

Edgeworth's treatment of the country gentleman clearly refutes such a view, and it reworks and develops an older, pre-revolutionary vision of the proper-tied gentleman and (re)presents him to the reader as the effective guardian of the national and imperial order.[19] '[O]ne of the best chances for restoring a national spirit of independence and honest patriotism', according to Edgeworth, is to educate country gentlemen 'to understand and to pursue their real inter-ests, and the interests of their country' (293). To this end, such men should acquaint themselves with all ranks of people, 'but chiefly … the middle and lower classes' (298). They should also conduct agricultural experiments 'for the advantage of their tenants, for the benefit of their estates, and of their coun-try' (303). As Edgeworth would to all intents and purposes have it here and throughout her writing, the country gentleman symbolizes and regulates Britain's honour; his person synecdochically reflects the condition of Britain and of the British way of life. In *The absentee*, for example, Edgeworth notes that the edu-cation of Mr Berryl, the hero's friend,

> fitted him exactly for the station which he was destined to fill in society
> – that of *a country gentleman*; not meaning by that expression a mere eating,
> drinking, hunting, shooting, ignorant, country squire of the old race,
> which is now nearly extinct; but a cultivated, enlightened, independent
> English country gentleman – the happiest, perhaps, of human beings.

Significantly, when 'called upon to give her decisive judgement between a town and a country life', Mr Berryl's future wife, Miss Broadhurst, declares 'she should prefer a country life, as much as she should prefer Robinson Crusoe's diary to

---

18 Barrell, *English literature*, 35, 38–9 and 49. Although Smollett's *The life and adventures of Sir Launcelot Greaves* was first published in 1762, Barrell's reading of this novel usefully illuminates this part of his argument. Smollett's text 'has as its central character a baronet who, before the opening of the novel, had been the ideal of the benevo-lent paternalist landowner' (200). Unhinged by the mistaken belief that Aurelia Darnel has rejected him, Launcelot Greaves sets out to redress what he perceives as grievances, and an essential point of Smollett's narrative is that this is hugely bound up with his greater ambition to serve his country. The difficulty for the reader, Barrell remarks, is to decide whether or not to dismiss Greaves as a lunatic knight errant 'for it is clear that he has a more complete grasp of the condition of England and of the virtues necessary to its government than anyone else in the book' (200).   19 The fact that Edgeworth is acutely conscious of the potential difficulties and post-Revolutionary implications of this project peculiarly manifests itself at one particular moment in *Essays on pro-fessional education*. Attaching a proviso to her insistence that future soldiers and sailors should read Thomas Day's *Sandford and Merton* (1783–89), she observes that the text's 'prejudice against *gentlemen*' is the result of the fact that it 'was written before the French revolution, and at a time, when there was reason to dread, that the luxurious and effeminate manners, which were then fashionable in France, should spread to the nobility of England, and debase the manly character of Britons' (138).

the journal of the idle man in the *Spectator*'.[20] In so doing, she effectively links the country gentleman to romance, thereby exposing the imaginative nature of this emphasis in Edgeworth's work. In order to maintain both his own honour and that of his nation, Edgeworth therefore insists in *Essays on professional education* that the country gentleman must steadfastly refuse to succumb to the temptations of either city or court. These temptations are expensive, she observes, and, as he is unable to 'stoop' to trade, he would have to sell his vote and engage in dubious parliamentary activity in order to support them (279). 'Instead of being their country's pride and the bulwark of her freedom', profligate country gentlemen would consequently 'become the wretched slaves of a party, or the despicable tools of a court' (279).

To underline the point she is making, Edgeworth significantly contrasts the policy of James I on this matter with that of 'Lewis the Fourteenth, and the arbitrary monarchs of France' (315). King James, she notes, was astonished that country gentleman should choose to leave behind their spheres of influence in order to embrace court life. 'It is singular', she remarks, 'that a sovereign, who was fond of arbitrary power, should ... have given advice, which tended to secure the independence and freedom of a large class of his subjects, and, through their means, probably of the whole body of the nation' (315). The French kings, on the other hand, drew 'round them all the gentry and nobles of the kingdom, to make the luxuries and pleasures of a court and of a capital city necessary to their existence, to inspire them with a taste for expence beyond what their private fortunes could afford, and thus to render them dependant on the sovereign for places and pensions to support their extravagance' (316). In this way, Edgeworth indicates that the country gentleman must take steps to protect himself from financial profligacy. Excessive expenditure is a national as well as a personal menace, she warns, and it threatens to undermine the very fabric of Britain's social and political life: 'The great, the brilliant, and the solid virtues of integrity, patriotism, and generosity, cannot long subsist, unless they be supported and protected by the seemingly insignificant and homely habits of prudence and economy' (279–80).

Although she is here explicitly addressing her remarks to the country gentleman, Edgeworth's assertions have a far wider significance in terms of her desire to disguise and control all of the pecuniary, mercantile desires that impel national and imperial expansion. 'In every rank and situation', she observes,

> there is a certain style in living, in houses, equipage, furniture, which is
> usual to persons of that class. Whoever in any of these things vies with

20 *Novels and selected works*, 5: 40.

persons of a superior station, and passes the bounds of his rank and fortune, may be justly accused of being luxurious and extravagant. Those
who consider the wealth of nations as the first object, are right in wishing to encourage this species of luxury, and to speak of it as tending
only to the quick transfer of property and division of estates; but those
who consider the happiness of nations as an object far preferable to their
wealth, will wish rather to preserve their moral independence, which
must be sacrificed in the indulgence of these tastes for extravagance. (281)

Again, this stress upon the need 'to preserve [the] moral independence' of the
British populace is directly related to Edgeworth's conviction that it is necessary
to construct the notion of an abstract 'honour' in Britain. This honour, she hopes,
will control the pecuniary realities that impel national and imperial expansion,
and disguise the less salubrious aspects of Britain's colonial and imperial life. By
educating their children properly, Edgeworth insists, parents can ensure that they
will later avoid 'that petty emulation in expense which ruins the happiness of
families, and prepares the destruction of kingdoms' (282). The text stresses that
the pursuit of money and of the 'luxury' that it can buy is not wrong as such; an
assertion, of course, that is entirely necessary if mercantile expansion is not to
be endangered. Instead, such acquisitive desires become harmful only when they
spiral out of control and prompt the individual to aspire to a standard of living
that is beyond his or her 'station.' This, Edgeworth avers, will necessarily lead the
individual to compromise his or her 'moral independence', and this, in its turn,
will erode the very fabric of Britain's socio-political life.

   In placing the English country gentleman at the very heart of the nation,
however, Edgeworth insists that it is positively essential that he should guard
against becoming 'a fixture in his own house; he should occasionally visit friends
in different parts of the empire, and of Europe at large, that he may change the
habitual course of his ideas, and that he may avoid acquiring local prejudices'
(314). Once more, this emphasis in *Essays on professional education* is important for
several reasons. Firstly, it demonstrates yet again that Edgeworth is drawing
upon early-eighteenth-century notions by insisting that the country gentleman
must make himself thoroughly familiar with other races and lands. This assertion also manifests itself in Richard Steele's definition of the gentleman in a
1713 edition of *The Guardian*, for example, where he similarly argues that such a
man 'must travel to open his Mind, to enlarge his Views, to learn the Policies
and Interests of foreign States, as well as to fashion and polish himself, and to
get clear of National Prejudices; of which every Country has its Share'.[21] In the

21 R. Steele, *The Guardian*, 34, 20 April 1713, quoted in Barrell, *English literature*, 37.

first place, this insistence can be linked to my earlier point regarding the early-eighteenth-century's preoccupation with the 'comprehensive view of the gentleman'; in order for a view to be properly comprehensive, after all, it must gaze upon the widest possible representation of human life. Barrell for his part suggests that it is this, perhaps, that is 'the crucial theme' of Smollett's *The adventures of Roderick Random* (1748): the hero's peripatetic experiences, he notes, give him ' a more comprehensive grasp of the society he lives in, than a gentleman brought up in more fortunate circumstances could have acquired'.[22]

Secondly, this argument in Edgeworth's work is significant because it illuminates her conviction that the country gentleman will play his part in helping Britain to 'appropriate' the wealth and ideas of other races and lands. Like the soldier and sailor, she predicts, he, too, will cast an acquisitive (colonial and imperial) eye over all that he sees. This anticipation of the appropriation of the physical resources and cultural wealth of other nations is a theme that recurs throughout Edgeworth's writing and, in this context, it might be useful to draw here again upon Perera's arguments. In light of the 'nationalizing imperative' that she maintains is discernable in the various sub genres of the early-nineteenth-century novel, Perera remarks that there was also a process of 'incorporation' at work in which other nations, such as India, were *incorporated* into the British historical narrative. James Mill's 1815 essay, 'On education', she notes for example, 'cites as a blueprint for general education in England a plan originally developed by Baptist missionaries in India.' As Mill's essay addresses matters as diverse as the solar system and geography, Perera's contention is that it finally amounts 'to no less than a cultural remapping of the cosmos, with geographical, historical, and theological "compendiums" of knowledge converging to establish England in its proper place of absolute centrality'.[23]

This 'absolute centrality' of England is decisively encoded within *Essays on professional education*. It manifests itself in the country gentleman's journey out from the heart of the empire and home again, and in the voyages and travels that Edgeworth anticipates will be undertaken by the future sailor or soldier. It also, of course, patently informs the journeys abroad that the treatise argues are absolutely essential for the education of a future statesman or prince. Thus, Edgeworth insists, the young statesman 'must ... study mankind. He must see his own and foreign countries ... He must make himself acquainted with the government, views, policy, resources, habits, education, and institutions of every country he visits' (436–7). Similarly, if the nation is at war, the young prince 'should serve abroad. The British empire affords generals, who are inferior to no men in education, and a camp has ever been the nursery of great princes'

22 Ibid. 196. 23 Perera, *Reaches of empire*, 37–9.

(484). In times of peace, on the other hand, the prince should travel and 'acquire more knowledge of men and manners; of the real state of his own and foreign countries, their resources, opinions, and customs; than he possibly could from books' (484–5).[24]

As is the case with the young soldier or sailor, according to Edgeworth, the young statesman's or prince's travels will convince him of the incontrovertible superiority of his native land. Like all British travellers, these will perceive 'that the misfortunes, which have befallen the countries of Europe, must be attributed to their political corruption, their party struggles, the errors of judgement of their rulers, or their total want of integrity; [and] to the duplicity and ineptitude of those, who call themselves negotiators and diplomatists' (448). Similarly, the young statesman or prince will learn to count himself lucky that

> [t]hough England is a commercial nation; and though the maxims of the trading part of the community have insensibly risen with their riches, and mixed with those of our aristocracy, yet there still exists a large portion of liberal disinterested virtue in these countries [*sic*], which the great motives, and great occasions of the times must call forth to public service, and public admiration. (451)

This passage in Edgeworth's work is clearly idealized, demonstrating yet again that her desire is to cultivate the (romantic) notion of the existence of an entirely disinterested British honour or virtue in her readers. This ambition is highlighted by the fact that she further insists that only those who believe that 'the reward of "an honest fame"' is 'the most glorious of all rewards' should step forward to 'become Minister[s] of the British Empire!' (453–4). Men such as these commit themselves to the 'exertions' and 'sacrifices' of an entirely noble existence (454).

All of this patently amplifies my earlier comments regarding Edgeworth's use of romance in *Essays on professional education*, for her argument once more is that reading will be the primary inspiration for all of these travels. As she so eloquently puts it in relation to the young statesman, he must study mankind 'after having studied books' (436). Similarly, Edgeworth further intimates that the first books that such a young man reads should be romances, or, in other words, works that will 'inspire' his 'noble ambition ... to serve, [and] to save his country' (411). So inspired, these readers should move on next to the perusal of history and geography, and 'the geography of a statesman', Edgeworth insists,

---

24 Edgeworth advances the same point in relation to the country gentleman who is waiting to inherit his estate. If the nation is at peace, he should travel at home and abroad; if it is at war, he should go into the army (298).

'must comprise more than a mere knowledge of countries and nations' (424). Instead, this individual must study a distinctly colonial or imperial geography: one that teaches him, that is, that geographical 'statistics' are not necessarily 'fixed, immutable, immortal words' (424).[25]

The preoccupation of *Essays on professional education* with the need for the individual to acquaint himself with the 'facts', 'figures', and 'resources' of other lands may clearly be related to the British nation's increased concern with the process of surveying throughout the eighteenth century. For her part, Katie Trumpener connects the measuring and mapping of land in Britain and Ireland in the name of agricultural improvement with the development of government ordnance surveying, declaring that this is 'clearly linked to the consolidation of British military control in Scotland and Ireland, North America and India.' Moreover, and echoing Perera's arguments, she observes, 'In domestic as in overseas territories under occupation, such surveys functioned quite explicitly as acts of incorporation.' For example, she notes, the final third of Arthur Young's landmark text, *A tour in Ireland* (1780),

> sketches a pioneering political economy of Ireland, illustrating the effects of absenteeism and analyzing the causes of political unrest, advocating large-scale bog reclamation and economic union with Britain, and calculating the advantages of both for Anglo-Irish landowners. The book's first five hundred pages, in contrast, consist of virtually raw data, reproducing in minute detail Young's notes from three years of fact-finding travel, farm for farm and field for field.[26]

In *Essays on professional education*, reading is always the first step that must be taken towards such 'acts of incorporation', and this is why Edgeworth's insistence that future soldiers or sailors should move on to the study of travel accounts after *Robinson Crusoe* is so important. By the end of the eighteenth and beginning of the nineteenth century, this species of literature was 'a well-established genre, closely connected, through its emphasis on first-hand experience, with a tradition of history writing that ran all the way back to Herodotus and

---

25 *Essays on professional education* similarly insists, 'A boy intended for the army or navy should be as soon as possible initiated in geography' (134).   26 Trumpener, *Bardic nationalism*, 25 and 37–8. We will explore how Edgeworth treats this process of incorporation/appropriation in her tales relating to Ireland in the next chapter. However, it is appropriate to note here Deane's observations regarding what he calls Edgeworth's 'dramatizing' of the England/Ireland relationship 'as an early form of imperial romance – one in which a "utilitarian" adventure is undertaken in a romantic territory in order to conquer it, remap it, domesticate it' (*Strange Country*, 30). The arguments of Trumpener and Perera have clear implications for what Deane is asserting here, as do Rose's contentions about the way in which 'discovering, or seeing, the world is equivalent to controlling, or subduing, it' (*The case of Peter Pan*, 58).

Thucydides.'[27] While people have always travelled and recorded those travels for a variety of reasons, 'a chief, if not the chief, reason for traveling has been for trade', and this imperative took on a greater consequence after 1600 as the competition between European nations for the control of other markets and lands became more intense. In this context,

> just as trade inspired businessmen and ministers of state to send out expeditions overseas or embassies to other nations, the books and let-ters produced by these groups made it easier for others to follow but [also] inspired a longing for exotic goods that quickly became necessi-ties. As a result, accounts written by men engaged in such travel were often propagandistic … As propaganda for international trade and for colonization, travel accounts had no equal.

Although the recreational and educational qualities of travel literature contin-ued to be of significance, the important point is that these were increasingly subsumed into the greater service of nation and empire. For example, records of long voyages were so much in demand in the eighteenth century 'that the British Admiralty followed the practice of confiscating all journals written on government-sponsored sailing expeditions so that an official version could be produced by careful editing'.[28]

For Edgeworth, travel writing finally 'represents literary work of the high-est political consequence',[29] and it is certain that a work like 'To-morrow' in *Popular tales* expertly illustrates the primary significance of accounts of voyages and travels. Overtly, this tale warns against the dangers of procrastination, for it is this bad habit that causes Basil, its hero, much personal distress and suf-fering. At the same time, the tale examines how the shortcomings of the indi-vidual can adversely affect the spread of empire, and it intimates that every individual must properly conduct his (or her) self abroad in order to facilitate the expansionist ambitions of the British nation. The father of one of Basil's college friends secures for him a place at the British embassy in China, and Basil's father significantly consents to this journey only 'upon condition that [he] should promise to write a history of [his] voyage and journey, in two vol-umes octavo, or one quarto, with a folio of plates.' Basil begins by literally missing his boat to China, and his poor organisational skills, coupled with his predisposition to procrastination, dog every step of his adventures. In the first

27 J. Brewer, *The pleasures of the imagination* (1997), 630–1.   28 P.G. Adams, *Travel literature and the evolution of the novel* (1983), 57, 77 and 42.   29 Trumpener, *Bardic nationalism*, 58. Trumpener suggests that the writing of such literature is, for Edgeworth, 'too often undertaken by the arrogant or ignorant, with lasting damage to cross-cultural under-standing', and she cites the case of Craiglethorpe, the self-styled travel writer in *Ennui*, by way of illustration (58).

instance, he leaves behind him on the ship on which he eventually does sail the notebooks in which he intended to record his observations, and is thereby reduced to jotting down rough notes on random scraps of paper. Secondly, having won the confidence of a French Jesuit mandarin, Basil fails to capitalise on the singular advantage he enjoys of having 'a companion who was able and willing to instruct [him] in every minute particular of the manners, and every general principle of the government and policy, of the people'.[30] Although himself aware that this circumstance ideally places him to engage in the kind of minute observation of the 'views, policy, resources, habits, education, and institutions' of a country in which Britain, and her empire, are keenly interested, Basil disgracefully throws this opportunity away. Instead, he is responsible for an accident with gunpowder that results in the British embassy being ordered to leave China and, in this way, he directly damages the expansionist interests of the British race.

Basil's indirect effect upon the future of England's expansion is equally as serious, however, and it is represented by his failure to produce an account of either his time in China or of his voyage. Such works are inordinately valuable, the tale implies, for they function as the tools that facilitate Britain's wider imperial project. Basil's failure in this regard is made even more pointed due to the closeness of his friendship with the French Jesuit mandarin. This individual represents a society that amassed an 'unbelievably large body of letters, journals, and summaries of travels written, collected, and published ... between 1540, the date the Society [of Jesus] was chartered, and 1773, when it was dissolved by papal decree.' Basil's friendship with the French Jesuit mandarin therefore amounts to a virtual apprenticeship to one who is a master in the art of travel writing; a master, moreover, who has a potentially vast network of contacts at his command. Furthermore, the Jesuit also represents a body of men 'who were assigned early in the eighteenth century to survey much of China'.[31] Through his friendship with this individual, Basil is in theory ideally placed to either access this information or to ascertain how best such information can be obtained. His failure to capitalize on this relationship is compounded by his ultimate inability to produce any account of his travels at all, for 'Sir George Staunton's history of the Embassy to China, in two volumes quarto' finally beats his half-hearted scribbling to the presses.[32] In this way, Edgeworth intimates how an individual's failings may seriously compromise the colonial and imperial ambitions of the British race.

This recognition in the first instance leads us back to the greater preoccupation with education that frames all of Edgeworth's writing, but it especially

---

30 *Popular tales*, 3: 256 and 271.   31 Adams, *Travel literature*, 55 and 65.   32 *Popular tales*, 3: 299–300.

illuminates her anxiety to promote the education of the professional classes. Professional men like Basil, she maintains, will be peculiarly implicated in Britain's national and imperial expansion, so they must be carefully educated so that their very persons are symbolic of the irrefutable superiority of the British nation. This will directly facilitate Britain's colonisation of other peoples and lands, as these will perceive that they are in fact lucky to be colonised by such a superior race. This strategy of explanation and of justification of the presence of the coloniser, Richardson points out, is a consistent feature of those works that adopt and adapt the themes of racial superiority that underpin Robinson Crusoe's adventures. 'Even in children's texts which explicitly condemn slavery', he notes, 'the Crusoe scenario typically includes a justification of European colonialism based on superior technology and the moral qualities that presumably go with it, such as industriousness and intellectual curiosity.'

Richardson's further point is: 'The figurative equation of children (especially poor children) and "primitives" is all too common within the educational discourses of the eighteenth and early nineteenth centuries'.[33] This first of all underpins Rose's arguments concerning the process through which the colonizer discovers and sees the native in order to finally control and subdue him, but it further reveals that not only race, but also class and gender issues variously inform Edgeworth's writing. Drawing upon Rousseau's strategy in *Émile*, Rose suggests, the usual first step in such figuring is to heap onto the child the responsibility for saving humanity from the degeneracy of modern society; a notion of childhood that manifests itself where Rousseau sets up childhood in his work 'as a primitive state where "nature" is still to be found if only one gets to it in time.' Childhood is thus transformed into 'the place where an older form of culture is preserved (nature or oral tradition), but the effect of this in turn is that this same form of culture is *infantilised*.' This has the result that, 'At this level, children's fiction has a set of long-established links with the colonialism which identified the new world with the infantile state of man ... the child is assumed to have some special relation to a world which – in our eyes at least – was only born when we found it'.[34]

While Richardson focuses in particular upon the class issues that are raised by such figuring, Kelly observes that 'the late-eighteenth-century cultural revolution' in fact grouped together 'women, children, the lower classes, and the

<hr />

33 Richardson, *Literature, education, and Romanticism*, 155–7. 34 Rose, *The case of Peter Pan*, 44 and 50. Just such a figuring of the primitive child features in 'The little merchants', for example, where the primitive culture of Naples and its inhabitants are newly discovered and reborn in the eyes of Arthur, an English servant. As my next chapter will demonstrate, the profound political repercussions of all of this are even more marked in a tale like 'The grateful negro', where a British plantation owner is portrayed as a benevolent father figure who watches over and protects his childlike slaves.

peoples Britain seemed destined to protect and "civilize".' These groups, he states, 'were often treated in the same way or made figures for each other as intellectual inferiors, social dependents, and moral wards of a professional middle class figured as a professional European or British man.'[35] This theme of the lower classes portrayed as either children or savages surfaces repeatedly in Edgeworth's work, but it is nowhere more strikingly illustrated, perhaps, than in the chapter devoted to the country gentleman in *Essays on professional education*. Explicitly, the members of the lower classes are here equated with savages, and savages, in their turn, are depicted as childlike and in need of the 'parental' guidance of their superior (colonial) lord. Urging the country gentleman to engage in agricultural experiments for the good of his country, Edgeworth insists that, with careful encouragement, he can overcome 'what is called obstinacy in the lower classes' (305). What is most remarkable about this argument is that Edgeworth's text proceeds from the members of the lower classes to native savages and all without missing a beat. Squires, the treatise therefore asserts, must make it their business to study the accounts of missionary societies; they must familiarize themselves, that is, with precisely how these societies succeeded, or otherwise, in (re)educating the (childlike) natives of other lands. One such account is represented by that of the Methodist South Sea missionaries, who 'began by preaching to the poor savages of things which they could not comprehend, and who blamed them for not having habits, which they had no means and no motive to acquire' (305–6). Of these 'tutors', the 'South Sea auditors ... acutely said, "Massas give us a great deal of good talkee, but very little of knives and scissors"' (305–6). The Quaker missionaries, on the other hand, decided to lead by example to promote 'the improvement and gradual civilization of the North American Indians' (306). Thus, they first of all cultivated ground for themselves 'and, without exhorting the natives to industry, showed them its advantages' (306). Although Edgeworth concludes by asking whether, if this can be achieved 'among ignorant and prejudiced tribes of savages', what may not be achieved among the 'civilized inhabitants' of England, her initial response to these 'civilized inhabitants' is to categorize them alongside savages or North America's native race (307).

While this is a particularly striking example of the 'figuring' of the lower classes in a work of Edgeworth's, all of her writing is ultimately involved in a process that tries to (re)shape and contain the lower orders. In the broadest sense, the key to this containment is always the construction of an educational romance, which impresses upon the individual the benefit of being educated for his or her 'station' in life. This anxiety of Edgeworth's does not limit itself to the lower orders, of course: her further point is that the acquisitive desires of the middle and upper classes must also be contained. In this context, and as we saw earlier, Edgeworth emphasizes that these desires are not wrong as such: they only become so once they encourage the individual to forget his or her 'place.' Once again, Edgeworth assigns a crucial role to woman in this regard, asserting that it is primarily woman's responsibility to act as a check upon such acquisitive compulsions. As she puts it in *Practical education*, 'Economy is in women an essential domestic virtue ... [Y]oung women, when they see in stubborn figures what must be the consequence of getting into situations where they must be tempted to exceed their means, will probably begin by avoiding, instead of braving, the danger.'[36]

Edgeworth expertly illustrates all of these themes in 'Madame de Fleury', which was published in the 1809 series of *Tales of fashionable life*. The overall purpose of this tale, the preface tells us, is 'to point out some of those errors to which the higher classes of society are disposed',[37] but the crucial point of Madame de Fleury's story is that it illustrates how she, an upper class woman, helps to contain the acquisitive desires of the lower orders. In founding a school for lower class girls, Madame de Fleury is therefore careful to refrain

> from giving any of her little pupils accomplishments unsuited to their situation. Some had a fine ear for music, others showed powers of dancing; but they were taught neither dancing nor music – talents which in their station were more likely to be dangerous than serviceable. They were not intended for actresses or opera-girls, but for shop-girls, mantua-makers, work-women, and servants of different sorts; consequently they were instructed in things which would be most necessary and useful to young women in their rank of life.[38]

In this way, Madame de Fleury's school guards against the inculcation of inappropriate or overly acquisitive desire in its pupils, and the relationship between the upper and lower classes is carefully managed.

'Out of debt out of danger', on the other hand, provides a colourful illustration of what happens when woman gives way to rampant acquisitive desires, and the fact that this threatens both nation and empire is central to Edgeworth's narrative. Leonard Ludgate, a haberdasher's son, rejects his late father's maxim of 'Out of debt out of Danger', replacing it, instead, with 'Spend to-day, and spare tomorrow'.[39] He also ignores his father's conviction that 'Miss Belle Perkins

36 M. Edgeworth and R.L. Edgeworth, *Practical education*, 2: 701 and 705.   37 R.L. Edgeworth, preface, *Tales of fashionable life* (1809) in *Novels and selected works*, 1: 159.   38 *Novels and selected works*, 5: 226.   39 *Popular tales*, 1: 311. Further

[was] a would-be fine lady, whom he advised his son never to think of for a wife', and the couple soon marry (1: 312). Leonard and his new wife immediately embark upon a spendthrift lifestyle that very quickly leads them into financial difficulties, and this culminates in Leonard being sent to the gallows for having passed counterfeit notes. Although Leonard and Belle each play their part in their eventual ruin, Edgeworth intimates that Belle's sin is by far the greater. By encouraging her husband to move into a fine house, and by piling up ever more debts in her relentless quest to keep up with their fashionable neighbours, she singularly fails to manifest any traces of 'domestic virtue.' Indeed, Leonard asserts as much himself when he is finally arrested: '"Cursed, cursed woman! you have brought me to the gallows, and all for this trumpery!" cried he, snatching her gaudy hat from her head, and trampling it under his feet. "For this – for this! you vain, you ugly creature, you have brought your husband to the gallows!"' (1: 374–5).

Crucially, 'Out of debt out of danger' also indirectly indicates why unbridled economic excess poses a threat to national and imperial expansion by tracing the wider (colonial) implications of Belle's inability to discharge her financial obligations. Called upon to settle a debt by an upholster, who is, significantly, 'fitting out one of his sons for the East Indies', Belle persuades one of his employees, Lucy, to leave her wages on his hands for another month (1: 338). At the end of that time, Belle tells her former companion, she will certainly be in a position to pay. Two months pass, however, and Lucy resolves to call on Belle, for her imminent marriage means that she really needs her wages. As the tale pointedly observes, 'she wished to put into her husband's hands the little fortune which she had hardly earned by her own industry' (1: 248). In this way, Edgeworth demonstrates that the effects of Belle's extravagance reach out far beyond her own home, and she simultaneously reiterates her point about how important it is for the individual to preserve his or her financial (and moral) independence.[40] The profligate Belle, she reveals, adversely affects not only her own home, but also the future prosperity of Britain's colonial and imperial project.

The details of 'Out of debt out of danger', or 'Madame de Fleury,' therefore demonstrate the efficacy of the argument that, throughout the nineteenth

references to this tale are cited parenthetically in the text. **40** Edgeworth highlights this point by contrasting the Ludgates with Lucy and her future husband, Allen, throughout the story. These come to the aid of the Ludgates' children, whom they 'educated … with their own children, in habits of economy and industry' (1: 383). This means the young Ludgates are ultimately able to retrieve 'the credit of their family, by living according to their grandfather's … maxim' (1: 384). This emphasis in the tale illustrates Michals' argument that, for Edgeworth, 'the family has a corporate personality, one underwritten by the market value of its members' good characters rather than by its inheritance of land, the traditional basis of such a corporate personality' ('Commerce and character in Maria Edgeworth', 1–2).

century, 'women were increasingly defined as the ideological and cultural foundation of society, state, nation, and empire, in fact serving the interests and
identity of the professional middle class and their allies in other classes'.[41] They
also, however, help to clarify Edgeworth's evident anxiety to offer a romanticized version of education, one that will diffuse and contain the potential social
problems caused by the newly upwardly mobile masses. As *Essays on professional
education* would have it, education is in this way transformed into a tool that regulates the individual even as it empowers him; it intimates that he can enjoy all
of the advantages of social advancement so long as he continues to respect the
boundaries that have traditionally delineated the social classes. Recounted in
the treatise, thus, is the story of a Yorkshire country gentleman who foolishly
put himself into debt in order to procure a statue of Venus. Edgeworth remarks,
'It is true, that the understanding cannot in any class of man be too much
enlarged; but it may be too much refined; it may be misapplied to subjects of
little use to the possessor, in the situation in which he is destined to live: this
must lead to the neglect of substantial duties, consequently to the degradation
of the character of the individual' (288).

These several themes recur throughout Edgeworth's writing, but, to illustrate further how romance and an appropriate education are linked by her in
the service of both nation and empire, I wish to turn next to 'Lame Jervas', and
to examine how the principles of romance which are detailed in *Essays on professional education* manifest themselves in this instance of her clearly imperial and
colonial writing. As one of Edgeworth's *Popular tales*, 'Lame Jervas' is part of a
work that is itself predicated upon a very specific didactic promise. Aimed at
the less 'polite' classes, it 'promises' these lower classes that their newly obtained
access to books and education will offer them the means through which they
can become upwardly mobile. At the same time, it also tries to guarantee the
stability of society by persuading these newly empowered readers that their
interests continue to be bound up with their proper observance of the existing
social order. 'Lame Jervas' therefore traces the hero's relentless social climb, and
his equally relentless acquisition of property, while simultaneously underlining
the fact that the English way of life guarantees such opportunities to all who
similarly apply themselves and work hard.

Richardson for his part reads 'Lame Jervas' as 'an educational romance',
whose 'discursive center resides in the treatment of property'.[42] If this tale is an

---

41 Kelly, *Women, writing, and revolution*, 173.   42 'Lame Jervas', he writes, 'is a story of self-help which looks back to
Dick Whittington and forward to Samuel Smiles' (*Literature, education, and Romanticism*, 225). Once Jervas arrives in
London and is taught to read and write, 'The narrative ... becomes an educational romance, as [he] pursues
"useful information" through self-directed reading' and thereafter experiences a number of extraordinary adventures (225). As the hero of 'an educational romance', it is entirely appropriate that Jervas shares his name with a

educational romance, though, it is manifestly a colonial and imperial one as well, for the hero has to travel to India to acquire his property. Jervas begins his working life as a virtual child-slave in the Cornish tin mines and his desire for property is first awakened when he is convalescing following an accident in the mine. He remembers that he 'began to desire to have … a little garden, and property' of his own for which he knew that he must 'work hard'.[43] While indicating that all may desire to acquire property, the tale takes pains to link this desire to the continued regulation of the social order. Jervas thus significantly takes his first steps towards amassing his fortune when he protects his master's property from the designs of dishonest miners who seek to conceal their discovery of a load. For this, his master financially rewards him, and he is also taken out of the mine and placed under the care of Dr Y—, who oversees his future education. What Jervas' schooling makes clear, however, is that education is both an empowering and a regulating tool. When he begins to have visions of earning his living by writing, Dr Y— tells Jervas it was 'not likely, … [he] should ever either earn [his] bread or equal those who had enjoyed greater advantages of leisure and education' (1: 39). In other words, Dr Y— informs Jervas that his education will only take him so far: he must still remember his 'place.'

A lot of hard work and honesty later, Jervas eventually ends up in India where he works firstly as an assistant in Dr Bell's school in Madras, and then in Tippoo Sultan's court where he is asked to instruct Prince Abdul Calie, the sultan's eldest son. Jervas notes that the prince was 'of a most amiable disposition, unlike the imperious and capricious temper which [Jervas] had remarked in his father. Prince Abdul Calie had been, when he was about twelve years old, one of the hostage princes left with Lord Cornwallis, at Seringapatam' (1: 91). In this manner, Edgeworth's tale directly links Prince Abdul's superior qualities to his earlier English education. The superiority of the English system which offers the benefits of such education to 'all' is further underlined when Jervas observes, 'Thus an obscure individual, in a country like England, where arts, sciences, and literature are open to all ranks, may obtain a degree of knowledge which an eastern despot, in all his pride, would gladly purchase with ingots of his purest gold' (1: 93–4). Equally, the opportunities through which Jervas amasses his subsequent wealth are also the result of the English system. The sultan first asks him 'to visit the tin-mines in his dominions, to instruct his miners how to work them, and to manage the ore according to the English fash-

---

translator of Cervantes' *Don Quixote*. Charles Jervas, or Jarvis, was probably born in Dublin in 1675, and was a portrait painter of some repute. His translation of *Don Quixote* was not published until three years after his death in 1739, but 'was frequently reprinted, and maintained its popularity, even against Smollett's translation (1755).' See the entry on Charles Jervas in the *DNB*. 43 *Popular tales*, 1: 15. Further references to this tale are cited parenthetically in the text.

ion' (1: 98). Having made a success of this, Jervas is made responsible for one of the largest of the sultan's diamond mines in Golconda. Jervas' eye is always to the future, though, and so the tale emphasises that he carefully manages whatever he earns: 'The five years salary due to me by the East India Company, which I had never touched, I had put out at interest at Madras; where sometimes the rate was as high as twelve per cent … I was in a fair way to get rich' (1: 107–8).

The narrative device with which Edgeworth frames this story renders the moral of the tale peculiarly effective. Jervas returns a wealthy gentleman to Cornwall and, at a celebration that his former master organizes in his honour, relates his own story to his former workmates. In this way the moral of Edgeworth's tale is expertly illustrated: it implies that all who 'hear' Jervas' story can similarly transform their lives. From here, perhaps, we can trace Edgeworth's anxiety to assert that the tale is no mere fantasy or romance. Of his voyage to India, for example, Jervas asserts, 'I am sorry that I have not, for your entertainment, any escape or imminent danger of shipwreck to relate' (1: 78). Similarly, he has no 'wonderful adventures' to recount of his time in Madras, as he only led 'a quiet regular life' (1: 79). What Edgeworth is attempting, of course, is to convince her readers that 'Lame Jervas' is not a romance. Instead, she implies, it is an instructional tale, whose moral is carefully drawn from real life.

There are some fundamental points which must be made about this 'rags-to-riches' story, points which are directly implicated in Edgeworth's treatment of both nation and empire in her writing. In the first place, and as I have remarked above, Jervas' rise in the world is inextricably linked to the rise of the British empire. It is a director of the East India Company who secures for him his position with Dr Bell in Madras, and Dr Bell's asylum for orphans, the tale observes, is 'an establishment which is immediately under the auspices of the East India Company, and which does them honour' (1: 72). This, as Albert Memmi would have it, illustrates but one example of the process that supports ongoing colonization. Of the future colonizer, Memmi notes, 'One protector sends him, another welcomes him, and his job is already waiting for him.'[44] Through his faithful service of the East India Company, Jervas amasses, or appropriates, a personal fortune while at the same time assisting in the spread of British interests in India. It is therefore significant that Jervas essentially replicates with his pupils in Madras the type of education that he himself received at the hands of Dr Y– in England. This preceptor taught Jervas that education can take the individual only so far and that the social status quo must at all times be main-

---

44 A. Memmi, *The colonizer and the colonized*, tr. Howard Greenfield (1990), 112. As we have already seen, this process is also in evidence in 'To-morrow' where the father of one of his college friends secures Basil's place at the embassy in China for him.

tained. In teaching the native orphans, Jervas similarly instructs them in the art of being docile and obedient subjects who will accept and serve the British presence in India. Once again, education acts as a tool of regulation.

Jervas' desire for property in this tale also mirrors that of the British nation itself and, while it is portrayed as both admirable and justifiable, the Tippoo Sultan's ambition to profit from his diamond mines is represented as a different case entirely. The fact that it is in the supervision of the draining of these mines than he employs Jervas, however, invites the making of a comparison in the tale between the sultan's project and the question of Britain's own long-standing preoccupation with bog reclamation. As Trumpener points out, the bog is 'the locus of a long-running struggle between improvers and nationalists, beginning already with the Elizabethan colonization and settlement of Ireland ...When bogs are cleared in an imperial context ... the activity openly augurs exploitation, not regional economic salvation ... [T]he empire can be profitable only because it siphons off profits from the peripheries and redirects them into the home economy.'[45] The reality of this 'exploitation' is what Edgeworth's tale seeks to avoid, and so the Tippoo Sultan's desires, which precisely parallel British desires to 'siphon off' the wealth of India, are portrayed in 'Lame Jervas' as resting upon unrestrained greed and blatant injustice. Further, the obvious correlation that can be made between the slaves in the Sultan's mines and those in the tin mines of Jervas' Cornish master is never admitted by the narrative, and it actually deflects potential criticism away from the owner of the Cornish mines and on to his workers. Thus, although Jervas was a child slave from about the age of five or six and had, as he tells us, 'a hard life of it', his insistence is that his 'good master ... never knew any thing of the matter; but [Jervas] was cruelly used, by those under him' (1: 8). In this way, the Cornish mine owner is cleared of any responsibility for a system of mining that clearly exploited people in the same manner as that of the Tippoo Sultan. As the tale would have it, Jervas suffers as a consequence of the avarice of the master's lower class hirelings, and not as a result of the master's own desire to extract the maximum profit from his holdings.

In his introduction to Memmi's text, Jean-Paul Sartre points out that the economic wealth of any colonizing nation will finally rest upon the systematic exploitation of native labour: '[T]he colony sells produce and raw materials cheaply, and purchases manufactured good at very high prices from the mother country. This singular trade is profitable to both parties only if the native works for little or nothing'.[46] This recognition is one that Edgeworth is anxious to avoid in 'Lame Jervas', and so she steps back from the painful fact that the wealth

45 Trumpener, *Bardic nationalism*, 46 and 51. 46 Jean-Paul Sartre, introduction, *The colonizer and the colonized*, 21.

of the British nation and empire rests upon slave labour. Instead, she attempts
to produce a (romantic) vision of an English greatness, which guarantees fair
treatment and justice to all walks of life. What she is aiming at is similarly
encoded in the sentiments expressed by the English visitor to Prussia in 'The
Prussian vase' in *Moral tales*. Observing the reluctance of the workers who are
forced to toil for King Frederick, he remarks, "Tis the way with all slaves. Our
English manufacturers ... work in quite another manner – for they are free.'[47]
It is also echoed in the trip that Rosamond makes to a cotton manufactory in
Continuation of Early lessons (1814). The factory to which her father takes his children is a model establishment 'managed by a very sensible, humane man, who
did not think only of how he could get so much work done for himself; but he
also considered how he could preserve the health of the people, who worked
for him, and how he could make them as comfortable and happy as possible'.[48]
This is far removed from the reality of Jervas' childhood as a worker, where
'[b]uried under ground in a mine ... from [his] infancy, the face of nature was
totally unknown to [him]' (1: 29). When he is taken out of the mine as a result
of protecting his master's property from the dishonest miners, Jervas to all intents
and purposes emerges into a world that he has never seen before. Consequently,
he stuffs his hat 'with weeds, and ... all sorts of wild flowers; and ... [his] coat
and waistcoat pockets ... with pebbles, and fungusses' (1: 32).

In his concern for the slaves of the Tippoo Sultan, Edgeworth indicates
that Jervas' attitude precisely reflects that of any Englishman who finds himself in a similar situation in a foreign land. Jervas thus endeavours to secure the
release of the slaves from the sultan's diamond mines to the great puzzlement
of Omychund, a Hindu merchant: 'They are not Europeans. What concern are
they of your's?' (1: 119). It is evident from the tale that Edgeworth's anxiety is
to counter Omychund's further observation to Jervas: 'Once in your native country, you will dream of them no more. You will think only of enjoying the wealth
you shall have brought from India' (1: 119). As Edgeworth tries to have it, Britain's
desire to accumulate, or to appropriate, wealth overseas is absolutely untainted
by either greed or injustice: it is always secondary to the overwhelming desire
of Britons to bring enlightenment to the inferior native. This leads us back once
more not only to how texts like 'Lame Jervas' work to base Britain's empire upon
moral and cultural superiority, but also to the part that they simultaneously
play in assisting the process of incorporation and appropriation in which the
British nation is ultimately engaged. This recognition adds an extra dimension
to Edgeworth's insistence in *Essays on professional education* upon the need to thoroughly master all of the details pertaining to other races and cultures, and it

47 Edgeworth, *Moral tales*, 1: 201.   48 M. Edgeworth, *Continuation of Early lessons* (1816), 1: 259.

ultimately represents the manifestation in her work of one part of the ideological forces that underpin the spread of empire. By learning everything possible about the facts, figures and resources of other nations, the would-be colonizer at the same time begins to appreciate how to reshape this information in his favour. In this context, Edgeworth's emphasis is that understanding the 'other' represents a vital first step in the process of colonization.

This particular reality peculiarly manifests itself at that point in *Essays on professional education* where Edgeworth considers whether or not a young man destined for the bar should acquaint himself with foreign languages. Her conclusion is that this is in fact positively crucial, as legal men will directly facilitate colonial and imperial expansion by helping Britain to 'master' the native's words. In the main part of her treatise, Edgeworth refers to William Jones, oriental scholar and judge of the high court of Calcutta, observing, 'How far it would be worth while for young lawyers to study the Sanskrit or Arabic with the hope of becoming judges in India, is a speculation foreign to this essay' (341). While significantly insisting that this is a 'speculation' that is foreign to her essay, Edgeworth amplifies her argument in an appendix to the treatise. Here, she quotes the remarks of one of Sir William's biographers who observed that the eminent judge and scholar learned Sanskrit and Arabic 'to promote the administration of justice in India, by detecting the misrepresentations of the Hindu or Mahommedan laws, and by correcting the impositions in the form of administering oaths to the followers of Brahma and Mahommed' (498). Although in his case referring specifically to the novel, the arguments that Said advances about how 'the structure of attitude and reference raises the whole question of power [in the text]' can also usefully be applied to what is at stake at this instance in *Essays on professional education*. Novels, Said asserts,

> participate in, are part of, contribute to an extremely slow, infinitesimal politics that clarifies, reinforces, perhaps even occasionally advances perceptions and attitudes about England and the world. It is striking that never, in the novel, is that world beyond seen except as subordinate and dominated, the English presence viewed as regulative and normative.[49]

In both 'The little merchants' and 'The Prussian vase', as we have already seen, Edgeworth inscribes this interpretation of the English presence as both regulative and normative, where the gaze of an English visitor imposes strict justice upon a foreign scene. What *Essays on professional education* to all intents and purposes implies is that the presence of Sir William Jones in India offers a sim-

---

49 Said, *Culture and imperialism*, 89.

ilar guarantee to the native; native law benefits enormously, Edgeworth avers, because Sir William's ability to detect and correct misrepresentations means that it is possible to administer the code much more effectively. What I am suggesting here echoes the type of arguments put forward by Kelly in relation to Elizabeth Hamilton's brother, Charles, who went to India in 1772. Charles Hamilton, according to Kelly, was part of the 'professional middle-class cultural revolution, led by Sir William Jones and his fellow Orientalists in the Asiatic Society at Calcutta, and dedicated to reform of both colonial administration and the empire's subject peoples.' Like Jones, Hamilton was an Oriental scholar, and he was 'given five years' leave in England by Warren Hastings to translate the Persian code of Islamic law for use by the colonial administration.' Kelly concludes that Hamilton's approach to the Indian law code 'implicitly subordinates the Islamic law code itself to the superior viewpoint of an implied reader who will be applying the code mitigated by the reason and moderation of the benevolent imperialist'.[50]

Hiding behind the apparently disinterested 'reason and moderation of the benevolent imperialist' are the harsher realities of a rampant mercantile and colonial desire, of course, and it is these unappealing realities that compel Edgeworth to harness the transformative power of romance throughout her writing. Edgeworth's strategy in *Essays on professional education* is to try to reshape this aspect of the British presence overseas so that it rests upon a cultural and moral rather than a military superiority. In this way, the true desire of British power in relation to the native is concealed, and it is less difficult for the colonizer both to justify and engage in the appropriation, or incorporation, of the wealth of other lands. In this context, it may be useful to quote from the entry for Sir William Jones in the *Dictionary of national biography*. This notes, 'As a great jurist Jones understood that the power of England in India must rest on good administration, and that the first requisite was to obtain a thorough mastery of the existing systems of law in India, and to have them codified and explained.' Thus, 'he decided to prepare a complete digest of Hindu and Muhammadan law, as observed in India; and to assist him in the colossal labour he collected round him learned native pundits and Muhammadan lawyers.' Such mastering and effective rewriting of native law patently smoothes the way for Britain's appropriation and incorporation of the resources of other nations; as the *Dictionary of national biography* significantly observes, for instance, Jones 'was on terms of intimate friendship with the successive governors-general of India, ... and the directors of the East India

<hr />

50 Kelly, *Women, writing, and revolution*, 128 and 130. Kelly notes that following Charles' death in 1792, Elizabeth, although devastated, 'wished to continue her brother's work as a cultural revolutionary', and did so as 'a fictionalized version of him, his career, and his work as an Orientalist' (129). For an overview of the life and works of Elizabeth Hamilton, see *Dictionary of British women writers*, 311–13.

Company ... recognized the value of his labours'.[51] It also, however, represents but one part of that process through which the colonizer attempts to transform what Memmi calls '*The Usurper's Role.*' In pursuit of this ambition, Memmi declares, the colonizer 'endeavors to falsify history, he rewrites laws, he would extinguish memories – anything to succeed in transforming his usurpation into legitimacy'.[52] In other words, and in my terms, he constructs an elaborate romance of a real versus an imaginary power,[53] which leaves the way clear for him to transform the geographical statistics that Edgeworth insists are only supposedly 'fixed, immutable, immortal words.'

It is therefore highly appropriate that *Essays on professional education* demonstrates Edgeworth's perception that words themselves will play a vital role in facilitating this process of appropriation. 'Brian Edwards, in the preface to his History of Jamaica', she observes, 'mentions, that an English judge, in trying a cause relative to the produce of a West India plantation, was utterly at a loss to know, what was meant by *molasses*' (352).[54] The inability of the judge to understand this one word, Edgeworth implies, seriously endangered Britain's chances of extracting the maximum profit from Jamaica, for, in order to successfully appropriate from the native, it is first of all necessary to master the language of his race. This immediately amplifies my earlier comments regarding Edgeworth's treatment of Sir William Jones' (linguistic) career as an oriental scholar and jurist, but it also illuminates my greater contention regarding why she is so emphatic that harnessing the power of romance will immeasurably facilitate Britain's colonial and imperial expansion. As she would have it, the (transformative) power of romance transcends all barriers, including, by implication, those of idiom or race. By harnessing the power of colonising romances, Edgeworth's work avers, Britons will therefore facilitate their very particular ambition: specifically, they will succeed in imposing their vision of reality across the face of the earth.

My intention in this chapter has been to begin to examine the ways in which Edgeworth attempts to reshape romance in the interests of both nation and empire. To this end, I have concentrated mainly upon *Essays on professional education*, suggesting that it is in this, perhaps Edgeworth's most blatant work of

51 See entry on Sir William Jones in the *DNB*. 52 Memmi, *The colonizer and the colonized*, 118. 53 Said also addresses this notion of a real versus an imaginary power in *Culture and imperialism*, where he considers E.M. Forster's *A passage to India* (1924). 'Part of the extraordinary novelty of Aziz's trial [in the novel] is that Forster admits that "the flimsy framework of the court" cannot be sustained because it is a "fantasy" that compromises British power (real) with impartial justice for Indians (unreal)' (89). 54 Bryan Edwards (1743–1800) was a West India merchant, who published several influential works tracing the history and implications of colonial life. One of these, *The history ... of the British colonies in the West Indies* (1793), features particularly in Edgeworth's 'The grateful negro', and we will be exploring it in detail in the next chapter. For an overview of Edwards' biographical details, see the entry on Bryan Edwards in the *DNB*.

empire, that she most clearly reveals the principles of romance upon which much of her writing finally rests. In this context, it might be argued, my approach has been to read Edgeworth's harnessing of the power of romance as an example of what Frye terms 'kidnapped' romance: romance, that is, that is used as a tool of ideology in the service of the 'ascendant values' of a particular social order.[55] Such a reading is entirely possible, particularly given the fact that Edgeworth's membership of the Protestant Ascendancy in Ireland itself lends an extra dimension to any consideration of how she treats the idea of the British nation or empire in her writing. After all, each of the complex ideological formations that impel her work ostensibly facilitates one greater didactic contention: that the colonizing British are necessarily representative of a superior morality and way of life. While this emphasis in Edgeworth's work is obviously important, it should not be allowed to efface other, more ambivalent instances in her writing, which appear to hint at some of the harsher realities of Britain's mercantile and colonial expansion. I have touched lightly upon such a moment in 'Lame Jervas', where I commented upon Edgeworth's anxiety in relation to the issue of slavery and the fact that much of Britain's wealth finally rested upon slave labour. If this recognition causes Edgeworth difficulty in this tale, it presents her with a near insurmountable obstacle in 'The grateful negro.' In this tale, she must somehow reconcile Britain's involvement in slavery and the slave trade with her romance of the British nation's incontrovertible honour or virtue. It is to this dilemma, and its effects upon Edgeworth's treatment of romance, that we will next turn our attention.

55 Frye, *Secular scripture*, 29 and 177.

CHAPTER THREE

Romance as an ideological weapon

Edgeworth uses complex ideological formations, or romances, to construct a vision of British moral and cultural superiority in her work, we have seen, and she primarily predicates her representation of national identity upon her concept of Britain's disinterested 'honour' or 'virtue.' According to Edgeworth, Britain's national and imperial expansion is impelled by altruistic rather than pecuniary considerations, and Britons principally engage in colonization so as to share the benefits of their superior way of life with other peoples and lands. In this context, Edgeworth insists that each of the men who contributes to Britain's expansionist project will ultimately prove to be nothing less than 'a noble adventurer, [or] a righteous pioneer';[1] inspired by 'noble ambition,'[2] he will help to spread the light of Britain's munificence across the face of the earth.

This emphasis in Edgeworth's work is clearly important for several reasons, but it in the first instance demonstrates why her (re)construction of both nation and empire is so heavily dependent upon her use of romance as a narrative form. As we saw earlier, critics point out that romance is by definition a prophetic genre; that it allows the author, or reader, to deny the reality in which he finds himself and to impose his romanticized or idealized perceptions upon what he sees.[3] It is in this context that Don Quixote insists upon 'imagin[ing]' that Aldonza Lorenzo/Dulcinea del Toboso is 'exactly as [he] say[s], without addition or diminution', for example, and it is why he defends his as yet unperformed exploits to Sancho Panza by emphasising that he 'look[s] upon [them] as already done'.[4] By behaving at all times *as if* what he envisions is real, Cervantes' hero anticipates making what he envisions *become* real; to put this another way, he simultaneously refuses to acknowledge and endeavours to close the gap that exists between his 'transfiguring imagination'[5] and life.

In order that this may be accomplished, though, Don Quixote first of all constructs an elaborate theory of reality, 'arguing that things "are" what they

---

1 Memmi, *The colonizer and the colonized*, 69.   2 R.L. Edgeworth, *Essays on professional education*, 411.   3 Beer, *The critical idiom*, 79 and 41.   4 Cervantes, *Don Quixote*, 289. Further references to this edition are cited parenthetically in the text.   5 Beer, *The critical idiom*, 41.

appear to be only by virtue of having been transformed from their true, romance state by an enchanter.' There are numerous consequences to this strategy, but it particularly facilitates Don Quixote's ambition to propound a 'conservative interpretation of history'; to insist, in other words, 'that it would be of inestimable benefit [to Spain] if the Golden Age of knight-errantry' were brought back.[6] 'I [do not] set myself up for a wise man, being really not so', Don Quixote remarks to Sancho Panza, 'all I aim at is, to convince the world of its error in not reviving those happy times, in which the order of knight-errantry flourished' (528). '[S]ince I have been a knight-errant', he insists, 'I am become valiant, civil, liberal, well-bred, generous, courteous, daring, affable, [and] patient', and his implication, of course, is so will all who follow his example (492).

This emphasis in the first place immediately appears to facilitate the arguments of critics who maintain that Don Quixote finally functions as a social visionary in Cervantes' narrative, but it also supports the contentions of those who insist that Don Quixote's desires are not primarily altruistic. For example, Michael McKeon maintains that an important point about Don Quixote is that he is not a don at all but a '*hidalgo*', or 'gentleman', and that, as such, he is attracted to chivalric romances because he anticipates that they will enable him 'to reconcile … the requirements of aristocratic ideology' with the lowly circumstances of his birth.[7] 'Doubt it not Sancho', Don Quixote observes, 'knight-errants do rise, and have risen to be kings and emperors', and, plainly, this is precisely what he believes will happen to him once he can impress the fame of his exploits upon a suitable monarch and his daughter:

> For you must know … there are two sorts of lineages in the world. Some there are, who derive their pedigree from princes and monarchs, whom time has reduced, by little and little, until they have ended in a point, like a pyramid reversed: others have had poor and low beginnings, and have risen by degrees, until at last they have become great lords … and who knows but I may be one of the former, and that upon examination, my origin may be found to have been great and glorious; with which the king, my father-in-law, that is to be, ought to be satisfied: and though he should not be satisfied, the infanta is to be so in love with me, that, in spite of her father, she is to receive me for her lord and husband, though she certainly knew I was the son of a water-carrier … (178–9)

6 McKeon, *Origins of the English novel*, 280 and 285.   7 Ibid. 284. McKeon observes, 'The first thing we know about Don Quixote, after all, is that he is a country gentleman with a small farming estate, a modest household, and a penchant for hunting; and the first thing we learn of Sancho is that he is a neighbor of Don Quixote's and a country laborer' (283).

Don Quixote's skilful use of romance in this way allows him to re-write both his future and his past, but an important point is that it simultaneously enables him to impress upon Sancho Panza his version of the social order. As he would have it, he acts as he does in order to fulfil his (natural) duties and obligations and, for his own good and that of Spain as a whole, Sancho Panza must embrace his master's (feudal) view of life. '[I]n all the books of chivalry I ever read', he observes,

> I never found that any squire conversed so much with his master as you do with yours. And really I account it a great fault both in you and me; in you, because you respect me so little; in me, that I do not make myself respected more ... [T]here ought to be a difference between master and man, between lord and lackey, and between knight and squire. (168)

Similarly, Don Quixote counters Sancho Panza's inquiry regarding how he shall be paid 'if perchance the time of ... favours should not come', observing that squires of old did not receive 'stated wages' (169). Rather, they 'relied on [their masters'] courtesy' and so, he infers, must Sancho Panza (169). In this context, *Don Quixote* demonstrates the efficacy of the argument that romance frequently functions 'as a narrative veil that hides "the language of ideology"';[8] through his use of romance, after all, Cervantes' hero disguises the feudal connotations of his discourse and persuades Sancho Panza that he should embrace his master's view of the world. What *Don Quixote* ultimately reveals, therefore, is that romance is an incredibly powerful ideological weapon. It allows the individual who controls it to 'imagine that everything is exactly as [he] say[s]', or, as we noted in the introduction, to impress upon others a complex 'medley ... of truth and lies' (226, 489).

In light of this recognition, Edgeworth's use of romance in her work takes on an added significance, for it enables us to appreciate better the extent to which her preoccupation with the concepts of 'nation' and national 'identity' is both informed by, and contributes to, the prevailing ideological debates of the time at which she was writing. The period between 1780 and 1830 witnessed unparalleled overseas expansion by Britain, with the result that, by 1820, roughly one quarter of the world's population was under British control. Alongside this, Britain experienced very real socio-political difficulties during

---

8 Elam, *Romancing the postmodern*, 20. 9 A. Richardson and S. Hofkosh, introduction in idem (eds), *Romanticism, race, and imperial culture* (1996), 3. Apart from the socio-political difficulties generated by the effects of both the French Revolution and the subsequent years of war with France, Richardson and Hofkosh note, Britain had to weather the crisis that was caused by the loss of its American colonies, along with the difficulties that arose both out of its early mismanagement of Bengal and the slave rebellions in the West Indies (3).

this era,[9] particularly as contemporaries increasingly began to question whether the methods that facilitated this expansion were consistent with the supposed moral and cultural superiority of the British nation and the British way of life. Inevitably, writers like Edgeworth became crucially implicated in this debate, and their works played a vital role in creating, reflecting, or disguising those ideologies that either facilitated, or interrogated, Britain's expansionist project.[10]

One of the most wrenching aspects of this debate revolved around slavery, as pro-abolitionists vied with the defenders of the plantocracy in order to expose the true implications of this facet of Britain's colonial life. While abolition was 'a persistent and significant literary concern' from the 1750s onwards,[11] the issue took on a particular significance '[f]rom the American Revolution onward ... [for] abolitionist attention to the empire automatically invoked the problem of domestic freedoms and political institutions.' During the 1790s, for instance,

> radical abolitionists helped to establish the Corresponding Societies and modeled them on abolitionist organizations. In their admiration of the political independence effected by the American Revolution (despite its concession to slaveholding interests), as well as in their deployment of a Painite rhetoric of the rights of man, British Radicals often drew parallels between domestic and imperial despotism.

This had the result that the 'rhetoric of the interdependence of domestic and colonial interests' became used 'across the political spectrum, by defenders of plantocracy as well as by radical abolitionists.'[12] In this context, Katie Trumpener maintains that a novel like Jane Austen's *Mansfield Park* (1814) requires an 'historicizing reading', which 'might well see its [famous] moment of silence about the slave trade as politically hard-hitting rather than evasive, a moment at which Austen's reader will know to fill in contemporary debates about abolition'. Singling out Edward Said's analysis of Austen's novel for particular criticism, Trumpener maintains his readings are 'neither broad nor narrow enough in their scope. Oddly foreshortened, they lack historical, political, and generic context; [his] *Mansfield Park* continues to stand in splendid isolation from its immediate surroundings'. In contradistinction to this, she insists that the moment of silence in *Mansfield Park* must be read in context of the wider fiction of the period:

10 My reading here is indebted to various critics, including, of course, Katie Trumpener. In her analysis of the British novel from the 1790s to the 1820s, she states that it 'is both caught up in a wide-reaching experiment with new and old narrative coordinates and engaged in an unprecedented reflection of extranovelistic intellectual and political trends, especially the expansion and consolidation of a worldwide British empire' (*Bardic nationalism*, 164).
11 Perera, *Reaches of empire*, 23.   12 Trumpener, *Bardic nationalism*, 163–4.

'Indirection ... is the key to Austen's treatment of abolitionist concerns and what gives the novel its subtlety and its power'.[13]

My intention is to subject Edgeworth's treatment of slavery to just such an 'historicizing reading', and to suggest that she responds to such awkward textual silences evasively, introducing extremely complex ideological formations, or romances, into her writing. Fashioned from the disparate strands of the abolition debate, these romances are manifestly intended to reconcile Britain's supposed moral and cultural superiority with the nation's economic dependence upon the slave trade and slave labour. Although variously informed, we shall see that these romances all have one thing in common: namely, they seek to sustain the fiction of Britain's moral pre-eminence by stressing the paternalistic nature of the nation's relationship to slavery. Thus it is, for example, that 'Lame Jervas' draws particular attention to its hero's efforts to secure the release of the Tippoo Sultan's slaves. Unlike the despotic potentate, it observes, Jervas is able to perceive not only the sensibility of the slaves, but also that they have a moral right to be free. Ultimately, this emphasis allows Edgeworth to elevate Jervas (and Britain) over the Tippoo Sultan (and Mysore), as it intimates both the moral superiority of Jervas and of the British way of life. Recalling the moment of the slaves' release, Jervas therefore significantly remarks, 'never will the expressions of joy and gratitude be effaced from my memory, which lighted up the black faces of these poor creatures! who, say what we will, have as much sensibility, perhaps more, than we have ourselves'.[14]

Crucially, Edgeworth is only able to sustain this argument in 'Lame Jervas' by carefully excluding from her tale the true nature of Britain's relationship to slavery. At the time that *Popular tales* was published, Britain still controlled 'well over half the Atlantic slave trade', but this fact is resolutely ignored, or silenced, in her story.[15] Similarly, Edgeworth has her hero impress upon Saheb, a native boy, that there are 'no slaves' in England and that, 'as soon as any slave touched the English shore, by our laws, he obtained his freedom'.[16] In the first place, this represents an extremely romantic reading of the celebrated Mansfield judgment of 14 May 1772,[17] and it completely ignores the vast numbers of slaves

---

13 Ibid. 163 and 175. Austen's heroine recalls this moment of silence when Edmund Bertram, her cousin, urges her to talk more freely with Sir Thomas, his father. Pointing out that she does 'talk to him more than [she] used', Fanny asks Edmund whether he heard her ask Sir Thomas 'about the slave trade last night?' Edmund replies he did, but he had hoped her question 'would be followed up by others.' 'I longed to do it', Fanny declares, 'but there was such a dead silence! And while my cousins were sitting by without speaking a word, or seeming at all interested in the subject, ... I thought it would appear as if I wanted to set myself off at their expense, by shewing a curiosity and pleasure in his information which he must wish his own daughters to feel': Jane Austen, *Mansfield Park*, ed. Tony Tanner (1966), 213. For Said's reading of *Mansfield Park*, see his *Culture and imperialism*, 95–116. **14** Edgeworth, *Popular tales*, 1: 124. **15** Perera, *Reaches of empire*, 21. **16** *Popular tales*, 1: 131. **17** Handed down in the case of James Somerset, a black slave who had been brought to England, versus his master, a Mr Stewart of Virginia,

that laboured upon Britain's colonial plantations. Although it is possible for Edgeworth to sustain this stance in 'Lame Jervas', it is patently impracticable in a work like 'The grateful negro', where the slaves in question labour for Britons in the West Indies. Here, as in 'The two guardians', one of her *Comic dramas in three acts* of 1817,[18] Edgeworth is positively compelled to confront the darker side of Britain's colonial and imperial expansion. While the issues at stake in this confrontation manifest themselves differently throughout her writing, they are nowhere more clearly revealed, perhaps, than in *Continuation of Early lessons*. In this text, Harry and Lucy read Anna Laetitia Barbauld's *Hymns in prose for children* (1781), and Harry's quoting aloud of his favourite hymn introduces into Edgeworth's narrative arguments that challenge Britain's colonizing prerogative: 'Negro woman, who sittest pining in captivity, and weepest over thy sick child; though no one seeth thee, God seeth thee; though no one pitieth thee, God pitieth thee: raise thy voice, forlorn and abandoned one: call upon him, from amidst thy bonds, for assuredly he will hear thee.'

Like Edgeworth in 'Lame Jervas', Barbauld here explicitly acknowledges and underlines the sensibility of the native other, but, unlike Edgeworth, she directly links the desire that impels national and imperial expansion to native suffering. By echoing the opening line of William Cowper's famous poem 'Verses, supposed to be written by Alexander Selkirk, during his solitary abode in the island of Juan Fernandez' (1782) at the beginning of her next verse,[19] Barbauld therefore engages with the type of colonizing romances that propel the expansionist project, while simultaneously exposing the connections that exist between these formations and the perpetuation of the slave trade and slavery: 'Monarch, that rulest over a hundred states, whose frown is terrible as death, and whose armies cover the land, boast not thyself, as though there were none above thee – God is above thee; his powerful arm is always over thee! And, if thou doest ill, assuredly he will punish thee'.[20]

---

this held that England was 'a soil whose air is deemed too pure for slaves to breathe in.' Widely interpreted to mean that slavery had effectively been abolished in England, the judgment did not result in the immediate emancipation of all of the slaves already upon English soil, and it 'ended neither the slave trade nor the institution of slavery in the colonies.' Rather, it functioned as a romantic benchmark against which Britain could continue to assert her moral and cultural pre-eminence, while simultaneously continuing to ignore the true implications of her relationship to slavery. My reading here is indebted to A. K. Mellor's consideration of the Mansfield Judgment in 'Am I not a woman, and a sister?', 311. **18** *Comic dramas, in three acts* represents one of only two sets of plays that Edgeworth ever published. The other is *Little plays for children*, which was published in 1827. Apart from 'The two guardians', *Comic dramas* includes two Irish plays, 'Love and law' and 'The rose, thistle, and shamrock', and these rehearse the themes of her more substantial Irish work. See M. Edgeworth, *Comic dramas, in three acts* (1817). **19** The first stanza of Cowper's poem begins: 'I am monarch of all I survey, / My right there is none to dispute, / From the center all round to the sea, / I am lord of the fowl and the brute' (1–4): J. D. Baird and C. Ryskamp (eds), *The poems of William Cowper* (1980), 403. **20** A.L. Barbauld, 'Hymn VIII', quoted in Edgeworth, *Continuation of Early lessons*, 2: 148–9.

Percy G. Adams ably demonstrates the complexities of the relationship between colonizing romances and slavery in his consideration of the extensive use that Daniel Defoe makes of travel accounts in his fiction. He points out, for instance, that Woodes Rogers' *The cruising voyage round the world* (1712) 'provided a chief impetus for Defoe's ambitions to open a British South Sea trade, but it also contains the first and basic account of the most famous of all real island castaways, Alexander Selkirk.' Underlining the fact that it is Selkirk's name, and not Crusoe's, that appears in the title of Cowper's celebrated poem, Adams suggests, 'Cowper's notion of the solitary ruler could have come from Woodes Rogers, who not only tells how the crew nicknamed Selkirk "Governour" but suggests that he was also "absolute Monarch of the island".'[21] In this way, Selkirk's real-life adventures are revealed variously to inspire Rogers' journal, Defoe's novel, Cowper's poem and Barbauld's hymn.[22] Unlike the other three, however, Barbauld's intention is not so much to stimulate colonial and imperial ambition, as it is to ensure that the fruits of its manifestation do not subsequently compromise the moral integrity of the British nation and race.

Although Harry's quoting of Barbauld's hymn raises the spectre of slavery in Edgeworth's narrative, it simultaneously provides her with the means through which to sustain the romance of Britain's moral and cultural superiority. Effectively, what Barbauld's hymn suggests is that the colonizing process is not in itself immoral; it only becomes so once the colonizer fails to exercise the type of moral integrity that ought to be expected of a Briton. This argument also infuses 'The colonists' and 'The kidnappers', two of the tales that appear in *Evenings at home; or, the juvenile budget opened* (1782–6). Produced for children by Barbauld and her brother, Dr John Aikin, this was a work that Edgeworth and her family 'admire[d] … extremely'.[23] In 'The colonists', Mr Barlow plays a game with his children, casting himself as 'the founder of a colony' and his sons as the representatives of different trades and professions who are coming to offer their services.[24] When one son offers himself as a soldier, Mr Barlow remarks, 'We are peaceable people, and I hope shall have no occasion to fight. We mean honestly to purchase our land from the natives, and to be just and fair in all our dealings with them' (351). This emphasis in 'The Colonists' amplifies the moral of 'The kidnappers', wherein Mr B reads his children a narrative from 'Churchill's

21 Adams, *Travel literature and the evolution of the novel*, 126 and 131. Defoe's hero insists on being called 'governour' by the English sailors on the ship that eventually conveys him back to civilisation (*Robinson Crusoe*, 264). 22 Significantly, as we saw in chapter one, it is Cowper's poem, not Defoe's novel, that inspires Frank's inappropriate emulation of Robinson Crusoe in *Frank*. 23 See Maria Edgeworth to Mrs Ruxton, 8 May 1794, letter 111. Edgeworth's admiration for Barbauld's work is evidenced not only by the frequent references that she makes to Barbauld in both her own writing and letters, but also by the Catalogue of the library of the Edgeworth family, which reveals that the family had copies of most of Barbauld's work. 24 Dr J. Aikin and Mrs Barbauld, *Evenings at home* (London no date), 348. Further references to this edition are cited parenthetically in the text.

voyages' that recounts how Danish sailors kidnapped Greenlanders and brought
them to Denmark as slaves (117). Noting that the Danes justified this by arguing that they instructed their captives in Christianity and then sent them back
to their own country, Mr B argues that this can be a good thing only 'if it were
done by proper means; but to attempt it by an act of violence and injustice could
not be right; for they could teach them nothing good by themselves setting a
bad example; and the poor people were not likely to learn willingly from those
who had begun by injuring them so cruelly' (118). Of colonization by force, Mr
B observes, 'a more impudent mockery of all right and justice cannot be conceived' (119). If one obvious implication of Barbauld and Aikin's tales is that
Britain ought to be 'just and fair' in all of her dealings with native peoples,
another is that this inevitably reaps the would-be colonizer a verifiable reward.
In 'The colonists', Mr B remarks, 'William Penn, the founder of Pennsylvania,
followed that plan; and when the Indians were at war with all the other European
settlers, a person in a Quaker's habit might pass through all their most ferocious
tribes without receiving the least injury' (351).

In this way, Barbauld and Aikin reveal that their ambition in *Evenings at home*
is to construct a paradigm of colonization that simultaneously defends Britain's
economic interests while protecting the moral integrity of the nation. In their
tale entitled 'Master and slave', they present their readers with a dialogue between
a plantation-owner and a slave who has made two attempts to escape. The point
of the story is to demonstrate that benevolence succeeds far better than cruelty in a colonial situation and, moreover, to illustrate that a liberated work-
force is the best guarantee of a colony's stability and prosperity. In this context, the slave emphasizes, 'It is impossible to make one who has felt the value
of freedom acquiesce in being a slave', thereby revealing the fundamental difficulty that confronts any colonial power (416). Eventually having convinced
his master to give him his liberty, the erstwhile slave goes on to delineate the
inherently untenable nature of the master/slave relationship. Slave owners 'are
surrounded by implacable foes, who long for a safe opportunity to revenge upon
[their masters] all the miseries they have endured' (417). 'The more generous
[the slaves'] natures, the more indignant they feel against that cruel injustice
which has dragged them to perpetual servitude' (417). Similarly, slave owners
delude themselves if they believe that kind treatment can 'soften the obduracy
of their [slaves'] resentment' (417). 'Superior force alone can give [slave-owners]
security', the former slave notes, 'As soon as that fails, [they] are at the mercy
of the merciless. Such is the social bond between master and slave!' (417).

This argument in Barbauld and Aikin's work, namely, that the social bond
between master and slave demands renegotiation if only on the grounds of the
security and economic well-being of the colony, is rehearsed repeatedly in late-

eighteenth- and early-nineteenth-century texts. In his *The interesting narrative of the life of Olaudah Equiano, or Gustavus Vassa, the African, written by himself* (1789), for example, Olaudah Equiano is emphatic that the practice of leaving plantations in the hands of overseers is singularly self-defeating. The cruelties of these men, who are 'for the most part persons of the worst character of any denomination of men in the West Indies', inevitably drive the slaves to 'retaliate on their tyrants!' Benevolent gentlemen planters who reside on their plantations, on the other hand, invariably find that 'benevolence [is] their true interest.' Equiano focuses upon the inevitable anxiety of the colonizer, insisting that equitable treatment of native workers would do much to diffuse the undercurrent of fear that informs colonial life: 'Are you not hourly in dread of an insurrection? … by changing your conduct, and treating your slaves as men, every cause of fear would be banished. They would be faithful, honest, intelligent and vigorous; and peace, prosperity, and happiness would attend you'.[25]

When we consider how Edgeworth (re)reads this master/slave relationship in her work, it rapidly becomes apparent that her writing is hugely influenced by the ideological formations, or cultural romances, with which the late-eighteenth- and early-nineteenth century British nation tried to (re)negotiate its relationship to slavery. While these romances are exceedingly complex, they all draw upon what have been defined as 'stereotypes of slaves and slavery, as well as Africans and Africa, that had become part of an orthodox perspective during one hundred and fifty years of anti-slavery protest.' In *Oroonoko* (1688), for instance, Aphra Behn constructed 'a paradigm of slavery, aspects of which became constitutive elements in colonial discourse for the next century and a half until the Emancipation Bill passed in 1834.' 'First of all, Behn affirms an abolitionist and emancipationist perspective in Oroonoko's famed speech', where the noble-born slave questions by what right the British colonists in Surinam condemn their slaves to a lifetime of labour and suffering.[26] Oroonoko declares,

> why … should we be slaves to an unknown people? Have they vanquished us nobly in fight? Have they won us in honourable battle? And are we, by the chance of war, become their slaves? … No, but we are bought and sold like apes, or monkeys, to be the sport of women, fools and cowards, and the support of rogues, runagades, that have abandoned their own countries, for raping, murders, thefts, and villainies … shall we render obedience to such a degenerate race, who have no one human virtue left, to distinguish them from the vilest creatures?

25 O. Equiano, *The interesting narrative and other writings*, ed. Vincent Carretta (1995), 105 and 112.   26 M. Ferguson, *Subject to others* (1992), 4 and 49.

Although this emotive speech prompts the slaves to rebel, they ultimately prove unfaithful to Oroonoko, and, rather than risk further punishment by the British, they abandon him and return to their masters. This circumstance underpins what is an essential point in Behn's text: namely, that Oroonoko is an exceptional savage. As such, even he becomes convinced and 'ashamed' of 'the rashness and inconsiderateness of his action ... in endeavouring to make those free, who were by nature slaves, poor wretched rogues, fit to be used as Christians' tools', and he announces that 'he had rather die than live upon the same earth with such dogs'.[27] In this way, *Oroonoko* 'ends up implicitly privileging plantocratic ideology, inflaming Eurocentric attitudes toward Africans, and bolstering the colonial status quo'.[28]

The terms of the 'colonial discourse' that Behn produced in *Oroonoko* variously manifest themselves throughout Edgeworth's work. Like Oroonoko, for example, the slave-hero of 'The grateful negro' is also a Koromantyn slave who is (re)named Caesar by his white masters, and his function in the narrative is similarly that of 'the sanctified hero, the slave-icon idealized by scared Britons'.[29] In contradistinction to Behn, however, Edgeworth's evident ambition to produce a consistent defence of Britain's colonial prerogative fundamentally transforms her tale, so that it functions as something much more significant than the story of one grateful, but exceptional, slave.[30] Instead, 'The grateful negro' operates as an elaborate romance, which is manifestly intended to impress upon the reader that it is possible to reconcile the notion of Britain's superiority with

---

27 A. Behn, *Oroonoko, The rover and other works*, ed. Janet Todd (1992), 126 and 130–1. 28 Ferguson, *Subject to others*, 49. 29 Ibid. 233. This type of idealization of the native other recurs repeatedly in texts of this period. As we will see below, it is clearly encoded in Bryan Edwards' *The history ... of the British colonies in the West Indies*, but it also evidences itself in an instance of peculiar significance in a later text of his in which he details the history of the slaves' rebellion in San Domingo. In this text, which was also in the Edgeworth family library, Edwards records the story of the Baillons, who 'were apprized of the revolt by one of their own slaves, who was himself in the conspiracy, but promised, if possible, to save the lives of his master and his family.' Edwards describes the three attempts that the slave made to secure the safety of his erstwhile masters, noting that, once he had finally conducted them to safety, he 'took his leave for ever, and went to join the rebels': B. Edwards, *An historical survey of the French colony in the island of St. Domingo* (1797), 75–6. Edgeworth clearly rehearses such an example of 'unexpected and affecting' loyalty in a slave in 'The grateful negro', and it is entirely possible that she incorporates ideas from *both* of Edwards' texts into her story. For an analysis of the comparisons that can be drawn between Edwards' and Edgeworth's figuring of the rebellious native other, see note number 49 below. 30 Behn's treatment of slavery in *Oroonoko* is different from that of Edgeworth in two crucial respects. Firstly, Behn figures Oroonoko as exceptional, while Edgeworth's argument in 'The grateful negro' and throughout her writing is that, with kindness, it is possible to make a 'Caesar' out of any slave. Secondly, although Behn's narrator insists that she admires Oroonoko and enjoys a special relationship with him, the fact that she is implicitly fearful of him challenges this assertion in her text. Thus, she observes, 'when the news was brought ... that Caesar had betaken himself to the woods, and carried with him all the Negroes, we were possessed with extreme fear, which no persuasions could dissipate, that he would secure himself till night, and then, that he would come down and cut all our throats' (*Oroonoko*, 132). As we shall see below, Edgeworth insists that Mr Edwards' professed affection for Caesar is genuine and consistent, and that he is literally willing to trust Caesar with his life.

the realities of colonial life. Thus, although the tale is 'named' for the grateful Caesar, it primarily revolves around the benevolent planter, Mr Edwards. An enlightened gentleman, he is at first unable to understand why the terms of the Mansfield judgment are confined to England. If it is on economic grounds, he observes, why cannot the goods in the colonies 'be produced by freemen, as well as by slaves? If we hired negroes for labourers, instead of purchasing them for slaves, do you think they would not work as well as they do now? Does any negro, under the fear of the overseer, work harder than a Birmingham journeyman, or a Newcastle collier; who toil for themselves and their families?'[31] By the time the tale closes, Mr Edwards has learned precisely why freedom is a 'Glorious privilege' that cannot be summarily 'extended to all [of England's] dominions': he realizes, that is, that the presence of the British colonizer is absolutely necessary in order to regulate the worst excesses of native life (3: 203).

As in Behn's *Oroonoko*, the question of how to manage the evident intelligence and sensibility of the native/slave is one of the primary concerns in 'The grateful negro', and it is in this context that Edgeworth presents two types of plantation owners to her reader. On the one hand, there is the benevolent Mr Edwards and, on the other, the negligent Mr Jefferies, who 'considered the negroes as an inferior species, incapable of gratitude, disposed to treachery, and to be roused from their natural indolence only by force: he treated his slaves, or rather suffered his overseer [Durant] to treat them, with the greatest severity' (3: 193). Originally owned by Mr Jefferies, Caesar and Clara, his betrothed, are seized along with other of the plantation owner's goods in order to help discharge his debts. Bought by Edwards, Caesar finds himself in the service of a man who 'treated his slaves with all possible humanity and kindness', and the narrative stresses that this benevolence has an immediate and identifiable impact upon the slave (3: 195). Thus, when Edwards shows Caesar the cottage and provision grounds that will be his, calling him his 'good friend' and stressing that he can henceforth work hard without the fear of either his earnings being taken from him or of his being sold, the tale notes, 'tears gushed from his eyes. Tears which no torture could have extorted!' (3: 206). Trusted later by Edwards with a sharp knife in order to trim the branches of a tamarind tree that overhangs his cottage, Caesar falls to his knees on the planter's departure 'and, in a transport of gratitude, swore that, with this knife, he would stab himself to the heart, sooner than betray his master!' (3: 224).

This avowal is of particular importance in a tale that is evidently preoccupied with the dangers of native rebellion, and Edgeworth stresses the sincerity of Caesar's emotional response to Edwards by emphasizing that it transcends

---

31 *Popular Tales*, 3: 202. Further references to this tale are cited parenthetically in the text.

even the loyalty that he feels for Hector, his particular friend and fellow-slave, who was brought with him on the same ship from Africa. Hector is one of the main conspirators in the plot against the planters on the island, and the cruelties he has suffered as a slave have left him incapable of understanding Caesar's loyalty to the master whom he now calls his 'benefactor … [and] friend!' (3: 211). The several conflicts that torment Caesar are carefully detailed in the tale,[32] with the narrative noting in one instance how his 'mind was divided, between love for his friend [Hector], and gratitude to his master: the conflict was violent, and painful. Gratitude at last prevailed: he repeated his declaration, that he would rather die than continue in a conspiracy against his benefactor' (3: 212). For his part, Richardson emphasizes the comparison that can be made here between Caesar and Lame Jervas, remarking: 'Colonialism, property, and the shift from horizontal to vertical allegiance, from solidarity with fellow laborers to identification with the master's interest' are obvious features of both of these tales.[33] While this is true, the greater significance of Edgeworth's treatment of this 'shift from horizontal to vertical allegiance' in 'The grateful negro' is that it demonstrates why native 'identification with the master's interest' is positively essential in a colonial situation where the threat of rebellion is ever-present. More than this, and echoing the sentiments of either Barbauld and Aikin's 'Master and slave' or Equiano's *Interesting narrative*, Edgeworth's assertion is that benevolence always succeeds far better than despotism in securing such identification.

This emphasis in 'The grateful negro' plainly accounts for Edgeworth's treatment of the miserable career of the negligent, insensitive, Mr Jefferies. By failing to properly fulfil his moral responsibilities to his slaves, this planter exposes the entire colony to danger. His indifference facilitates the cruelties of Durant, his overseer, whose actions are inevitably self-defeating.[34] Durant's ill treatment of the slaves 'made him constantly suspicious: he dreaded that the slaves should combine against him' (3: 213–14). This fear causes him to treat the slaves ever more cruelly, and it is this that leads to the eventual rebellion upon the Jefferies estate. The greater point that Edgeworth is making is underlined, firstly, by the fact that the intended rebellion does not confine itself to this one plantation alone and, secondly, by the further recognition that only for Mr Edwards the insurrection would have spread over the entire island: '[Durant]

32 The fact that Caesar has to struggle against his affection for Clara, his betrothed, is also emphasized in Edgeworth's tale. Terrified by the threats that Esther, the obeah woman, makes against Caesar's life, Clara begs him to join the conspirators. Instead of his life, Caesar tells her to think of his 'honour' (3: 222).   33 Richardson, *Literature, education, and Romanticism*, 226.   34 Remarking that 'Mr Jefferies might perhaps have forbidden such violence to be used, if he had not been at the time carousing with a party of jovial West Indians', Edgeworth's narrative implies that the planter's character has been adversely affected by contact with the representatives of an inferior culture (3: 199).

was the principal object of [the slaves'] vengeance: he died in tortures, inflicted by the hands of those who had suffered most by his cruelties. Mr Edwards, however, quelled the insurrection before rebellion spread to any other estates in the island. The influence of his character, and the effect of his eloquence upon the minds of the people, were astonishing' (3: 239). In its turn, Mr Edwards' intervention is in itself only possible as a result of his benevolent treatment of his slaves. The fact that this secures their loyalty is repeatedly noted in the tale,[35] but it manifests itself most significantly where Caesar decides to turn his back on freedom and instead warn his master of the impending rebellion. 'The principle of gratitude conquered every other sensation', the narrative observes, 'His heart beat high at the idea of recovering his liberty; but he was not to be seduced from his duty, not even … by the dreadful certainty that his former friends and countrymen, considering him as a deserter from their course, would become his bitterest enemies' (3: 224).

Unable to recover his losses, or to conquer his fear of future insurrection, Jefferies returns with his family to Britain, and continues to '[rail] at the treachery of the whole race of slaves' (3: 240). In so doing, the planter demonstrates his final inability to learn from his experiences on the island, for he fails to appreciate that it was his negligence and Durant's ill treatment that provoked the rebellion. This emphasis obviously echoes my earlier observations regarding the implications that Barbauld's hymn has for the colonizing process, but it also indicates the extent to which 'The grateful negro' itself functions as a plantocratic romance, which is intended to demonstrate for the reader how to secure the status quo in the colonies. Early in her story, Edgeworth treats the benevolence of Mr Edwards at length, noting how he

> wished that there was no such thing as slavery in the world; but he was convinced, by the arguments of those who have the best means of obtaining information, that the sudden emancipation of the negroes would rather increase than diminish their miseries. His benevolence therefore confined itself within the bounds of reason. He adopted those plans, for the amelioration of the state of the slaves, which appeared to him the most likely to succeed without producing any violent agitation, or revolution. (3: 195).

A footnote attached to this important passage states that 'these ideas are adopted – not stolen' from a text entitled *The history …of the British colonies in the*

---

35 Details of the conspiracy are known to all of the slaves on the island except those on the Edwards' estate (3: 208). Once informed by Caesar of the rebellion, moreover, Edwards arms the slaves as well as the whites on his plantation as 'they were all equally attached to him' (3: 236).

West Indies (1793) by Bryan Edwards (3: 173). Critics who comment upon the part played by Edwards' work in Edgeworth's tale in general confine themselves to remarking upon the liberal use that she makes in one of her footnotes to his consideration of '*Obeah* practice' in Jamaica (3: 216). I will be elaborating upon this myself below, but what I want to underline here is that Edgeworth does more than 'adopt' Edwards' ideas into her tale: she draws upon them to the extent that they become the very bones upon which she constructs her planto-cratic romance. For example, 'The grateful negro' declares that it is positively immoral for a slave to be seized in order to help discharge the debts of his or her master. A slave such as this often finds himself sold on to strangers, the narrative notes, sometimes ending up as a labourer in the mines of Mexico, 'and all this without any crime or imprudence on his part, real or pretended. He is punished because his master is unfortunate' (3: 195). This preoccupation is clearly modelled upon that of Edwards, whose text likewise observes that this practice in the West Indies 'unhappily ... occurs every day'; the slave 'is pun-ished because his master is unfortunate'.[36]

The greater import of Edgeworth's reliance upon Edwards' text, though, lies in the fact that it itself is a carefully constructed romance, or fiction, which aims to prove that the 'independent spirit' of the West Indian planters is entirely representative of the greater superiority of the British race (2: 8). As such, Edwards' strategy echoes that of Edgeworth's father in his prefaces to her works. He insists, in other words, that the work that follows is the result of 'personal knowledge and actual experience', and that it is faithfully drawn from real life (1: xiv). Edwards' particular desire in writing his text is to counteract 'the malig-nant and unmerited aspersions which are daily and hourly thrown upon the planters, for supposed improper and inhuman treatment of their African labour-ers' (1: xvii). The unwarranted result of such 'false' accusations is that the planters' 'characters' and 'honour' have been 'most cruelly traduced' (1: xvii–xviii). While this is in itself bad enough, Edwards' further point is that this circumstance has had profoundly detrimental national and imperial consequences. Britons have allowed themselves to forget that the West Indies 'are become the princi-pal source of the national opulence and maritime power' and, as such, that 'these little dependencies' are crucially implicated in the stability and prosperity of

36 B. Edwards, *The history ... of the British colonies in the West Indies* (Dublin 1793) 2: 141. Further references to this edi-tion are cited parenthetically in the text. Edgeworth's preoccupation with Edwards' text in 'The grateful negro' also manifests itself in the names of her characters. In the first place, the fact that Edgeworth's 'Mr Edwards' is clearly 'named' for Bryan Edwards is a point so obvious that it might be overlooked. Similarly, Clara, Caesar's betrothed, is evidently named for one of Bryan Edwards' slaves who was 'a most faithful well-disposed woman ... brought from the Gold Coast to Jamaica the latter end of 1784' (2: 62–3). The significance of Edgeworth's choice of the name 'Abraham Bayley' for her benevolent overseer is discussed in greater detail below.

British life (1: 450).[37] For the good of the nation, Edwards implies, his readers must correct their mistaken impressions about slavery: specifically, they must recognize that the irrefutable integrity of the British colonists entitles them to keep slaves.

To support his argument, Edwards draws upon many of the prevailing cultural romances with which the British nation tried to justify and excuse its career as an owner and trader of slaves. For instance, he contends that most Africans were already enslaved in Africa, an argument typically advanced by proponents of slavery.[38] He further insists, 'a good mind may honestly derive some degree of consolation in considering that all such of the wretched victims as were slaves in Africa, are, by being sold to the Whites, removed to a situation infinitely more desirable, even in its worst state, than that of the best and most favoured slaves in their own country' (2: 99). This contention, namely, that being enslaved to whites is far superior to anything that the native might have experienced in his or her own land, represents a crucial part of the (pro-slavery) colonial discourse upon which Edwards finally pins his text and, as we shall see below, it also informs Edgeworth's treatment of slavery. Edwards' avowal, however, is that this recognition has even been made by 'The Reverend Society established in Great Britain for propagating the Gospel in foreign parts' (2: 34). This 'venerable society' holds

> a plantation in Barbadoes under a devise of Colonel Codrington; and they have found themselves not only under the disagreeable necessity of supporting the system of slavery which was bequeathed to them with the land; but are induced also, from the purest and best of motives, to purchase occasionally a certain number of Negroes, in order to divide the work, and keep up the stock. They well know that moderate labour, unaccompanied with that wretched anxiety to which the poor of England are subject, in making provision for the day that is passing over them, is a state of comparative felicity: and they know also, that

---

37 Edwards dedicated his history to 'The King's Most Excellent Majesty', observing that, 'under his mild and auspicious government', Britain's West Indian dominions 'are become the principal source of the national opulence and maritime power' (n.p.).   38 According to Edwards, he questioned 25 of his own slaves, newly arrived from Africa, and discovered that 15 'were born to slavery, and were either sold to pay the debts, or bartered away to supply the wants of their owners' (2: 97). Of the 10 remaining, 5 had been 'kidnapped ... and sold to black merchants, while the other 5 had fallen victims to some of those petty wars' periodically instigated throughout Africa (2: 97). As Mellor points out, merchants, traders and planters typically sought to defend slavery and the slave trade on the grounds that both 'were necessary to Britain's economic survival', and supported their arguments with the further observation that both practices were also 'morally justified' as many Africans 'had been slaves in their own countries and ... were savages or heathen[s] incapable of rational thought or moral feeling and hence unfit for freedom' ('Am I not a woman, and a sister', 312).

men in savage life have no incentive to emulation: persuasion is lost on such men, and compulsion, to a certain degree, is humanity and charity. (2: 34–5)[39]

This significant passage further demonstrates Edwards' anxiety to distance the West Indian plantocracy from the worst charges of the abolitionists. He contends that the society's holdings in Barbadoes are effectively 'accidental'; they were bequeathed the Codrington estates. This, he insists, has been the unfortunate lot of many of the planters: 'Much the greatest part of the present inhabitants of the British West Indies came into possession of their plantations by inheritance or accident' (2: 34).[40] Edwards stresses that thus many planters, 'unacquainted with local circumstances, and misled by the popular outcry, have humanely given orders to emancipate all their slaves, at whatever expence; but are convinced that their benevolent purposes cannot be carried into effect consistently even with the happiness of the Negroes themselves' (2: 34). He professes that he, too, was once in favour of the complete suppression of the 'reprobated commerce' of the slave trade, but that a 'fuller enquiry and better information' has lead him to 'fear that a direct and sudden abolition by one nation alone, will not serve the purposes of humanity in Africa' (2: 105). If Britain abolishes its part in the trade, some '38,000 of these miserable people (the present annual export in British shipping) [will be] thrown upon the market' (2: 101). The inevitable result of this, Edwards emphasizes, is that either the Dutch or the French 'will encrease their trade in proportion to the encreased supply, or, having the choice and refusal of 38,000 more than they have at present, will become more difficult to please; confining their purchases to such only as are called prime slaves' (2: 101–2). For humanitarian reasons, then, Britain must not abolish slavery; its part in the trade guarantees old and sick slaves a better life.

All of the complex ideological formations in *The history … of the British Colonies in the West Indies* contribute to one greater argument: namely, however abhorrent slavery may be in theory, in practice it has always existed. Amelioration, and not abolition, thus represents the best way for Britain to regulate her involvement in the keeping and trading of slaves:

39 For a consideration of the Church of England's 'conservative' approach to slavery in the East Caribbean, see Ferguson, *Subject to others*, 100.   40 Edwards also tries to distance the West Indian plantocracy from the charges of the abolitionists by insisting that planters are 'entirely innocent and ignorant of the manner in which the Slave Trade is conducted … so it is equally consonant to their interest and their wishes, that effectual means should be pursued for preserving the health of the Negroes, by securing to them proper and reasonable accommodation on the passage' (2: 113). Edgeworth's treatment of the mine-owner's lack of responsibility for the conditions under which Jervas laboured as a child clearly echoes Edwards' assertion that the high mortality rate on some of the ships is directly attributable to 'the criminal rapaciousness of many of the ship-masters' (2: 110).

Perhaps, like pain, poverty, sickness, and sorrow, and all the various other calamities of our condition, [slavery] may have been originally interwoven into the constitution of the world, for purposes inscrutable to man. Of this I am certain, that an immediate emancipation of the slaves in the West Indies, would involve both master and slave in one common destruction. Thus much however is allowed; the miseries we cannot wholly remove, we may in some cases mitigate: We may alleviate, though we cannot cure. (2: 138)

It is upon this plantocratic romance that Edgeworth ultimately constructs 'The grateful negro', and her Mr Edwards therefore adopts the ameliorative schemes recommended by his namesake in real life. These include paying the slaves wages for their extra labour, securing to them the cottages in which they live and the provision grounds with which they supply their table, and guaranteeing that property they might amass will never be taken from them (3: 195–8).[41] What is obvious in first Edwards' and then in Edgeworth's writing, though, is that all of these schemes are rooted in something much more than philanthropic ambition: each one is also manifestly intended to contribute to both the future profit and the security of Britain's colonial presence in the West Indies. For this reason, Edwards' work observes that the practices it describes are 'calculated to awaken a spirit of emulation and industry, which the dread of punishment can never produce' (2: 139). 'The grateful negro' echoes these sentiments, insisting: 'Those who are animated by hope can perform what would seem impossibilities, to those who are under the depressing influence of fear' (3: 196). Similarly, Edwards maintains that the system whereby a slave's cottage and provision ground is secured to him is 'universally allowed to be judicious and beneficial; producing a happy coalition of interests between the master and the slave' (2: 123). In recognition of this, the slaves of Edgeworth's Mr Edwards have 'their property … secured to them by the prudence as well as by the generosity of their master' (3: 197–8).

Edgeworth's insistence upon this need for a prudent benevolence on the part of the planter/colonizer is clearly drawn not only from her reading of Edwards' work, but also from the terms of the wider colonial discourse that surrounded slavery from the late seventeenth century onwards. It also, however, illustrates the efficacy of the argument that, '[f]or any state, the greatest test of its hegemonic powers is posed by its colonial subjects. For though hegemony is not just a cultural affair, there is no doubt that culture is vital to its work-

---

41 Edwards suggests that the work of slaves should be 'certain and determinate' (2: 138). They should be paid 'wages for extra labour … At the same time, it will be necessary to secure to the Negroes by law, the little property or *peculium* which their own industry may thus acquire' (2: 139).

ings; and winning the consent of men and women to be governed is a more precarious business when there is an embarrassing cultural rift between rulers and ruled'.[42] Edwards wins this consent because, firstly, he recognizes his slaves' sensibility and, secondly, puts into practice schemes explicitly designed to ameliorate the conditions in which they live. In reality, of course, the schemes that Bryan Edwards suggests and Edgeworth adopts expertly illustrate what Memmi identifies as the paternalistic, or, 'charitable racism' with which the colonizer typically treats the colonized. This type of racism, according to Memmi, is impelled by the colonizer's desire to ensure the continued profitability of the colonial relationship and, as such, it is entirely dependent upon the colonized's on-going co-operation with the colonizing project. In looking after the colonized, in granting him wages, the colonizer always insists that 'these are gifts and never duties. If he recognized duties, he would have to admit that the colonized have rights'.[43] It is precisely this rationale that underpins Edgeworth's treatment of slavery in her work, and this in the first place demonstrates the extent to which her writing is informed by the arguments of those who sought to defend slavery on economic grounds. It also illustrates the logic that informs her evident anxiety to re-shape the sensibility of the native, so that, rather than being a moral right, freedom becomes a gift that the colonizer can bestow or withhold. As I have already intimated, this is exactly what Mr Edwards discovers in 'The grateful negro.' Native sensibility, he comes to realize, must never be left entirely to its own devices; it must continue to be carefully regulated by Britain's moral and cultural pre-eminence.

It is in this context that Edgeworth systematically reshapes what is in fact a fight for freedom in her tale until it represents nothing so much as the manifestation of an infernal desire upon Britain's West Indian estates. As she would have it, the slaves' rebellion effectively constitutes a demonic attack upon the sanctity of Britain and the British way of life. Edgeworth's strategy here again owes much to Bryan Edwards, particularly to his analysis of the part played by 'Obeah Practice' in the 1760 slave rebellion in Jamaica (2: 88). This uprising was primarily due to 'the influence of the professors of the *Obeah Art*', according to Edwards (2: 91). These 'induce[d] a great many of the Negroe slaves in Jamaica to engage in the rebellion' and, finding themselves 'invested with command, [they gave] full play to their revengeful passions; and exercise[d] all the wantoness of cruelty without restraint or remorse' (2: 91, 74). By figuring obeah in this fashion, Edwards succeeds in demonising a vital part of native culture, and implies that the 1760 rebellion had less to do with the colonists' behaviour than with the deluded actions of a superstitious race.

---

42 T. Eagleton, *Heathcliff and the Great Hunger* (1995), 28.   43 Memmi, *The colonizer and the colonized*, 142.

This emphasis peculiarly facilitates Edwards' ambition to conclusively demonstrate that the benevolence of the British planter will necessarily protect him from the effects of such demonic power, but it is unable to totally disguise the fact that the institution of slavery will always provide reason enough for insurrection. Edwards' first reference to the 1760 rebellion is thus preceded by his observations regarding the Koromantyn or Gold Coast slaves: 'there cannot be a doubt that many of the captives taken in battle, and sold in the European settlements, were of free condition in their native country, and perhaps the owners of slaves themselves' (2: 59). In light of this, Edwards acknowledges,

> It is not wonderful that such men should endeavour, even by means the most desperate, to regain the freedom of which they have been deprived; nor do I conceive that any further circumstances are necessary to prompt them into action, than that of being sold into captivity in a distant country. I mean only to state facts as I find them. Such I well know was the origin of the Negro rebellion which happened in Jamaica in 1760. (2: 59)

This, of course, blatantly contradicts his later contention that Africans are somehow unaffected by slavery:

> Although there is something extremely shocking to a humane and cultivated mind, in the idea of beholding a numerous body of our unfortunate fellow creatures, in captivity and exile, exposed naked to public view, and sold like a herd of cattle, yet I never could perceive ... that the Negroes themselves were oppressed with many of those painful sensations which a person unaccustomed to the scene would naturally attribute to such apparent wretchedness. The circumstance of being exposed naked, is perhaps of little account to those who were never sensible of the necessity or propriety of being clothed. (2: 116)

Edwards brings this part of his argument to a distinctly colonial conclusion by insisting that prospective slaves are typically eager to be sold after their long voyage from Africa. When buyers are few, he observes, they present themselves 'with cheerfulness and alacrity for selection, and [appear] mortified and disappointed when refused' (2: 118).

The recognition that even the most ignoble savage yearns for freedom, however, undermines the prevailing implication of his work, which is that amelioration is an effective guarantee against revolution. The 1760 rebellion, he notes, 'arose at the instigation of a Koromantyn Negro of the name of Tacky ... [and on the plantations involved] ... I do not believe that an individual amongst [the slaves] had received the least shadow of ill treatment from the time of their arrival there' (2: 59–60). Edwards observes that he can personally attest to this in the case of the estate belonging to one of his relatives, Zachary Bayly:

> I can pronounce of my own knowledge that [these slaves] were under the government of an overseer of singular tenderness and humanity. His name was Abraham Fletcher, and let it be remembered, in justice even to the rebels, and as a lesson to other overseers, that his life was spared from respect to his virtues. The insurgents had heard of his character from the other Negroes, and suffered him to pass through them unmolested. (2: 60)[44]

Where Edwards is unable to argue, as in the case of Abraham Fletcher, that benevolence inevitably affords the planter some protection from the worst excesses of the native slaves, he carefully excludes from his writing the reality that the actions he is describing in fact represent the struggle of an oppressed people for freedom. Instead, he emphasizes the horrors visited upon the white population by the rebels, noting that at one overseer's house colonists found 'eight or ten White people ... in bed, every one of whom [the rebels] butchered in the most savage manner, and literally drank their blood mixed with rum ... In one morning they murdered between thirty and forty Whites, not sparing even the infants at the breast, before their progress was stopped' (2: 60–1). Significantly, these graphic descriptions precede Edwards' account of the barbaric punishments meted out to the leaders of the rebellion, and are obviously partly intended to justify the ferocity of the colonists' reprisals. One rebel, he notes, was chained to an iron stake on the ground and burned alive: 'He uttered not a groan, and saw his legs reduced to ashes with the utmost firmness and composure; after which one of his arms by some means getting loose, he snatched a brand from the fire that was consuming him, and flung it in the face of the executioner' (2: 61).[45] By stressing here that the native slave neither feels

---

44 Zachary Bayly, of Jamaica, was one of Edwards' mother's two rich brothers in the West Indies. When she found herself a widow in 1756, Bayly took her and her 6 children under his protection. See the entry on Bryan Edwards in the *DNB*. It is, of course, entirely significant that the benevolent overseer in 'The grateful negro' is named in part for Zachary Bayly, Edwards' uncle, and for that gentleman's overseer, Abraham Fletcher. Thus, Edgeworth's 'Abraham Bayley' is 'a man of a mild but steady temper' (3: 196).   45 This figuring of the African as being somehow impervious to pain played a vital part in the process through which colonists denied the humanity of the native other, and Edwards' account of the terrible fortitude with which the ringleader met his horrendous death has clear parallels with Behn's description of the death of Oroonoko. According to Behn's narrative, Oroonoko calmly smoked a pipe while an executioner hacked him to pieces. Only when his second arm was cut off, it notes, did 'he [give] up the ghost, without a groan, or a reproach' (*Oroonoko*, 140).

pain nor fears death in the same way as his white master, Edwards encodes a two-fold inference in his text. Firstly, he intimates that Africans are savages whose barbarity is beyond anything that could be imagined by his readers and that this barbarity, by implication, excuses any methods adopted by the whites in order to secure the stability of colonial life.[46] Secondly, Edwards further implies that the worst treatment of the white planters is as nothing compared to what the Africans experience in their own countries. To support this, he appends a footnote to the text, which details how one of his slaves expressed a preference for Jamaica rather than her native land: '[asked by Edwards] which country she liked best, Jamaica or Guiney? She replied, that Jamaica was the better country, *"for that people were not killed there as in Guiney at the funeral of their masters"'* (2: 63).

The overwhelming significance of Edwards' description of both the atrocities committed by the rebels and, in particular, of the scarcely credible fortitude with which their leaders met their deaths, is that they combine to effectively undermine the humanity of the slaves and the moral integrity of their rebellion. When this is added to his interpretation of the infernal part that '*Obeah art*' played in inspiring the insurrection, Edwards effectively succeeds in demonising both Africans and that part of their culture that enables them to mount some resistance to the colonizing British race.[47] Not surprisingly, Edgeworth replicates Edwards' treatment of obeah in 'The grateful negro', rehearsing his arguments that the practice of this art represents a fundamental threat to not only the British colonists' continued ability to extract a profit from their plantations, but also to Britain's continued presence in the West Indies. First of all, she appends a long footnote drawn from Edwards' history to her tale, which includes the account of a planter in Jamaica who was initially unable to discover why a large number of his slaves was falling into a mysterious illness and dying. One slave finally confides to his master that it was all due to the malevolent influence of an obeah woman, whose house the planter subsequently pulls asunder. The text notes, 'The total of his losses, in

---

46 Edgeworth's treatment of Hector encodes a similar proposition in 'The grateful negro': 'Even in his dreams, Hector breathed vengeance. "Spare none! Sons of Africa, Spare none!" were the words he uttered in his sleep' (3: 210). 47 Remarking that *Belinda* is 'a novel of significant political interest [that is too] easily dismissed as a conventional tale of courtship and fashionable life in the metropolis', Perera traces the significance of the character of Harriet Freke being explicitly equated with that of an obeah woman in the novel: 'Representing as it did the survival of African religion and culture on the plantations, obeah was immediately recognized by slave owners as a vehicle of resistance and defiance, and brutal measures were taken to crush its (often female) practitioners. To the West Indian plantocracy so heavily represented in *Belinda* – Percival, Vincent, and the father of Belinda's rival, Virginia, are all owners of Caribbean properties, and Virginia's lover, Captain Sunderland, has helped to suppress a slave revolt there – the obeah woman is a frightening portent indeed' (*Reaches of empire*, 15–16). As in 'The grateful negro', a footnote in *Belinda* directs the reader's attention to Edwards' treatment of obeah in his history of the West Indies (209).

the course of about fifteen years preceding the discovery, and imputable solely to the *Obeah practice*, he estimates, at least, at one hundred negroes' (3: 218). Having indicated that obeah is in fact an efficacious practice that poses an insidious danger to the entire colonial project, Edgeworth, like Edwards, chooses to respond by demonising this aspect of the enslaved natives' culture. She thus disguises the moral connotations of the Africans' insurrection, and implies that it is the colonist's (Christian) duty to banish this malicious art from the face of the earth.

In this context, Edgeworth's tale stresses that Esther, 'the chief instigator' of the rebellion was considered a 'sorceress' by the African slaves and, further, that she 'had obtained by her skill in poisonous herbs, and her knowledge of venomous reptiles, a high reputation amongst her countrymen' (3: 216–18). Esther is, in fact, repeatedly 'named' as a sorceress throughout the 'The grateful negro' and is portrayed as the visible manifestation of the infernal part of native life. When Caesar finds Clara an apparent corpse on the ground of Esther's habitation, the tale therefore notes, 'The sorceress had thrown her into a trance, by a preparation of deadly night-shade. The hag burst into an infernal laugh, when she beheld the despair that was painted in Caesar's countenance' (3: 232–3). Similarly, when Caesar pretends to yield to the rebels' cause, it observes, 'The sorceress clapped her hands, with infernal joy in her countenance' (3: 235). The climax of this negative figuring of the native and, consequently, of the natives' rebellion occurs where Edgeworth describes the arrival of Mr Edwards at the rebel's hut: '[The planter] looked through a hole in the wall; and, by the blue flame of a cauldron, over which the sorceress was stretching her shrivelled hands, he saw Hector and five stout negroes standing, intent upon her incantations. These negroes held their knives in their hands, ready to dip them into [a] bowl of poison' (3: 237).[48] It is, of course, entirely significant that Mr Edwards has to peer 'through a hole in the wall' in order to view the insurrectionists: the final implication of the tale is that his exemplary gaze confers order upon all that he sees.

This (re)figuring of the native other in 'The grateful negro' ultimately provides Edgeworth with the means through which she is able to argue for the continued (ameliorative) presence of the British in the West Indies. Her argument, which manifests itself in all of her work, is that the native's freedom is a privilege best managed by a benevolent colonizer. The several steps

48 In his account of the San Domingo rebellion in his *An historical survey of the French colony in the island of St Domingo*, Edwards similarly (re)interprets a fight for freedom so that it represents nothing so much as the manifestation of demonic desire in what was, formerly, a vision of paradise. During the rebellion, he writes, 'savage man … committ[ed] crimes which [were] hitherto unheard of in history', turning 'the most fertile and beautiful plains in the world … into one vast field of carnage; – a wilderness of desolation!' (xviii and 64).

that contribute to this romance are perhaps best illustrated in her play 'The two guardians', where Edgeworth transforms the British prerogative to grant or withhold the native's freedom into a type of magic that is far greater than obeah power. Published ten years after the abolition of Britain's slave trade and seventeen years before the slaves on British colonial plantations were finally freed, the play relates the story of St Albans, a young, rich, West-Indian planter who comes to London with his mother in order to settle the final details concerning his guardianship until he comes of age. The two possible candidates for the position of acting guardian are Mr Onslow, a quiet country gentleman, and Lord Courtington, who lives with his family at the very heart of fashionable society. One of the first actions that St Albans performs shortly after arriving in England, however, is to free his native slave, with Edgeworth once more encoding an oblique reference to the Mansfield judgment within her text. St Albans thus tells Quaco there are 'No slaves in England. From the moment that you touched English ground, Quaco, you ceased to be a slave.'[49] When Quaco is left alone, he celebrates his newfound freedom with a song that praises British superiority, transforming it into a type of magic that directly challenges obeah power. Again, the song amplifies Edgeworth's wider point: namely, that nobly inspired Britons inevitably project their imaginations upon reality, thereby transforming it as a result of their innate virtue and benevolence:

> Freedom! freedom! happy sound,
> Magic land this British ground;
> Touch it slave, and slave be free,
> 'Tis the Land of Liberty.
>
> Indian *Obee's* wicked art,
> Sicken slow poor negro's heart,
> English *Obee* makes the slave
> Twice be young, and twice be brave.
>
> Quick the magic, strong the pow'r –
> See man changing in an hour!
> For the day that makes him free,
> Double worth that man shall be.
>
> Massa, grateful Quaco do
> Twice the work of slave for you;

49 *Comic dramas*, 160. Further references to this play are cited parenthetically in the text.

Fight for Massa twice as long;
Love for Massa twice as strong. (162–3)

As well as setting Quaco free, St Albans also pays him the value of his 'former labor', but he at the same time urges his erstwhile slave not to let the money spoil him (161). Don't, he insists, 'spend [it] in drinking … Shew me, Quaco, that you are a reasonable being, and fit to be free' (162). Once more, Edgeworth's insistence is that the native does not enjoy an unconditional right to freedom and, moreover, that the freeing of slaves need not necessarily pose a threat to the economic stability of Britain's empire. The freed native will do twice the work of a slave, she avers, and this freedom will be directly linked to the native's continued submission to the moral superiority of his or her (British) master and the British way of life. Again, this represents another part of the colonial discourse surrounding slavery at the end of the eighteenth and beginning of the nineteenth century. For example, having literally bought his freedom from Robert King, his master in the West Indies, Olaudah Equiano recalls that his immediate desire was to make his way to London. Pressed by King to remain in his service, Equiano remembers that 'gratitude bowed [him] down', so that he felt compelled to make several more voyages on behalf of the trader.[50] In 'The two guardians', Quaco's acceptance of his liberty is revealed to be explicitly conditional, as he accepts his freedom only once he is assured that he can remain in the service of St Albans. This serves a crucial (colonial) function in Edgeworth's narrative, allowing her to imply that even a childlike native is capable of recognizing the incontrovertible superiority of his British master and of the British way of life:[51]

Quaco: (*Clapping his hands and capering.*) Free! Free! Quaco? – But no, Massa –
           (*Changing his tone, and kneeling to his master*) – me will be Massa's slave
           alway.
St Alb.:   My servant, henceforward – not my slave. Now if you stay with me,
           it is from choice. – You may go when, and where you please – you
           may chuse another master.
Quaco: Quaco never have no other massa. – Good massa – love him – kind
           to Quaco, from time leetle piccinini boy. – Oh, let Quaco stay wid
           massa.

---

50 Equiano, *Interesting narrative*, 138.   51 This theme also informs Amelia Opie's *Adeline Mowbray*, where an act of kindness on the heroine's part secures the unceasing loyalty of Savanna, a mulatto woman. Having insisted upon working for Adeline 'for noting [*sic*] but [her] meat and drink', Savanna remains loyal to her mistress in the face of ever worsening misfortunes and it is upon the faithful servant's bosom that Adeline eventually expires: A. Opie, *Adeline Mowbray* (1999), 144.

St Alb.:   Stay, and welcome, my faithful fellow, – but remember you are at lib-
           erty. (160–1)

In granting the native's sensibility, and his freedom, in 'The two guardians',
Edgeworth therefore skilfully perpetuates that process through which he or she
is necessarily figured as childlike and dependent. Thus, while Quaco demonstrates both a singular sensibility and a capacity for rational thought,[52] he effectively remains in the same position at the end of the play as he was at the beginning: he still serves a West Indian planter. As Anne K. Mellor has it:

> By constantly contrasting Quaco's loyalty, compassion, and rectitude
> to the cruel duplicities of the young lords and ladies "of fashion,"
> Edgeworth insists on the moral superiority of the "childlike" black to
> the self-indulgent cruelties of the spoiled European youths ... At the
> same time, she defines Quaco as *only* a child, one who eagerly seeks to
> sustain his dependence upon his superior white master.[53]

This emphasis upon the slave's refusal to leave the service of his or her
(English) master also manifests itself in one of Edgeworth's *Moral tales*. In 'The
good aunt', the exemplary Mrs Howard sells her property in the West Indies,
as she 'did not particularly wish, to be the proprietor of slaves.' She also gives
orders that the oldest of the slaves on her plantation should be freed and some
provision provided for them. When Augustus Holloway causes a coach to be
over-turned, a 'mulatto woman' is injured, and she eventually proves to be Cuba,
one of Mrs Howard's former slaves. Not having received the land provided for
by Mrs Howard's instructions, she has come to London in search of her former
mistress. At the tale's close, Cuba decides not to return to the West Indies, elect-
ing to remain, instead, in Mrs Howard's employ.[54] Tracing the connection that
can be made here between 'The grateful negro' and Barbauld and Aikin's 'Master
and slave', Moira Ferguson suggests, 'Edgeworth's young readers learn [from
Cuba] that slaves work willingly when freed in London as well as in the
Caribbean'.[55] The greater significance of Cuba's actions, however, is that once

---

52 When the eyes of St Albans and his mother are finally opened to the perfidy of the Courtingtons, for instance,
Quaco's innate integrity is treated in terms that explicitly contest the notion of the 'savage heathens'' inability to
experience sensibility. His honesty and generosity are thus examined in relation to the deceit and selfish behaviour of Juliana Courtington, who for her part is forced to stand 'in contrast with this negro boy!' (252). 53 Mellor,
'Am I not a woman, and a sister', 322. 54 M. Edgeworth, *Moral tales*, 2: 14 and 50–1. An essential point of this tale
is that, unlike the exemplary Charles Howard, Augustus Holloway is unable to perceive the sensibility of Oliver,
a Creole boy and fellow pupil at school. He consequently tells the horrified Charles, 'I will make a slave of [Oliver],
if I choose it – a negro slave, if I please!' (2: 33). 55 Ferguson, *Subject to others*, 234.

again Edgeworth intimates that the native other will inevitably appreciate the superiority of his or her British master, and, as a result, desire to remain in that master's employ for the rest of his or her life.

This insistence within these works demonstrates how closely Edgeworth draws upon the ideological formations, or romances, with which merchants, traders and planters sought to defend Britain's relationship to slavery. Although nearly thirty years separate the two works, for example, the central contention of 'The two guardians' clearly echoes that of Thomas Bellamy's pro-West Indian planters play, *The benevolent planters*, which was first performed in 1789. In Bellamy's work, Oran, a slave, is reunited with his beloved Selima through the actions of his generous owner, Godwin, and he says 'under subjection like yours, SLAVERY IS BUT A NAME'.[56] This romance, which links the (freed) native's sensibility to his/her inevitable desire to remain in the service of the (British) master, obviously infuses 'The two guardians', but Godwin's reuniting of Oran and Selima is also mirrored by Edgeworth in 'The grateful negro', where Caesar begs Mr Edwards to purchase both himself and his beloved Clara: 'Will you be my master? Will you be her master? Buy both of us. You shall not repent of it. Caesar will serve you faithfully' (3: 177). Caesar's entreaties imply that to serve Edwards is to be a slave in name only, and this constitutes the reason why he finally refuses to participate in the slaves' rebellion.

In weaving a complex plantocratic romance around Britain's relationship to slavery in the West Indies, Edgeworth's manifest ambition is to diffuse and contain the deep-rooted fears of the British colonizer. The well-treated native will positively refuse to rebel against his British master, she declares, for he will recognize that he is in fact fortunate to serve a representative of such an honourable nation and way of life. This emphasis clearly had a very particular significance for a British nation still reeling from the implications of the 1791 slave rebellion in the French colonies on San Domingo. As Ferguson points out, 'San Domingo itself – the word, the geographical territory, its alleged inhabitability, its progress – became synonymous with Anglo-Africanist barbarity that terrified most Britons, regardless of abolitionist commitment'.[57] Perera for her part agrees, observing that it is to the 'terrifying possibility of a Haiti-style rebellion in the English slave colonies' that 'The grateful negro' finally 'bears witness.'[58]

While all of this is obviously important, Edgeworth's work is clearly haunted by the prospect of a far closer rebellion: specifically, one by Ireland's discontented native race. Edgeworth and her family directly experienced such an insurrection in 1798, after all, so it is hardly surprising that 'the theme of

56 Quoted in Mellor, 'Am I not a woman, and a sister', 313.   57 Ferguson, *Subject to others*, 230.   58 Perera, *Reaches of empire*, 20.

colonist insecurity'[59] informs her Irish fiction and her letters.[60] Although it is true that the Edgeworths emerged effectively unscathed from the United Irishmen's rebellion, they were forced to flee to Longford for protection, and did experience days of real anxiety and danger. Only a fortunate delay prevented them from being blown up with an ammunition cart,[61] for example, and an angry mob at one point threatened the life of Edgeworth's father.[62] Similarly, the psychological impact of what the Edgeworths experienced in 1798 cannot be underestimated, and their shock is best illustrated, perhaps, by Edgeworth's expression of her inability to believe in what had transpired: 'It all seems like a dream', she wrote to her cousin, Sophy, shortly after returning to Edgeworthstown, 'a mixture of the absurd, the ridiculous and the horrid'.[63]

While Edgeworth is keen to stress in her father's *Memoirs* that his response to 1798 was entirely pragmatic,[64] we shall see in the next chapter that hers was extraordinarily complex. In the first instance, it manifested itself in her (redoubled) efforts to '(re)write' Ireland:[65] that is, to produce a romance of both nation and national identity that would diffuse and contain the socio-political difficulties of Irish life. Secondly, it was hugely informed by her greater ambition to celebrate her father's achievements in her work: specifically, to convince

---

59 I am drawing here upon Tom Dunne's suggestion that Edgeworth works 'show remarkable patterns of continuity and interaction. In particular, the theme of colonist insecurity in the face of the native threat recurs': T. Dunne, 'A gentleman's estate should be a moral school' (1991), 96. 60 Edgeworth's letters demonstrate that she grew increasingly aware of the possible consequences of growing native discontent during the last decade of the eighteenth century. In a letter to her Aunt Ruxton in 1794, for example, she observes, 'There have been lately several flying reports of Defenders, near us, but we never thought the danger *near* till today – last night, a party of men, amounting to a sober 40? ... attacked a house of one Hoxey, about half a mile from us and took as usual their arms ... You will probably my dear Aunt be surprised at our making such a mighty matter of a first visit from Gentlemen Defenders – you who have had soldiers sitting up in your kitchen for weeks – but you will consider that it is our *first visit.*' References to Defender activity steadily increase in Edgeworth's letters, until, by April 1795, she is writing that there is 'a whirlwind in our county' with 'no Angel to direct it.' In the event, this 'whirlwind' did not manifest itself properly until May 1798, when the United Irishmen finally embarked upon their long-planned for insurrection. The 'dreadful disturbances' of which the Edgeworths read in newspapers did not reach Edgeworthstown until early September, but Edgeworth anxiously traced its approach in her letters. See Maria Edgeworth to Mrs Ruxton, 11 Aug. 1794, letter 114, and 20 Apr. 1795, letter 126. Also, Maria Edgeworth to Sophy Ruxton, 20 June 1798, letter 187. 61 Edgeworth's account of the family's lucky escape is contained in a letter to her Aunt Ruxton. Two officers and six dragoons who were escorting an ammunition cart to Longford offered the Edgeworths their protection. Detained by Edgeworth's father, the family thirty minutes later heard what they thought was 'a clap of thunder.' In truth, the ammunition cart had exploded and, if the Edgeworths had accompanied this cart, they 'must' have been killed. See Maria Edgeworth to Mrs Ruxton, 5 Sept. 1798, letter 194. 62 This occurred after a Protestant sergeant of militia convinced Longford's terrified inhabitants that Edgeworth's father had been signalling to the French from the town's goal. For Edgeworth's account of the family's experiences in 1798, see R.L. Edgeworth and M. Edgeworth, *Memoirs*, 2: 205–38. 63 Maria Edgeworth to Sophy Ruxton, 9 Sept. 1798, letter 195. 64 She writes in the *Memoirs* that he drew the conclusion 'that he ought to mix more with society, and make himself more generally known in Ireland' (2: 237). 65 Edgeworth, of course, did not wait until 1798 to begin writing about Ireland; *Castle Rackrent*, as Butler points out in her introduction to Castle Rackrent *and* Ennui, for example, was probably begun as early as 1794 (5).

her readers that his theories would *necessarily* offer the means through which to secure national and imperial reform. In advancing this argument, though, my intention is not to suggest that Edgeworth merely functioned as her father's Sancho Panza.[66] As my next chapter will show, yes, she faithfully rehearsed his theories in her work, but, in so doing, she simultaneously encoded her perception that these would ultimately prove entirely quixotic.

---

66 Michael Hurst makes the same point, albeit in a different context. 'Though [her father's] role had in some ways been that of a Don Quixote', he writes, 'it is strongly evident ... that Maria was no mere Sancho Panza. Frequent and deferential in tone as her references to her father always were, the contribution she made to the maintenance and improvement of conditions at Edgeworthstown and the thoughts she threw out on public affairs generally marked her out as a person of considerable intellect, outstandingly fine feeling and no mean practical skill as a manager of human beings': M. Hurst, *Maria Edgeworth and the public scene* (1969), 179.

Romancing Ireland

We have been exploring the romances, or colonizing fictions, with which
Edgeworth infuses her work in order to facilitate British national and imperial
expansion. These romances, we have seen, seek to disguise the darker side of
Britain's colonial desire by emphasizing that such expansion is necessarily predicated upon the greater moral and cultural superiority of the British nation and
race. The native other, Edgeworth's work implies, inevitably benefits from the
presence of the British colonizer; her writing emphasizes that the worst excesses
of the British colonial presence are as nothing compared to the barbarities of
the native cultures that it replaces. The truth of this, as Edgeworth would have
it, manifests itself firstly in the native's instinctive recognition of the British colonizer's innate superiority, and, secondly, in the freed native's reluctance to leave
the service of his or her British master. By figuring the colonial relationship in
this way in her work, Edgeworth facilitates her greater contention that liberty is
actually a privilege and not a right, and that, as such, it remains forever in the gift
of the morally superior colonizer. The native who refuses to accept this version
of the colonizing process, and who attempts to secure his or her emancipation,
thus commits an incontrovertibly immoral act; one constituted by Edgeworth in
her writing as nothing less than the manifestation of a demonic desire.

As numerous critics have suggested, Edgeworth's treatment of the relationship between the colonizer and the colonized is necessarily influenced by
her analysis of the social and political situation in late-eighteenth- and early-
nineteenth-century Ireland. Katie Trumpener, among others, makes this point,
suggesting that Edgeworth's 'affirmative account of paternalistic slavery in "The
grateful negro" and her negative depiction of slaves' agitation for their emancipation result partly from the way she has superimposed the economic and
political situation of the Irish estate onto the more extreme conditions of the
Jamaican slave plantation'.[1] In *The absentee*, for example, Edgeworth has a native
Irish innkeeper draw an analogy between Irish and West Indian society. He
remarks that the perpetually absent Lord Clonbrony 'might as well be a West

---

1 Trumpener, *Bardic nationalism*, 165.

India planter, and we negroes, for any thing he knows to the contrary – [he] has no more care, nor thought about us, than if we were in Jamaica, or the other world'.[2] Writing as a member of a Protestant Ascendancy family whose very presence upon its Irish estates in itself symbolizes the colonizer's dispossession of the native, this observation has a resonance in Edgeworth's work that it would not have, for instance, in the fiction of Jane Austen. Unlike Austen, Edgeworth and her Irish characters inhabit a world where the repercussions of colonial desire are experienced as a quotidian reality; theirs is a world where the dispossessed and subjugated native is physically and persistently present.[3] Faced with the difficulty of negotiating this uncomfortable situation in her writing, Edgeworth endeavours to deny or to disguise it, constructing a vision of Ireland in her works that justifies and facilitates the continuing presence of the colonizing class that she herself represents. In this context, my argument in this chapter will be that what she finally produces in her Irish tales peculiarly illustrates the efficacy of the contention that to 'narrate a history in Ireland is to promulgate a particular image of the nation, fashioning what you purport to describe'.[4] Edgeworth's Irish tales, we shall discover, are literally fictions: that is, Edgeworthian romances wherein she 'promulgates' a deliberately familial and colonial 'image' of her world.

Such a reading immediately supports the contentions of those critics who maintain that romance is less concerned with representing reality than with (re)creating it, but it also demonstrates why greater attention still needs to be paid to the significance of the mode that Edgeworth chooses in order to represent her family in her writing. In her reading of *The absentee*, for instance, Mary Jean Corbett identifies what she calls the 'familial plot' in this tale, suggesting how this narrative device is central to Edgeworth's study of the evils of absentee landlordism in Ireland. Corbett suggests that, 'in order to achieve narratively and ideologically the "harmonious alignment" between unequal partners with which the novel concludes, Edgeworth must also reform the families from which [the] would-be rulers of Ireland spring: she must establish modes of legitimate and normative behaviour for women and men.' Drawing upon Edmund Burke's analysis in his *Reflections on the revolution in France* of the need to reform and thence maintain 'proper familial relations,' Edgeworth, Corbett concludes,

> rewrites politics precisely as a familial plot: *The absentee* represents the
> struggle for imperial hegemony within the discursive terms of family

---

2 M. Edgeworth, *Novels and selected works*, 5: 101.   3 This illuminates Dunne's contention that a 'sense of being under siege from the native Irish world underlies all [Edgeworth's] Irish novels' ('A gentleman's estate should be a moral school', 98).   4 Eagleton, *Heathcliff and the Great Hunger*, 152.

and romance … In Edgeworth's view, the rehabilitation of Ireland
depends on the presence of its rehabilitated patriarch and his earnest
son, who would jointly recognize that their 'duty and interest' coincide
with the proper supervision and regulation of their tenants; their own
subsistence and their tenants' – as well as their mutual security – rest
on the father being restored to his proper place.[5]

'Romance' for Corbett here simply denotes rituals of courtship and wooing,[6]
and so her reading of the familial plot in Edgeworth's Irish fiction is reductive
for two reasons. Failing in the first instance to acknowledge that Edgeworth
does not merely rewrite politics as *a* family plot, but, rather, as *her* family plot,
it also fails to consider the fact that she draws heavily upon romance conventions in order to 'saturate' her texts with a deliberately *imprecise* version of her
family's past.[7] Fashioned from both Edgeworth family history and the history
of Edgeworthstown and its environs,[8] this version is crucial to Edgeworth's
purpose, for it allows her to imply that, like *Castle Rackrent*, each of her Irish
works is finally a 'plain round tale' that is 'taken from the life'.[9] Concentrating
in particular upon her father's 1782 return Ireland, Edgeworth uses romance in
order to (re)present this essentially familial event to her readers as an archetypal
quest with apocalyptic implications for national and imperial reform. By coming
'home', she avers, her father (re)discovered not only the truth of his (Protestant
Ascendancy) identity, but also the ontological nature of, and the solution to,
the socio-political difficulties threatening to destabilize national stability in
Ireland and the future of Anglo-Irish affairs.[10] In order to diffuse and contain
these difficulties, Edgeworth insists her readers must replicate her father's exam-

5 M.J. Corbett, 'Public affections and familial politics' (1994), 877, 883 and 893. The *Reflections*, according to Corbett,
'promotes the gendered ideals underpinning social and imperial order threatened, in his thinking as in Edgeworth's,
by feminine sociosexual impropriety' (878). 6 Corbett develops her analysis of the familial plot in Edgeworth's
fiction in her *Allegories of union in Irish and English writing* (2000), and one of her observations in this text particularly illustrates the way in which she reads romance: 'Throughout post-Union fiction, the marriage plot operates
as a rhetorical instrument for promoting colonial hegemony in making the private relations of romance and repro-
duction central to the public and imperial good … [T]his narrative structure … figures relations of domination
and subordination in a colonial context as coextensive with those of gender and class': M.J. Corbett, *Allegories of
union in Irish and English writing* (2000), 53. 7 I am drawing here upon Thomas Flanagan's study of the Irish novel,
wherein he argues that it is typically 'saturated with history … However tedious this preoccupation with history
became to others, however much it limited his own work, the Irish writer was yoked to it forever. His search for
identity drove him relentlessly into the past': T. Flanagan, *The Irish novelists* (1976), 16. 8 The sterling work of scholars such as W.J. McCormack, Tom Dunne, and W.A. Maguire, among others, has done much to illuminate the
extent to which Edgeworth draws upon not only her own family's history, but also that of her environs in her
writing. As Butler observes in her general introduction to the *Novels and selected works of Maria Edgeworth*, 'It is now
apparent that all four of Edgeworth's Irish tales, and to a lesser extent the *Essay on Irish bulls*, are sophisticated textual constructions of a small county in the heart of Ireland' (1: xxviii). 9 *Novels and selected works*, 1: 54. 10 R.L.
Edgeworth and M. Edgeworth, *Memoirs*, 2: 2.

ple, and she intimates that this is particularly important for Ireland's Protestant Ascendancy class. By absenting themselves from Ireland, these have effectively 'forgotten' their original identity and, in order to recover it, they must emulate her father and return to their estates.

As we noted in the introduction, though, 'all memory is selective',[11] and so what the Irish tales ultimately reveal is that what Edgeworth represents as an act of ontological remembrance on her father's part was actually an act of self-creation, one which enabled him to distance himself from both his own and his ancestors' failings and to simultaneously reconstitute his relations with the native Irish race.[12] Rather than recovering an 'original' identity, we shall see that Glenthorn, Colambre and Ormond all strike out on a decisively new path from that of their ancestors and, as *Castle Rackrent* demonstrates, Edgeworth's perception is that this is entirely necessary in order to diffuse the socio-political difficulties of Irish life.

Treating of these difficulties in a 1797 pamphlet addressed to the earl of Charlemont, Edgeworth thus rehearses the contention that is central to all her Irish fiction, implying that these are in the first place symptomatic of what we might term the 'ontological blindness' of the colonizing (English) race. Noting that 'the West Indies ... are obviously in the eyes of the [British ministry], the most valuable appendages of the British empire', her suggestion is that the English are only able to sustain this belief by refusing to gaze directly upon their neighbour; by persisting in viewing Ireland, instead, only 'accidentally ... by reflection.' Condemning those, like Gibbon, who dismiss Ireland as 'a remote and petty Province' in Britain's empire, she insists, 'Old prejudices in nations as well as in individuals, remain, in the mind and influence the conduct long after the circumstances, in which they originated, are changed. – A century ago, Ireland was a burthen to England, now she is her most useful ally'.[13] Here, and throughout her writing, Edgeworth casts the difficulties in the Anglo-Irish relationship in terms of identity; she emphasizes that time and circumstances have substantially altered the nature of Ireland's relationship to England, but that England and the English have proved incapable, or unwilling, to admit of this change.

---

11 Frye, *Secular scripture*, 175. 12 As Flanagan points out, for instance, Richard Lovell Edgeworth's 'long residence in England must have been responsible for some part of the conditions which greeted [the Edgeworth family upon their 1782 return to Ireland], though Maria would never have admitted that, but the root of the trouble was buried in the centuries' (*Irish novelists*, 62). 13 R.L. Edgeworth, A *letter to the right hon. the earl of Charlemont* (1797), 37 and 39–40. Although originally printed under her father's name alone, it is clear from family correspondence that Edgeworth wrote most, if not all, of the text. In a letter to her Aunt Ruxton in April 1795, for example, Edgeworth writes, 'My father says he will allow me to manufacture an Essay on the Logograph [that is, the telegraph] – He furnishing the solid materials & I spinning them.' See Maria Edgeworth to Mrs Ruxton, 11 Apr. 1795, letter 125.

As a mode, of course, romance is peculiarly concerned with identity; indeed, we saw in the introduction that Frye goes so far as to suggest that identity effectively constitutes 'reality' for this narrative form. The typical romance comes into being precisely because of the hero's or heroine's sense of ontological confusion, he remarks, and ceases to be when the identity of the hero or heroine has been (re)established within the text. To this end, 'Most romances end happily with a return to the state of identity, and begin with a departure from it'; the mode is inevitably concerned with fluidity or dislocation, and traces what he terms 'a cyclical movement' between two ontological states.[14] *Ennui, The absentee* and *Ormond* lend themselves most obviously to this model, but it is my contention that each of Edgeworth's Irish tales finally has its origins in her perception of the need to (re)establish identity in Ireland; that each is primarily impelled by her conviction that the identity of the nation has itself been confounded. In working out this argument in her writing, Edgeworth further insists that the fact that Ireland's national identity has been confused has led, in its turn, to the confounding of the identities of the individuals and classes that make up the nation, and it is this confusion that has engendered the social and political difficulties that threaten to overwhelm Anglo-Irish affairs. In considering these difficulties in her writing, Edgeworth traces the origin of this confusion back to that process through which England initially facilitated and justified the colonisation of its near neighbour. Her intimation, we shall see, is that, to satisfy its colonial desire, England deliberately transformed Ireland and the native Irish into a 'changeling' nation and race. One of Edgeworth's several ambitions in each of her Irish tales, therefore, is to clarify for the reader, in particular, the English and Protestant Ascendancy reader, the precise nature of Ireland's national identity; another is to identify the duties and obligations of the several classes that constitute the nation. This clarification is positively essential, for, in Edgeworth's paradigm of Anglo-Irish relations, it is only when each class in Ireland reassumes and properly discharges its responsibilities that social and political stability can be guaranteed. Once this moment is reached, Edgeworth's works assume that the (colonized) native Irish will inevitably realize that they are better off under their Protestant Ascendancy superiors, while the members of this latter (colonizing) class will simultaneously discover that the properly managed 'otherness' of the native Irish tenant represents no threat to national or imperial affairs.

These complex arguments clearly inform and impel all of Edgeworth's Irish work, but they are rendered peculiarly explicit in the *Essay on Irish bulls*,[15] the 1802

---

14 Frye, *Secular scripture*, 54. 15 The first edition of *Essays on Irish bulls* was carelessly printed and, in 1803, the Edgeworths brought out a new edition, which corrected many of the mistakes of the original and added some

text that, according to Edgeworth, represents the most perfect example of her literary partnership with her father.[16] In this text, it rapidly becomes apparent that the Edgeworths' patent ambition is to delineate and, thus, to obviate the several prejudices that exist between Ireland and England, thereby facilitating an ideological reformation in Anglo-Irish relations. Addressing themselves in the first instance to their readers in England, the Edgeworths begin by identifying language as a primary site for the inculcation of prejudice, emphasizing that the ridicule heaped upon the Irish for their efforts to speak or write English is singularly ill-founded. English is to the Irish 'a foreign language', they point out, 'it is scarcely within the limits of probability, that they should avoid making blunders both in speaking and writing'.[17] Much more significantly, they also propound the theory that the very characteristics for which the Irish are ridiculed are not actually peculiar to the inhabitants of Ireland; they suggest that they may, indeed, be the manifestations of the original, displaced identity of the English race. In truth, their recognition, which clearly echoes that of Jonathan Swift and others before them, is that the English may have projected onto their near neighbours 'those elements which [they] denied or despised in themselves'.[18] Tracing the etymology of Irish bulls, the Edgeworths therefore observe, 'We have a papal bull, and John Bull, the representative of the majesty of the people of England. It is a curious coincidence, that the name of that species of blunder, which is peculiar to the Irish, should be, to a letter, the same as the distinguishing appellation of the english [sic] nation' (11). 'It would be absurd', they suggest, 'to suppose, that John Bull could ever have been subject to blunder; although there is a passage in a letter of Swift's, obscurely hinting at some such idea: — "I have it in contemplation," says Swift, "to write an essay on english [sic] bulls and blunders"' (12). The Edgeworths thought of Swift that he either 'believed that bulls were of english [sic] origin', or 'was guilty of a barbarism in language' (12).

new material. In 1808, they published a third edition, but, as the textual note to the *Essay* in *The novels and selected works of Maria Edgeworth* observes, this involved 'the wholesale rearrangement of some of the chapters, and a completely new beginning' (1: iii). Although the editors of *The novels and selected works* have decided to use the 1808 edition of the *Essay* for their purposes, I feel that this version effaces many of the arguments of the original text. In particular, it removes many of those passages in which the Edgeworths most keenly reveal their perception that Britain's ability to 'change' the identity of other nations peculiarly facilitates those appetites that impel colonial and imperial life. For this reason, I have chosen not to use the Pickering and Chatto edition of the *Essay*, and so all of my references are to the 1803 edition of the text. 16 Recalling the production of the *Essay* in the *Memoirs*, Edgeworth explains, 'sometimes, what was spoken by him, was afterwards written by me; or when I wrote my first thoughts, they were corrected and improved by him; so that no book was ever written more completely in partnership' (2: 336). 17 M. Edgeworth and R.L. Edgeworth, *Essay on Irish bulls* (1803), 7–8. Further references to this edition are cited parenthetically in the text. 18 I am drawing here upon Declan Kiberd's reading of the several aspirations that underpinned England's stereotyping of the Irish from the time of the first settlers. 'Burke', he suggests, for example, 'contested English stereotypes of the Irish, because he saw in them projections onto a neighbouring people of those elements which the English denied or despised in themselves': D. Kiberd, *Inventing Ireland* (1996), 20.

What Edgeworth and her father are finally insinuating, of course, is that the etymology of any bull is so uncertain that it is impossible to definitely attribute the origins of any blunder to one particular nation. Pointing to Horace Walpole, they note how he 'records in his *Walpoliana* an irish [*sic*] bull, which he pronounces to be the best that he had ever heard – "I hate that woman," said a gentleman, looking at a person who had been his nurse, "I hate that woman; for she changed me at nurse"' (21). In this, the Edgeworths remark, 'such is the confusion of ideas, that … even personal identity is confounded' (21). In tracing the implications of this apparent bull in the *Essay*, the Edgeworths' desire, clearly, is to convince their readers that it is not only representative of one of the greatest of all metaphysical wonders, but also that it is, further, entirely 'destitute of originality', and 'by no means unprecedented in France, England, or ancient Greece; and consequently [that] it cannot be an instance of national idiosyncracy [*sic*], or an irish [*sic*] bull' (24). Quoting John Locke's observation in his *Essay concerning human understanding* (1690) that personal identity 'consists not in the identity of substance, but … in the identity of consciousness', they contend that the Irishman's ostensible blunder encodes the indisputably tenuous grasp that any individual has upon the 'reality' of his formative identity (22). They write:

> We may presume our Hibernian who was changed at nurse, was so like his foster brother, that the identity of substance could not easily be ascertained by his parents during his infancy; and when he arrived at man's estate, his own consciousness could not reach to the time when the act of changing at nurse was performed; consequently there was no continuity of identity between the infant who was changed at nurse, and the man who hated the nurse for perpetrating the change; ergo, the Irishman could not confound that which did not exist as to him, viz. identity. (23–4)

We shall see below that Edgeworth reserves her fullest treatment of this metaphysical conundrum for *Ennui*, that great Irish tale wherein she painstakingly unfolds the consequences of her hero's literal changeling status.

What is crucial for my purposes, however, is the fact that the *Essay on Irish bulls* finds 'a similar [ontological] blunder in Spain, in the time of Cervantes', recounting Sancho Panza's observation to the Duchess in Book Two of *Don Quixote*: 'I myself am that very squire of his, who is mentioned, or ought to be mentioned, in that history, *unless they have changed me in the cradle*' (24–5).[19] As a nar-

19 Catherine Gallagher's reading of the importance of the changeling device in Edgeworth's work similarly calls

rative device, I have already suggested, the importance of the changeling cannot
be underestimated, particularly in romance where the hero's or heroine's desire
to untangle his or her confounded identity frequently compels the fiction. As
an aid to colonization, it is positively crucial, for, as the *Essay on Irish bulls* reveals,
such confounding or stereotyping of the native other directly facilitates colonial and imperial expansion. I quote the following passage at length because of
its significance:

> That species of monopolising pride, which inspires one nation with
> the belief that all the rest of the world are barbarians, and speak bar-
> barisms, is evidently a very useful prejudice, which the English, with
> their usual good sense, have condescended to adopt from the Greeks
> and Romans. They have applied it judiciously in their treatment of
> France and Ireland. The maxim, that one Englishman can beat ten
> Frenchman, has undoubtedly gained many a battle both by sea and land;
> it forms a sort of succedaneum for the belief in predestination, which
> operates on the imagination of mahometan soldiers, as opium does on
> their physical powers, creating supernatural strength and courage. But
> it is a refinement of this sort of policy, to instil into a nation the belief,
> that they are superior in intellectual abilities to their neighbours. Impute
> a peculiar incurable mental disease to a given people, show that it inca-
> pacitates them from speaking or acting with common sense, expose
> their infirmities continually to public ridicule, and in time probably
> this people, let their constitutional boldness be ever so great, may be
> subjugated to that sense of inferiority, and to that acquiescence in a
> state of dependance, which is the necessary consequence of the con-
> viction of imbecility. (19–20)

There are several important points to be made here. In the first place, the
Edgeworths' arguments clearly illuminate the contentions of those critics who
contend that late-eighteenth- and early-nineteenth-century Britain defined its
'national identity' in terms of its 'Revolutionary and post-Revolutionary strug-

---

attention to this moment in the *Essay*. For her, the significance of the Edgeworths' treatment of Sancho Panza's
bull lies in the fact that it illuminates a wider contention of their essay, namely that 'when language calls personal
identity into question, property of all kinds, but literary property in particular, is soon at issue.' Gallagher's analysis of Edgeworth's use of the changeling device finally differs in several important respects from mine; for instance,
she does not recognize that one of the fundamental implications of the *Essay* is that the colonizing process changes
the colonizing as well as the colonized race. Nevertheless, her suggestion that 'Edgeworth implied, especially in
her turn-of-the-century works, that Anglo-Irish instabilities, as well as possibilities for self-creation, could be
traced to an intrinsic *Irish* changeableness' is useful, and has helped to inform my reading. See C. Gallagher, *Nobody's
story* (1994), 292–3, and 289.

gles against France, America, Russia, and other rivals.' As we saw earlier, this
meant that the British nation was increasingly 'constituted' in terms of its '"destiny" to rule and civilize alien peoples throughout the world, to "protect" them
from themselves and from predatory neighbours'.[20] While admitting that the
ability of one nation to undermine or to 'change' the ontological integrity of
another plays a crucial role in facilitating national and imperial expansion, the
Edgeworths' point is that the English are profoundly mistaken in continuing
to apply this strategy 'judiciously' to Ireland as well as France. Unlike the French,
the Irish are now allies, not rivals, and should no longer be treated as an inferior race. However useful this (colonizing) strategy may once have been, the
Edgeworths argue that the time has now come for England to admit a crucial
fact: namely, since the passing of the Act of Union, Ireland has constituted a
part of Britain's greater, imperial identity, and so it is in fact counter-productive for the English to continue to treat their near neighbour as an alien nation:

> Whatever might have been the policy of the english [*sic*] nation towards
> Ireland, whilst she was a separate kingdom, since the union it can no
> longer be her wish to depreciate the talents, or ridicule the language of
> Hibernians. One of the Czars of Russia used to take the cap and bells
> from his fool, and place it on the head of any of his subjects whom he
> wished to disgrace. The idea of extending such a punishment to a whole
> nation was ingenious, and magnanimous: but England cannot now put
> it into execution towards Ireland. Would it not be a practical bull to
> place the cap and bells upon her own imperial head? (307–8)

At this moment, the Edgeworths appear aligned with contemporary theorists who maintain that the success of any colonizing project is invariably dependent upon the colonizer's powers of (mis)representation. In his study of Irish
writing since 1790, for example, Seamus Deane suggests that, while Jonathan
Swift's analysis of the relationship between England and Ireland resulted in his
identification of 'an impasse' in British-Irish relations, 'Burke expanded that
local instance into a crisis in the relationship between two modes of civilisation.' For Burke, 'Ireland was ... that part of the British polity most vulnerable to the radical ideas of the Enlightenment and revolution precisely because
it had never known under British rule the virtues of the ancient civilization that
had collapsed in France.' Extending his analysis, Deane maintains, 'For over a
century after Burke, the same ambiguity prevailed – between the representation
of a country that is foreign and unknown, in which the conditions are phan-

20 Kelly, *Women, writing, and revolution*, 184–5.

tasmagoric, especially to the English reader, and a country that is, at the same time, part of the British system, perfectly recognizable and part of the traditional world that the French Revolution had overthrown.' In other words, Deane's suggestion is that, by (mis)representing Ireland, by refusing to view its cultural and linguistic 'difference' as the manifestations of an unfamiliar, but entirely authentic identity, England succeeded, instead, in stressing the 'unreal' or 'phantasmagoric' nature of its near neighbour. This, he avers, made possible its further insistence that '[r]eality will be restored to that phantasmal country only through the introduction into of that kind of civic stability which is characteristically British'.[21]

Edgeworth's Irish writing is manifestly predicated upon such ideological formations, for she similarly insists that the reformation of Ireland will only be accomplished once the nation's native inhabitants are brought to more nearly resemble an English form. Each of her Irish tales similarly stresses the phantasmagoric nature of Ireland,[22] insisting that visitors must protect their 'selves' when they visit this fantastic place. In this context, a cursory reading of Edgeworth's work might lead the unwary reader to deduce that she merely rehearses longstanding (English) arguments about what have been termed the 'amazing absorptive powers' of Ireland; that process, that is, through which successive English visitors to the island inevitably came to appear more Irish than the Irish themselves. England, increasingly frustrated by this, made '[a] number of attempts ... in turn desultory, sullen, and ferocious, to halt these transformations, and always with the intention of keeping the cultures separate'.[23] The crucial point about Edgeworth's treatment of this issue in her work, though, is that it reveals her keen perception that such 'transformations' are primarily contingent upon the colonizing process itself; as she would have it, the identity of any individual is necessarily changed the moment he decides to embrace the colonizer's life. It is in this context, then, that the Edgeworths argue in their *Essay on Irish bulls* that the 'maxim that one Englishman can beat ten Frenchman ... forms a succedaneum for the belief in predestination, which operates on the imagination of mahometan soldiers, as opium does on their physical powers, creating supernatural strength and courage' (19–20). Their recognition is that the would-be conqueror, or colonizer, inevitably changes his 'self' *as well as* that of the colonized in order to facilitate his desire to conquer, or colonize, other lands.

In order to further illustrate what I am suggesting here, it might be helpful to refer once more to *Don Quixote*, and to Cervantes' careful treatment of

---

21 Deane, *Strange country*, 3 and 16–18. 22 Joep Leerssen argues that this mode of narrating Ireland 'interposes itself between reader and subject matter, hides Ireland from view, indeed pushes it beyond the horizon ... Ireland is *made exotic* by the selfsame descriptions which purport to represent or explain Ireland' (*Remembrance and imagination*, 37). 23 Flanagan, *Irish novelists*, 4.

Sancho Panza's colonial desire in Book Two of that work. As I remarked earlier, one of Cervantes' most significant observations in this novel is that reading romance facilitates colonial expansion: his suggestion is that it leads directly
to the manifestation of expansionist desire. Sancho Panza puts it this way to
Don Quixote: '[I]f your worship reflects, you will find it was your worship that
put me upon the scent of governing; for I know no more of the government
of islands than a bustard'.[24] In tracing how Sancho Panza eventually secures his
'island', however, Cervantes places a singular emphasis upon the concept of
identity in his narrative, intimating that the entertaining of such desire necessarily poses a fundamental threat to the integrity of the squire's ontological
condition, or self. Thus it is, for example, that the bachelor Sampson Carrasco
doubts Sancho Panza's assertion that he will never forget his humble origins
should he be so fortunate as to secure his island. Discounting the squire's insistence that 'Sancho [he] was born, and Sancho [he] intend[s] to die', the scholar
points out, 'honours change manners; and it may come to pass, when you are a
governor, that you may not know the very mother that bore you' (549–50). He
anticipates, in other words, that, as a governor, Sancho Panza may forget, or
more properly perhaps, that he may wish to forget his original status.

This recognition also informs the eminently sensible advice with which
Don Quixote furnishes Sancho Panza before he sets out for his island; advice
that allows 'possibly the greatest figure in the history of romance [to recover]
his proper function as a social visionary'.[25] Having firstly instructed the future
governor to 'fear God; for, to fear Him is wisdom, and being wise, you cannot
err', Don Quixote thence urges him:

> *Consider who you were*, and endeavour to know yourself, which is the most
> difficult point of knowledge imaginable. The knowledge of yourself
> will keep you from puffing yourself up, like the frog, who strove to
> equal herself to the ox; for the consideration of your having been a
> swineherd in your own country will be, to the wheel of your fortune,
> like the peacock's ugly feet. (820) (my emphasis)

Don Quixote's insistence that Sancho Panza must try to remember who he was
once he becomes a governor charges Cervantes' writing with the recognition
that the satisfying of hegemonic desire invariably precipitates a transformation
of the newly empowered individual; specifically, that it usually results in that
individual's determination to 'change' or, more properly perhaps, to 'aggran-

---

24 Cervantes, *Don Quixote*, 828. Further references to this novel are cited parenthetically in the text.   25 Frye, *Secular
scripture*, 179.

dize' his original 'status.' An essential point of *Don Quixote*, therefore, is that Sancho Panza subsequently proves himself a good governor precisely because he resists such temptation. Upon arriving at his island, he thus refuses to (re)style himself a 'don', insisting, 'Don does not belong to me, nor ever did to any of my family: I am called plain Sancho Panza; my father was Sancho, and my grandfather a Sancho, and they were all Panzas, without any addition of Dons or Doñas' (839). Continuing to remember who he 'was' once he finds himself a governor renders Sancho Panza capable of identifying with his subjects; the former squire governs well because he forever perceives that 'while we are asleep, the great and the small, the poor and the rich, are all equal' (828). It is as a result of this identification, the narrative implies, that Sancho Panza is able to discharge his duties with 'discretion', putting his subjects' interests before his own and resolutely touching 'no fee ... nor any bribe' (892–3). Upon leaving his island, he is consequently able to observe to his assembled erstwhile officials: 'Gentlemen ... naked was I born, and naked I am; I neither win nor lose; I mean, that without a penny came I to this government, and without a penny do I quit it, the direct reverse of the governors of other islands' (907).

Edgeworth is a direct descendent of settlers herself, so it is clearly not her intention to persuade either her English or, more importantly, her Protestant Ascendancy readers that they should replicate Sancho Panza's action and leave the island of Ireland, nor is it her ambition to convince them that they should put the governance of Ireland back into native hands. It is, however, her desire to remind these readers that they, like Cervantes' squire, must exercise a greater ontological awareness in dealing with their 'subjects'; at the very least, that they must identify their interests with those of the native Irish and render themselves capable of perceiving the necessarily reciprocal nature of Anglo-Irish affairs. In order to facilitate this ambition, Edgeworth skilfully draws upon what Frye terms the 'motif of amnesia' in romance: namely, that 'break of consciousness' that 'often begins' the typical romance narrative.[26] To this end, she suggests that her English and, more particularly, her Protestant Ascendancy readers are not wilfully neglectful of Ireland, and that they have, instead, merely forgotten their duties and obligations as a governing class. Rewriting her father's experiences with his tenants in her fiction, Edgeworth effectively attempts to remind the would-be-rulers of Ireland that, in order to be successful, they must first of all manifest a similarly superior ontological form. As I noted in my introduction, her emphasis in 'her' volume of her father's memoirs is that such integrity will inevitably be recognized and appreciated by the native Irish. Richard Lovell Edgeworth's tenants immediately recognized that he was 'a good

26 Ibid. 102.

landlord ... [and] *a real gentleman*', Edgeworth stresses, and this ability to 'distinguish ... from every pretender to the character' is peculiar to the native Irish race.[27] In this context, we can see that Edgeworth's father is the true 'hero of [her] Irish novels'; he is 'the prototype' for all of the 'just, percipient, improving landlord[s]' in her fiction, who are 'rewarded for [their] many virtues by ... contented and grateful' tenants.[28]

Although Edgeworth is keen to stress the benevolent and paternal aspects of this relationship, the *Memoirs* clearly reveal that colonial and pedagogical preoccupations informed her father's endeavours to 'touch' his tenants' 'hearts.' Stressing that he 'took especial care, that they should be convinced of his strictness in punishing, as well as of his desire to reward', Edgeworth observes, 'This sort of power to encourage and reward, in the hands of the landlord, is advantageous in Ireland. It acts as a motive for exertion; it keeps up the connexion and dependance, which there ought to be between the different ranks, without creating any servile habits, or leaving the improving tenant insecure as to the fair reward of his industry'.[29] Amplifying my analysis of how she treats Mr Edwards' relationship with his slaves in 'The grateful negro', Edgeworth in this way figures the landlord/tenant relationship in Ireland in implicitly colonial terms throughout her writing, casting the former in the role of a benevolent patriarch who has a duty to educate, reward, and punish his childlike dependents. As Deane puts it, although Edgeworth 'was not the first novelist to have chosen Ireland as her "scene" ... she was the first to realize that there was, within it, a missionary opportunity to convert it to Enlightenment faith and rescue it from its "romantic" conditions. She defined that opportunity, as did so many others, as an educational one. Irish national character was to be brought to school'.[30]

One of Edgeworth's first attempts to 'bring Irish national character to school' is represented by 'The white pigeon', one of her lesser-known tales for young children that was published in *The parent's assistant* in 1796. Here, in miniature, are discovered the terms of the familial and colonial romance that frames and impels all of her more celebrated Irish fiction. On the simplest of levels, this tale tells the story of Brian O'Neill, an exemplary young Irish boy who lives with his equally commendable parents in a little town called Somerville in Ireland. Brian is given a pigeon as a present, and his treatment of the bird renders it so tame that 'it would hop about the kitchen, and eat off the same trencher with the [family's] dog'.[31] Learning of the discovery that pigeons can

---

27 *Memoirs*, 2: 37. 28 B. Hollingworth, *Maria Edgeworth's Irish writing* (1997), 114–15. 29 *Memoirs*, 2: 39, 31 and 26–7.
30 Deane, *Strange country*, 32. 31 M. Edgeworth, *The parent's assistant*, 3: 34. Further references to this tale are cited parenthetically in the text.

be used to carry messages, Brian hopes to earn money for his parents in this manner. The son of Mr Cox, an alehouse keeper, steals the pigeon, however, and his intention is to use the bird to convey messages for a gang of thieves. Once released, the pigeon returns to Brian, who discovers from the message attached to the bird's leg that the gang intend to rob the home of Mr Somerville to whom the town of Somerville 'belongs' (3: 25). Brian and his father alert the landowner, the plan is foiled, the gang is caught, and Mr Somerville rewards Brian's father by making him the master of the town's new inn, the White Pigeon. In so doing, Mr Somerville remarks to Brian: 'And I wish him joy of having such a son as you are. Those who bring up their children well will certainly be rewarded for it, be they poor or rich' (3: 41).

Ostensibly nothing more than a story designed to demonstrate, firstly, that obedient children are inevitably rewarded, and, secondly, that parents must properly educate their children, 'The white pigeon' not only rehearses the terms of the colonial and familial discourse that impels all of Edgeworth's Irish writing, but also intimates why the construction of this discourse is peculiarly facilitated by her use of the romance mode. An essential point of the tale is that Mr Somerville's benevolent paternalism legitimises his presence in Ireland, but another is that it also enables him to impose his 'transfiguring imagination' upon his environs:[32] it allows him, that is, to confer an English appearance upon his estates: 'The little town of Somerville, in Ireland, has, within these few years, assumed the neat and cheerful appearance of an English village. Mr Somerville ... wished to inspire his tenantry with a taste for order and domestic happiness, and took every means in his power to encourage industrious well-behaved people to settle in his neighbourhood' (3: 25). Patently informing all of Edgeworth's Irish fiction, this theme expertly illuminates what we might term the aspirational nature of her father's relationship with his tenants. It intimates, that is, that he treated them with benevolence in the anticipation of their reform. It is for this reason that Edgeworth places such a particular emphasis upon what we might term the 'ontological foresight' of her father in her volume of the *Memoirs*, insisting that, 'even' in 1782, he 'foresaw, and foretold, the happy change, which increasing intercourse with other countries, improving education, and the consequent progress of the diffusion of knowledge, would in a few years produce in Irish society'.[33] Edgeworth's fiction manifestly draws upon precisely this ideological formation, and it asserts that all of Ireland's landlords, or rulers, will similarly reap the rewards of their 'transfiguring' labours. The potentially rebellious native Irish will be contained, it avers, by treating them from the first as if they had already been changed. Recalling the alarms caused

32 Beer, *The critical idiom*, 41. 33 *Memoirs*, 2: 13.

by Defender activity in the late 1780s and early 1790s, Edgeworth thus emphasizes in *A letter to the right hon. the earl of Charlemont*:

> [Richard Lovell Edgeworth] built and improved ... [and] employed
> numerous tradesmen and labourers, *as if* the country were in perfect
> security; and in the dreadful scenes which afterwards occurred [in 1792],
> [he had] the satisfaction to say no tenant on [his] estate was ever con-
> victed or even accused – nor has a defender been found; even amongst
> [his] workmen. (my emphasis)[34]

Edgeworth echoes these sentiments in 'The white pigeon', insisting that Mr
Somerville's survival is a direct result of the ontological foresight he employs in
conducting his affairs. In this context, Brian and his father represent the first
examples of the various loyal native servants with whom Edgeworth populates
her later Irish fiction. They also, of course, symbolize her original fictional incar-
nations of the several faithful retainers who came to the assistance of the
Edgeworth family at various times during the course of its colonial career.[35]
Their presence in this story, like that of Jimmy Riley in *Ennui*, or of Moriarty
Carroll in *Ormond* is clearly crucial, for 'it was important for Edgeworth's [didac-
tic] purpose to show the capacity of the native Irish for loyalty, if treated properly'.[36] By convincing the natives and their masters that all of their interests necessarily coincide, Edgeworth's assertion here and throughout her work is that
an increasingly defensive Protestant Ascendancy class can pave the way for social
and political stability in Ireland. An essential point of the Irish tales, therefore,
is that 'Irish Protestants have to be recuperated from a long degradation which
has led to their impoverishment and irresponsibility. So restored, they will redeem
the other Irish from their native and unreliable, if endearing, romanticism'.[37]

The preface to *Castle Rackrent* anticipates this 'redemption', insisting that all
of Ireland's native inhabitants will cheerfully submit to such reform. The native
Irish, it emphasises, will uncomplainingly cast off their former 'consciousness',
and willingly embrace the 'habits' of a 'new' life.[38] As Catherine Gallagher
remarks, the final intimation of the preface is: 'Unlike the Irish gentleman in
the bull, these future former Irishmen will hold no grudge against anyone for
having "changed" them, and their laughter at their own dispossession will convince everyone of their complete complicity'.[39] The preface thus observes,

---

34 R.L. Edgeworth, *A letter to ... the earl of Charlemont*, 3. 35 During the rebellion of 1641, for example, one Edmond
MacBrian Ferrall saved the infant son of Captain John Edgeworth from 'a vast concourse of rabble, headed by
some Popish gentry and several Popish priests': H.J. Butler and H. Edgeworth Butler (eds), *The black book of
Edgeworthstown* (1927), 12–13. 36 T. Dunne, *Maria Edgeworth and the colonial mind* (1984), 17. 37 Deane, *Strange country*,
33. 38 *Novels and selected works*, 1: 7. Further references to this tale are cited parenthetically in the text. 39 Gallagher,

There is a time, when individuals can bear to be rallied for their past
follies and absurdities, after they have acquired new habits, and a new
consciousness. Nations as well as individuals gradually lose attachment
to their identity, and the present generation is amused rather than
offended by the ridicule that is thrown upon its ancestors.

Probably we shall soon have it in our power, in a hundred instances,
to verify the truth of these observations.

When Ireland loses her identity by an union with Great Britain,
she will look back with a smile of good-humoured complacency on
the Sir Kits and Sir Condys of her former existence. (1: 7)

For her part, Butler maintains that this 'was probably written' by Edgeworth's
father, 'though perhaps with her assistance',[40] and this would certainly account
for the curious tension that exists between the claims of the preface and the
subsequent content of the tale. The final point of *Castle Rackrent*, after all, is
that the members of the O'Shaughlin family never succeed in properly inhab-
iting their new consciousness, preferring to cling, instead, to the lineaments of
a by-gone feudal life. Like each of the Irish tales, as we shall see, *Castle Rackrent*
on the one hand rehearses Richard Lovell Edgeworth's vision of Ireland, while
on the other it implies that this vision may be defective. Despite all well-mean-
ing protestations to the contrary, it insists, the native Irish may prove to be
entirely incorrigible, and it may not be possible to repair the 'tainted' identity
of the nation's ruling (Ascendancy) class. Contrary to the didactic assertion of
the preface, *Castle Rackrent* is therefore finally haunted by Edgeworth's recognition that the passing of the Act of Union in Ireland may prove to be a detrimental act; one that will 'retard' rather than 'hasten ... the melioration of [the]
country' (1: 54).

Although *Castle Rackrent* and each of the Irish tales is obviously concerned
with the need to effect the reformation of the Protestant Ascendancy in Ireland,
it is, thus, entirely significant that Edgeworth chooses not to address this issue
directly in her writing, concentrating, instead, upon apostate native families in
each of her tales. While *Castle Rackrent* manifestly draws upon episodes drawn
from Edgeworth family history, for example, Edgeworth chooses to displace
the worst excesses of her ancestors onto the O'Shaughlin/Rackrents, representatives of Ireland's native race. In this context, the O'Shaughlin/Rackrents
function as the effective 'changelings' of *Castle Rackrent*, having heaped upon
themselves the less salubrious aspects of the Edgeworth family's early Irish life.
W.J. McCormack remarks that this is clearly a skilful piece of 'authorial self-

Nobody's story, 294.   40 Butler, endnotes, Castle Rackrent *and* Ennui, 347.

exculpation' on Edgeworth's part, for it allows her to tell, but simultaneously to disguise her family's (colonial) history. For instance, *Castle Rackrent* 'is almost innocent of sectarian allusion', while *The black book of Edgeworthstown*, from which Edgeworth drew many of her details, pays considerable attention to the marriage of Francis Edgeworth and Jane Tuite, his Catholic wife.[41] During the rebellion of 1641, *The black book* notes not only how MacBrian Ferrall come to the aid of the young Edgeworth heir and his mother, but also that 'the old castle of Crannelagh' was saved from certain destruction when Catholic rebels happened upon Jane's picture in the house.[42] Noting that a one hundred and seven year old former servant of the family ostensibly told this tale to Richard Edgeworth, Edgeworth's grandfather, McCormack claims,

> The value of a narrator, less than ingenuous, in holding together the details of a family's varied generations, was evident to Maria Edgeworth whenever she consulted *The black book*. And it is the mode of narrative, the semblance of history together with the discreet silences, which is significant rather than the reportage of betting coups and drinking bouts.[43]

Butler puts it this way: 'Maria Edgeworth was telling not just a family chronicle but her own family chronicle [in *Castle Rackrent*]; or rather she was not telling it, but conveying it circuitously to the reader via the profoundly unreliable Thady'.[44]

If all of this were not enough, the fact that the Rackrents are also apostates renders them changelings twice in the novel. Originally descended from 'the kings of Ireland', they have 'by act of parliament … take[n] … the surname and arms of Rackrent' (1: 10). This change of name, religion, and political allegiance amounts to the family's virtual renunciation of the fundamental pillars of its identity; their apostasy represents the O'Shaughlins' assumption of an inauthentic 'self.' Edgeworth of course, repeats this substitution of apostate changelings for Protestant Ascendancy families in each of her Irish tales. In *Ennui*, it is stressed that the aristocratic Glenthorns were O'Shaughnessys 'before they stooped to be *lorded*', and the hero, I have already remarked, discovers that he has himself been literally changed at nurse.[45] King Corny and Father Jos look 'with horror … [and] contempt' upon Sir Ulick O'Shane's apostasy in *Ormond*,[46] while the very title of *The absentee* itself explicitly condemns

41 W.J. McCormack, *Ascendancy and tradition* (1985), 99 and 104.   42 Butler and Butler, *The black book*, 13.   43 McCormack, *Ascendancy and tradition*, 105.   44 Butler, general introduction, *The Novels and selected works*, 1: xl.   45 *Novels and selected works*, 1: 175.   46 *Novels and selected works*, 8: 39.

apostate families who abandon their true selves, as well as their Irish estates, in order to affect a pseudo '*Henglish*' identity.[47]

The changeling device allows Edgeworth to develop her arguments of the *Letter* and the *Essay on Irish bulls*: namely, that nothing less than a profound onto-logical confusion is threatening the Ascendancy's pre-eminence in Ireland, the Anglo-Irish relationship, and, ultimately, the future of Britain's imperial affairs. It also, though, allows her

> to distance [her own class] from the patent evils of the system she
> described, while making the point that a native Irish landlordism, even
> if superficially anglicised, could neither improve the lives of the people,
> or cope with their subversiveness. This cleared the way for the main
> theme of her later novels, that an improving paternalistic English land-
> lordism, which would challenge peasant indolence and dishonesty, while
> harnessing peasant loyalty and appreciation of even-handed justice, was
> the only path to the achievement of a peaceful and prosperous colony.[48]

The changeling device has a further, crucial significance, of course: it enables Edgeworth to express how profoundly complicated the transformation of indi-vidual or of national identity is. Its outcome is always far from certain, she avers, and is particularly so in Ireland given the peculiar (colonial) tensions that inform Irish life. In this regard, the healing 'polarization' that Edgeworth aims to effect between Ireland's ruling class and its lower orders is both 'shaken with irony' and aspirational; it is 'energized more by ... desire' than by the percep-tion of what has truly been achieved.[49]

An essential point of *Castle Rackrent*, therefore, is that successive Rackrents cling to their notion of the family's 'true' identity, even when it is plainly in their interests to submit to ontological reform. Sir Patrick, the family's first apostate, or changeling, thus hastens his death and the decline of his family's fortunes by adhering to his concept of the O'Shaughlins' pre-apostate, feudal life. Rather than reforming his 'self', he wastefully expends his time, his energy and his resources, mounting lavish 'entertainment' and, fittingly, this 'hospital-ity is, literally, the death of him',[50] for he dies as a result of dashing off 'a

---

47 The theme of apostasy is also raised indirectly by the fact that Colambre '*will* have a prodigiously fine estate when some Mr Quin dies' (*Novels and selected works*, 5: 5–6). As W.J. McCormack and Kim Walker observe, 'the name [Quin] is not uncommon in Ireland, but thus spelled (with one 'n') is usually Protestant.' Although it is not directly stated in Edgeworth's narrative, it is therefore obvious that the Clonbronys have recanted their faith; as a Catholic, Colambre could not inherit Quin's estate. See endnotes by W.J. McCormack and K. Walker in *The absentee* (1988), 286.   48 Dunne, *Maria Edgeworth and the colonial mind*, 8. As we have seen from 'The white pigeon', this theme is not confined to Edgeworth's later novels.   49 McCormack, *Ascendancy and tradition*, 10.   50 C. Connolly, 'Uncanny

bumper toast' at table (1: 10–11). In this context, the sentiment that Sir Condy has inscribed upon the 'handsome marble stone' that he erects to 'his great ancestor' is entirely appropriate: Sir Patrick Rackrent did, indeed, '[live] and [die] a monument of old Irish hospitality' and of Irish life (1: 24).

Patrick's successor, the litigious Sir Murtagh, and his 'Skinflint' wife, pursue a course directly opposite to that advocated by Edgeworth's father in administering their affairs (1: 12). Sir Murtagh engages in endless, unproductive lawsuits, and he and his wife together delight in 'driving and driving, and pounding and pounding, and canting and canting, and replevying and replevying' their unfortunate tenants (1: 12). Their successor, Sir Kit, in two ways fails himself and the Irish nation. Initially adopting the lifestyle of an absentee, he leaves the Rackrent demesnes in the hands of an agent who 'ferreted the tenants out of their lives' (1: 16). Returning home, he brings with him an unsuitable *'Jewish'* wife who views her husband's estates with a mixture of ill-disguised amusement and disgust (1: 18). Recounting how she dismissed the bog of 'Allyballycarricko'shaughlin' as 'a very ugly prospect', for example, Thady Quirk, the family's steward, also notes how 'she fell to laughing like one out of their right mind' at its name (1: 19). Unlike Cecilia Delamere in *Ennui*, Grace Nugent in *The absentee*, or Florence Annaly in *Ormond*, as we shall see, the emphasis of *Castle Rackrent* is that this pseudo-matriarchal figure has no natural understanding of, or affection for Ireland and, consequently, that she is incapable of contributing to its reform.[51] In Edgeworth's terms, this is particularly catastrophic, for she believes that every marriage made in Ireland must reflect and contribute to the greater, harmonious Union that should exist between the Irish and the English nations.

Edgeworth's treatment of the final Rackrent, Sir Condy, is particularly significant, as it expertly illustrates the (subversive) contention that manifests itself in all of her Irish writing. In tracing Sir Condy's demise, Edgeworth simultaneously traces her perception that Ireland's is a peculiarly attractive ontological power and her conviction that the members of the Protestant Ascendancy class may not be able to resist its temptations, even if they reform. As a representative of 'a remote branch of the family', Condy is never expected to inherit the Rackrent estates, and he consequently receives an early education that is inappropriate to his eventual status (1: 25). By spending his childhood 'running through the streets of O'Shaughlin's town, and playing … with the boys of the town', he cultivates inappropriate associations (1: 25); in particular, he becomes

---

Castle Rackrent' (1998), 1: 214. 51 McCormack makes the point that, although the Rackrent estate changes hands five times in the course of the novel, only one inheritance is by primogeniture (*Ascendancy and tradition*, 109). Thus, Sir Patrick O'Shaughlin's wife, who is never even named, is the only mother in the tale.

too friendly with Thady's son, Jason, who, for Edgeworth, clearly symbolizes the predatory native Irish race. If the part that Jason ultimately plays in Condy's demise is significant, so, too, are the efforts of Thady, the old family steward. As Edgeworth would have it, Thady effectively engages in an 'ontological seduction' of the young Condy, inculcating in him the desire to replicate his ancestors' feudal behaviour. '[Condy] was ever my white-headed boy', Thady remarks, '[he] love[d] to sit on my knee, whilst I told him stories of the family, and the blood from which he was sprung, and how he might look forward, if the *then* present man should die without childer, to being at the head of the Castle Rackrent estate' (1: 25).

Although Edgeworth intimates that Thady's efforts were assisted by the 'old people [in the neighbourhood who] always told [Condy] he was a great likeness of Sir Patrick; which made him first have an ambition to take after him, as far as his fortune should allow', it is entirely significant that it is primarily the old steward's influence that directly and indirectly affects the destiny of the future heir (1: 26). As Gallagher puts it, 'the last of the Rackrents is Thady's creature, an imitation Sir Patrick produced by the servant who is supposed to "belong" to the family'.[52] In the first place, it is *because* Thady fills his head with stories that Condy becomes increasingly certain that he will inherit, and this, in its turn, leads him to abandon the studies through which he could have become his family's saviour. Further, an important point of Edgeworth's tale is that Condy's fortune does not 'allow' his endeavours to replicate his ancestor, so he effectively bankrupts himself, financially and ontologically, by succumbing to the influence of his steward. When he does finally 'become' Sir Condy, as Thady observes, he finds himself unable to 'command a penny of his first year's income; which, and keeping no accounts, and the great sight of company he did, with many other causes too numerous to mention, was the origin of his distresses' (1: 26). For once the notoriously ambiguous steward is here telling the literal truth: it *is* Condy's 'embarrassed situation' and his inability to confront it that facilitates Jason Quirk's creeping ascendancy over the Rackrent estates (1: 26). Rather than trying to remedy his present, Edgeworth intimates that Sir Condy instead chooses to take refuge in his (mythic) past, an act that eventually enables Jason to (inappropriately) occupy his former master's status.

Reviving 'the family intimacy that had been in Sir Patrick's time' with the 'Moneygawls of Mount Juliet's town', Condy worsens his already disastrous situation by marrying Isabella Moneygawl (1: 27). An affected, self-dramatizing woman, this Lady Rackrent spends 'as if she [has] a mint of money at her elbow', and turns Castle Rackrent 'topsy-turvy' (1: 30). If his wife's inability to control

52 Gallagher, *Nobody's story*, 297.

her excesses contributes to the Rackrents' demise, so, too, does the fact that Sir Condy ill advisedly puts himself forward as a candidate in a local election. This attempt to aggrandize his 'self' has a catastrophic effect upon his resources, for, in the first instance, 'all the gentlemen of [Sir Condy's election] committee, who managed all for him, and talked how they'd bring him in without costing him a penny … forgot to pay their subscriptions … so [that] all was left at his door' (1: 36). Sir Condy's ontological resources are also weakened, for he ultimately discovers that he is less of a man for having left his estates. '[V]ery ill used by the government about a place that was promised him and never given', as Thady puts it, Condy is 'greatly abused' for going 'against his conscience very honourably' (1: 37). This affects him very badly because he had 'the name of a great patriot in the country before' (1: 37). The overall implication of the tale, of course, is that it is, finally, Ireland that suffers because Sir Condy cannot resist the temptation to indulge in what he perceives as an opportunity for self-aggrandizement. Thady's description of an abandoned Castle Rackrent is, as a result, hugely important, and symbolizes much more than the Rackrents' abandonment of their estates:

> There was then a great silence in Castle Rackrent, and I went moping from room to room, hearing the doors clap for want of right locks, and the wind through the broken windows, that the glazier never would come to mend, and the rain coming through the roof and best ceilings all over the house for want of the slater, whose bill was not paid, besides our having no slates or shingles for that part of the old building which was shingled and burnt when the chimney took fire, and had been open to the weather ever since. (1: 36)

Having finally lost the control of Castle Rackrent to Jason, however, Condy nonetheless persists in his allegiance to his notion of his family's original status. Although this identity has essentially facilitated his destruction, it is still, in Condy's eyes, his authentic 'self'. For this reason, Condy shocks Thady with his desire to see his funeral 'afore' he dies, but, in fact, he is merely trying to bring his attempts to replicate Sir Patrick's adventures to their logical conclusion (1: 46). Assured by the old steward that his funeral will be 'as great … as ever Sir Patrick O'Shaughlin's was, and such a one as that had never been known in the county afore or since', Condy pretends to die, cheerfully anticipating the fine stories of 'himself' that will be told by those who mourn him (1: 46). Condy, though, finds 'his' wake intensely disappointing. In the first instance, it is nearly the literal death of him, for he finds himself smothering under the great coats that have been casually thrown by mourners upon the supposed corpse. Secondly, buried beneath these coats, Condy complains to Thady that he is unable to hear

'a word of all they're saying of the deceased' (1: 47); an extremely comical observation, this also denotes Condy's increasingly fractured sense of 'self.' Finally,
and as Thady remarks, 'Sir Condy was rather upon the sad order in the midst
of it all, not finding there had been such a great talk about himself after his
death as he had always expected to hear' (1: 47). In other words, having clung
to the lineaments of an assumed (and mythic) ontological condition, Condy
at the last discovers that this identity is wanting, or, more properly perhaps, he
realizes he has failed to properly inhabit his assumed state.

Forced from Castle Rackrent by Jason, Condy finds himself in exile in the
estate lodge, where he discovers the 'great horn ... that used to belong originally to the celebrated Sir Patrick, his ancestor' (1:52). Significantly, Thady recalls
that 'his honour was fond often of telling the story that he learned from me
when a child, how Sir Patrick drank the full of this horn without stopping, and
this was what no other man afore or since could without drawing breath' (1: 52).
Condy eventually succumbs to the desire to recreate this mythical feat, and one
(ironic) intimation of Edgeworth's tale is that he in this way finally succeeds in
his ambition to replicate Sir Patrick precisely: he kills himself, that is, by replicating the very act through which Sir Patrick died. Another, however, is that this
circumstance is the entirely predictable outcome of Thady's ontological seduction of the young heir; Sir Condy dies, that is, because, from childhood, the
steward has persistently encouraged him to replicate his ancestor's life.

Condy lingers for five days and nights in a fever as a consequence of this
act of foolish intemperance, but recovers his senses for just long enough to ask
Thady: 'where are all the friends?' (1: 53). Realizing that none are coming, he
poignantly remarks, 'Gone, hey? Ay, Sir Condy has been a fool all his days', and
Thady makes clear that these were 'the last word[s]' his master spoke before his
demise (1: 53). On the one hand illustrating for the final time Condy's fractured
sense of self, this comment also represents Edgeworth's expert summing up of
the fatal flaw of this character in her story. At the very last, Condy expresses
his realization that 'Sir Condy' has all along been a fool, or more properly perhaps, that he has made himself into somebody else's creature as a result of his
ill-advised desire to replicate Sir Patrick's life. Mercifully for Condy, the laws
of metaphysics prevent him from witnessing the final consequence of his
(mis)spent existence, and so he never sees that he had 'but a very poor funeral'
(1: 53). In a nation where the turnout at one's funeral was of considerable importance, this sad fact serves as the ultimate comment upon the way in which this
last Rackrent has pitifully (mis)managed the ontological affairs of his family;
it serves as 'the last disaster in the going down of the Rackrent line'.[53]

53 J. Moynahan, *Anglo-Irish* (1995), 21.

Edgeworth's treatment of the Rackrents' continuing adherence to their O'Shaughlin identity manifestly conflicts with the confident assertions of *Castle Rackrent*'s preface, and it illustrates her perception that the passing of the Act of Union may have an effect directly opposite to that which its supporters intended. In tracing the gradual ascendancy of the Quirks, Edgeworth intimates that, far from facilitating England's and the Ascendancy's desire to transform the native Irish, the Act of Union may simply further empower an already powerful and subversive race. Thus, while the question of Thady's loyalty to the Rackrents continues to vex Edgeworth's readers, I would suggest that one certainty of the tale is that the steward, unlike his masters, is immediately capable of appreciating the benefits of ontological reform. Recounting the career of Sir Murtagh, Thady recalls how he 'used to wonder to see [him] in the midst of the papers in his office! Why he could hardly turn about for them. I made bold to shrug my shoulders once in his presence, and thanked my stars I was not born a gentleman to so much toil and trouble; but Sir Murtagh took me up short with his old proverb, "learning is better than house or land"' (1: 13). By (indirectly) revealing the way in which Jason gradually secures his ascendancy over his family's erstwhile masters, Thady (implicitly) acknowledges that he fully understood the ontological import of Sir Murtagh's observation. He points out:

> Jason Quirk, though he be my son … was a good scholar from his birth, and a very 'cute lad; I thought to make him a priest, but he did better for himself: seeing how he was as good a clerk as any in the county, the agent gave him his rent accounts to copy, which he did first of all for the pleasure of obliging the gentleman, and would take nothing at all for his trouble, but was always proud to serve the family. (1: 16)

Encoded here, of course, is the realization of the colonizer's ultimate fear: that the colonized will eventually usurp the colonizer's place as a result of his colonial education. It is this perception that lends such peculiar import to Thady's observation that he 'love[s] to look upon' Sir Patrick's portrait (1: 10). McCormack maintains that this comment is important because it begs the question as to where the portrait hangs '*now*',[54] but of much more significance, surely, is where is *Thady*? By having the old retainer insist that Sir Patrick's picture is 'now opposite' to him, is Edgeworth inviting us to perceive that Thady has usurped his old master's place? (1: 10). It is precisely this (colonial) anxiety that finally informs the 'editorial afterward' that concludes the tale, for this recognizes that the enactment of the Act of Union may result in profound

54 McCormack, *Ascendancy and tradition*, 114.

ontological slippage: 'It is a problem of difficult solution to determine, whether an Union will hasten or retard the melioration of this country. The few gentlemen of education, who now reside in this country, will resort to England: they are few, but they are in nothing inferior to men of the same rank in Great Britain. The best that can happen will be the introduction of British manufacturers in their places' (1: 54). As well as anticipating that the Union will cause widespread confusion in Ireland, Edgeworth reveals her fear that this confusion will ultimately prove to be to the Protestant Ascendancy's disadvantage. Rather than facilitating the 'remaking' of the native Irish, she implies, the Union may simply ensure that it is the Protestant Ascendancy and the English who are 'remade': 'Did the Warwickshire militia, who were chiefly artisans, teach the Irish to drink beer? or did they learn from the Irish to drink whiskey?' (1: 54).

        This disturbing possibility is present in each of Edgeworth's Irish tales, but nowhere more clearly, perhaps, than in *Ennui*, which revolves around the profoundly complicated implications of the hero's literal changeling status. Bred up as 'the only son and heir of the earl of Glenthorn', Edgeworth's native Irish hero gives up this identity once he realizes that it is not rightfully his possession, and instead sets out to reform his 'Christy O'Donoghoe' self.[55] Having eventually proved himself to be of exemplary character, he mutates once more by the end of Edgeworth's narrative, this time 'tak[ing] and bear[ing] the name and arms of Delamere' following his marriage (1: 306). On the one hand merely illustrating the alacrity with which he facilitates his union to Cecilia Delamere, this act on the other hand also symbolizes the efficacy of Christy O'Donoghoe's reformation. The new 'Mr Delamere' is entirely worthy of his Ascendancy bride, the tale avers, and of the chance that he is ultimately given to (re)occupy the lineaments of his former life. If this appears simply to faithfully rehearse the didactic contentions that impel all of Edgeworth's writing, we shall see that *Ennui* also lends itself to a more subversive reading. Drawing upon and developing the themes of *Castle Rackrent*, this tale similarly intimates that it may not be possible for the Ascendancy to control the educated native Irish; by the end of the tale, after all, another 'Anglo-Irish estate has fallen into Irish hands'.[56]

        Purporting to represent the 'memoirs' of the earl of Glenthorn, Edgeworth's narrative begins by recalling his inappropriate early life and education, and claims that these have combined to render him incapable of properly discharging the duties and obligations of his aristocratic station (1: 161). 'Bred up in luxurious indolence', Glenthorn is 'surrounded by friends who seemed to have no

---

55 *Novels and selected works*, 1: 161. Further references to this tale are cited parenthetically in the text.   56 R. Tracy, 'Maria Edgeworth and Lady Morgan' (1985), 6.

business in this world but to save [him] the trouble of thinking or acting for [himself]', and these confirm him in his 'helplessness' by continually reminding him that he is a future earl (1: 161). Recalling the observation in the *Essay on Irish bulls* that '*nobody* is a word of very uncertain significance, varying according to time, place, and circumstance', Edgeworth's intimation here is that Glenthorn's time, place and circumstances have essentially stripped him of his identity (4). Although as an earl he should be somebody, Glenthorn occupies the mere outward trappings of his elevated status. Lady Geraldine's comment later in the narrative upon her mother's desire to 'match' her with Glenthorn is, therefore, singularly appropriate. 'Mamma', she observes, 'wants me to catch somebody, and to be caught by somebody; but that will not be; for, do you know, I think somebody is nobody' (1: 212). As Gallagher points out,

> This remark agrees with the first-person narrator's judgement of his own youthful self: an aristocratic upbringing ha[s] made him selfishly indolent and disdainful of all sorts of "business," characteristics that in turn [prevent] his personality from solidifying into anything definite. Ignorant and purposeless, Glenthorn is "nobody" in the first part of the book because he is unrealized and unsituated ... He has, in other words, no character.[57]

In order to give Glenthorn 'character', Edgeworth uses romance conventions to send him on a journey, which manifestly reworks the ramifications of her father's 1782 return home. Frye's reading of romance, we saw earlier, suggests that its heroes, or heroines, typically exist to symbolize a contrast between two worlds. There is an idyllic world and a demonic or night-world, he maintains, and most romances culminate in 'a return to the idyllic world, or to some symbol of it like a marriage'.[58] While Edgeworth clearly draws upon such a paradigm in *Ennui, The absentee*, and *Ormond*, she uses it to symbolize a contrast between, not two worlds, but two ontological states. In tracing the adventures of her heroes, her ambition is to impress the superiority of her father's identity upon her readers, and to convince them that they must replicate his example in order to facilitate their own and their nation's reform. Edgeworth therefore uses romance in order to impart to her readers her perception that Ireland can function as either an idyllic or a demonic realm; the difference, as she would have it, depends upon the condition of the individual's self. In this context, then, we might argue that *Castle Rackrent* finally differs from the other three Irish tales in that it effectively functions as an 'inverted' romance; one where the

57 Gallagher, *Nobody's story*, 300–1. 58 Frye, *Secular scripture*, 54.

Rackrents' fundamental lack of integrity, coupled with their inability to reform, plunges them into an underworld life.

This recognition that Ireland can represent either an idyllic or a demonic world first manifests itself in *Ennui* when Edgeworth introduces Ellinor, Glenthorn's old Irish nurse, into the tale. By suddenly appearing upon his English estates, Ellinor immediately prevents the earl from committing suicide, thwarting his resolution to 'shoot [himself] at the close of the day' (1: 170). At the same time, though, she is nearly responsible for his death, causing the horse that he is riding to plunge and throw him. Ellinor remains an equivocal character throughout *Ennui*; like the nation she so clearly represents, she has the capacity to either restore Glenthorn's 'self' or to destroy his peace of mind and reputation. Describing how she alone of his servants evidenced 'an agony of grief' at his apparent 'death' following his fall, Glenthorn therefore intimates that Ellinor succeeded in piercing the shell of his essential alienation (1: 172). 'The strong affections of this poor woman', as he puts it, 'touched me more than anything I had ever yet felt in my life' (1: 172). Edgeworth echoes her treatment of Thady Quirk's influence upon Sir Condy in *Castle Rackrent*, however, indicating that, at the same time as nursing Glenthorn back to health following his accident, Ellinor 'infects' him with an inappropriate admiration of his ancestors' feudal situation. When she sat up talking with him at night, Glenthorn consequently recalls, 'She was inexhaustible in her anecdotes of my ancestors, all tending to the honour and glory of the family' (1: 175). '[W]ell stored' with 'histories of Irish and Scottish chiefs', and with tales of 'fairies', '*shadowless witches*', '*banshees*', 'spirits and ghosts, and haunted castles without end', she 'excited' in his mind the desire 'to see' his castle (1: 175).

As well as implying here that Ellinor essentially functions as a repository wherein are stored the lineaments of the O'Shaughnessy family's original identity, or 'repressed collective unconsciousness', Edgeworth's further intimation is that, like Thady in *Castle Rackrent*, the old nurse effectively reminds Glenthorn of the pre-apostate, native Irish condition of his family. '[A]s the embodiment of an earlier, now-lost cultural epoch',[59] Ellinor's ambition is to use Glenthorn to avenge what she declares to be an ontological crime, or 'murder', and, in so doing, to bring *her* version of the O'Shaughnessy family back to life (1: 175). Insisting that he 'was only a lord ... in England; but [that he] could be all as

---

59 My reading here is indebted to Trumpener's analysis of the function of the nurse in Romantic literature. Romantic novelists, she writes, 'argue contra Rousseau [that] the nurse's disappearance from the early-nineteenth-century household fundamentally alters children's relationship to language and the day-to-day texture of class traditions. Once under official prohibition, indeed, the nurse (like the bard or the bog before her) begins to represent a repressed collective unconsciousness; her persistent return in fiction and in dreams ... represents a collective resistance against the order of banishment' (*Bardic nationalism*, 197).

one as a king in Ireland', Ellinor tries to tempt Glenthorn back to Ireland, impressing him 'with the idea of the sort of feudal power [he] should possess in [his] vast territory, over tenants who were almost vassals, and amongst a numerous train of dependents' (1: 175). Although she succeeds in exacting 'a vague promise' that he will *sometime or other*, visit Glenthorn Castle', it is not until Glenthorn attends a boxing match and witnesses the demise of Michael Noonan, an 'unfortunate Irishman', that Ireland is finally 'recalled to [his] thoughts' (1: 175, 182). Persistently remarked in *Ennui*, as in *The absentee* and *Ormond*, forgetfulness represents Edgeworth's skilful use of 'the motif of amnesia' in her writing. As she would have it, Ireland's absentee rulers are not wilfully negligent; instead, they have suffered a 'break in consciousness', and have temporarily 'forgotten' their duties.[60] Once reminded of these duties, Edgeworth implies, the Ascendancy will cheerfully embrace them, as they will perceive that their true destiny lies 'at home.'

When he describes his eventual return to his Irish estates, Glenthorn therefore stresses the therapeutic nature of his journey, emphasizing that Ireland, like Ellinor, reawakens his essential sensibility, and restores him to himself:

> [T]hough I complained bitterly, and swore it was impracticable for a gentleman to travel in Ireland; yet I never remembered to have experienced, on any journey, less ennui ... I should recommend to wealthy hypochondriacs a journey in Ireland ... [for] their best feelings cannot fail to be awakened by the warm, generous hospitality, they will receive in this country, from the cabin to the castle. (1: 187–8)

The nearer Glenthorn draws to his Irish 'dominions', though, the greater grows his perception that he is entering a phantasmagoric environ, one that will fundamentally challenge his very being. The approach to his 'maritime territories' was distinctly eerie, he notes,

> the cottages were thinly scattered, and the trees had a stunted appearance; they all slanted one way, from the prevalent winds that blew from the ocean. Our road presently stretched along the beach, and I saw nothing to vary the prospect but rocks, and their huge shadows upon the water. The road being sandy, the feet of the horses made no noise, and nothing interrupted the silence of the night but the hissing sound of the carriage-wheels passing through the sand. (1: 189)

60 Frye, *Secular scripture*, 102.

Glenthorn's sense of the desolate, magical nature of the place is further underlined for him (and his reader) by the fact that the postilions whom he has hired
in Dublin express themselves no less amazed than he by their environs. '[T]his
bees a strange Irish place', remarks one to the other, 'with no possible way o' getting at it, as I see' (1: 189). 'Dismayed and helpless', Glenthorn and the postil-
lion require the aid of a passing 'Irish carman' to reach Glenthorn castle, which
'seemed to rise from the sea, abrupt and insulated, in all the gloomy grandeur
of ancient times' (1: 189).

Upon entering the castle, Glenthorn immediately undergoes a sort of 'ontological transportation.' '[T]he multitude of servants and dependants' who rushed
to greet him, he observes, 'gave me an idea of my own consequence beyond any
thing which I had ever felt in England. These people seemed "born for my use"
... [and] more [like] vassals than tenants, and carried my imagination centuries
back to feudal times' (1: 190). Edgeworth's first point, of course, is that
Glenthorn initially delights in his new-found identity, as the feudal responses
of his tenants enable him to efface the 'nothingness' that has previously (neg-
atively) defined his sense of self. Her second point, though, is that Glenthorn's
response here is manifestly informed by his reading of Gothic romances, for
the fact that he draws upon such works in order to reconstitute his self is made
abundantly clear in the narrative. Having feasted upon 'one of the most pro-
fusely hospitable suppers that ever was prepared for a noble baron, even in the
days when oxen were roasted whole', Glenthorn recalls that he retired to a 'state
tower ... hung with magnificent tapestry ... [that] was so like a room in a
haunted castle, that if I had not been too much fatigued to think of any thing,
I should certainly have thought of Mrs Radcliffe' (1: 190–1). In Edgeworth's
terms, Glenthorn's revelation of his predilection for the works of Ann Radcliffe
(1764–1823) is highly significant, and helps to explain the remarkable ease with
which he is ontologically seduced by Ellinor and his native Irish tenants.[61] The
fact that Glenthorn's imagination has been inflamed by his reading is made particularly clear when he describes his sensations upon looking out of his window
the next morning: 'the whole prospect bore an air of savage wildness. As I con-
templated the scene, my imagination was seized with the idea of remoteness
from civilized society: the melancholy feeling of solitary grandeur took possession of my soul' (1: 191).

The efforts of Mr M'Leod and, ultimately, of Lord Y to reform Glenthorn
are nothing less than an ontological battle, one in which each man struggles to

---

61 Ann Radcliffe was 'the leading and best-known Gothic writer' of the late eighteenth century, with her name
being peculiarly associated with 'tales of the half-ruined medieval castle, reputedly Gothic, surrounded with striking, wild scenery and populated with a cast of characters made up of a lonely maiden, a middle-aged villain, a
loyal servant, and a virtuous hero' (*Dictionary of British women writers*, 550–1).

cast out the (native) demons that have taken possession of the earl's imagination and heart. For M'Leod, this proves particularly problematic, for Glenthorn
is at first deeply suspicious of his agent, believing his ambition is to 'cheat' him
out of the 'power' that properly belongs to himself (1: 195). Although M'Leod's
conduct gradually satisfies him that this is not the case, on Glenthorn's part at
least the relationship continues to be strained. Having initially rejoiced in an
authority 'seemingly next to despotic', Glenthorn is amazed to discover 'that
the feeling of benevolence is a greater pleasure than the possession of *barouches*,
and horses, and castles, and parks – greater even than the possession of power'
(1: 193–4, 198). Having 'tasted [this] species of pleasure', he is 'angry' with
M'Leod, 'irritated' and frustrated by the perpetual '*doubt*[s]' that the agent casts
on his ill-considered schemes (1: 199).

As is the case with Lord Y later in the narrative, M'Leod's ultimate function in *Ennui* is to demonstrate for Glenthorn and the reader why the assumption of an implicitly Edgeworthian identity is absolutely necessary in order to
control the potentially rebellious native Irish race. Doubting like Edgeworth's
father 'whether any thing effectual can be done till [the native Irish] have a better
education', M'Leod's desire is 'to teach men to see clearly, and to follow steadily,
their real interests'; an imperative, Edgeworth intimates, that applies to landlords just as much as their tenants (1: 202–3). Upon visiting M'Leod's holdings,
Glenthorn discovers from his agent precisely what can be accomplished in
Ireland, and is exposed to what is clearly an idyllic view of Irish life. Realizing
that M'Leod and his wife have 'actually created a paradise amid the wilds', he
observes, 'There was nothing wonderful in any thing I saw around me; but there
was such an air of neatness and comfort, order and activity, in the people, and
in their cottages, that I almost thought myself in England; and I could not fore-
bear exclaiming, – "How could all this be brought about in Ireland!"' (1: 220).
Intimating yet again that Ireland and the native Irish must be brought to more
nearly resemble the English in order to satisfy their (colonial) overlords' British
sensibilities, Edgeworth here rehearses the same ideological formations as in
Essays on professional education, where she details the efforts of the Quakers and the
South Sea missionaries with native races. M'Leod thus insists that he and his
wife succeeded with their tenants 'Chiefly by not doing and not expecting too
much at first'; that they instructed the native Irish by way of 'example', leading
where they 'could not have driven' (1: 220–21). Recognizing that they 'could not
expect to do much with the old, whose habits were fixed', M'Leod's and his
wife's primary concern has been 'to give the young children better notions' (1:
221). Admitting that their endeavours have taken some twenty six years, he
explains that they began 'with the children: a race of our own training has now
grown up, and they go on in the way they were taught, and prosper to our hearts'

content, and, what is better still, to their hearts' content' (1: 221). As in 'The white pigeon' or 'The grateful negro', the colonial imperative framing Edgeworth's narrative here is devastatingly apparent, and it is this fact that inspires Flanagan's contention that *Ennui* finally illustrates how the Edgeworths 'conspired' in the 'defeat' of their way of life. 'Only that bloodless paragon, M'Leod, could find nourishment in a social program which runs so athwart the temper of an entire people as that of which he is the mouthpiece'.[62]

The fact that it is not Mr M'Leod, but Lord Y[63] who completes Glenthorn's ontological reformation is highly important, particularly as this takes place only after the 'earl' discovers the truth about his changeling status. In the first instance demonstrating that Edgeworth is only able to sustain the didactic theories of her father in her fiction by resorting to romance, the text of *Ennui* intimates that this is something of which she is herself peculiarly conscious, for, on several occasions, the narrative seems deliberately designed to anticipate and to diffuse the criticism of the reader. At the beginning of the chapter immediately following his discovery that Ellinor is his mother, for example, Glenthorn observes, 'The romance of real life certainly goes beyond all other romances; and there are facts which few writers would dare to put into a book, as there are skies which few painters would venture to put into a picture' (1: 268). Similarly, before Lord Y introduces him to the woman who will eventually become his wife, Glenthorn overhears a conversation during which his future mother-in-law ponders the improbabilities of his changeling status. 'Can you conceive it?', the elderly lady remarks, 'Changed at nurse! One hears of such things in novels, but, in real life, I absolutely cannot believe it' (1: 289).

The overwhelming consequence of Glenthorn's discovery that he has, unwittingly, contributed to the crime that has 'wronged, and robbed' the true Lord Glenthorn of his 'rightful inheritance', or status, though, is that it allows Edgeworth to plunge her hero into a crisis from which he recovers only once he follows Lord Y's instructions as to how he should reconstruct his entire existence (1: 267). Following Ellinor's revelation that she is his 'lawful mother',[64] Glenthorn finds himself faced with the ultimate metaphysical dilemma: namely, he must decide whether to continue '[t]o be or not to be Lord Glenthorn', or, instead, to 'act honestly and honourably, and to relinquish what [he] could no longer maintain without committing injustice' (1: 266, 272–3). Having made the 'virtuous decision' to inform Christy O'Donoghoe of their mutually confounded identities, he once more 'change[s] places' with the rightful earl, and is thence

---

62 Flanagan, *Irish novelists*, 84–5.   63 Lord Y is 'an Irish nobleman, with whom [Glenthorn] was not personally acquainted, but for whose amiable character and literary reputation [he] had always, even during [his] days of dissipation, peculiar respect' (1: 285).   64 Ellinor makes this startling admission in the mistaken belief that her other son, Owen, is among a band of rebels seized by Glenthorn and M'Leod upon the Glenthorn estate (1: 266–7).

plunged into a chaotic world which he experiences and expresses in explicitly ontological terms (1: 273–4). Travelling for the first time in his life without attendants, for instance, he reveals that he was amazed to discover that he was both his 'self' and his servant now that he was no longer an earl:

> I once caught myself saying of myself, "that careless blockhead has forgot my nightcap." For some time I was liable to make odd blunders about my own identity; I was apt to make mistakes between my old and my new habits, so that when I spoke in the tone and the imperative mode in which Lord Glenthorn had been habituated to speak, people stared at me as if I was mad, and I in my turn was frequently astonished by their astonishment, and perplexed by their ease of behaviour in my presence. (1: 284)

At this point, Edgeworth introduces Lord Y into her narrative, and her message is clear: all of Glenthorn's difficulties can be effaced if he assumes an Edgeworthian self. Presenting himself in person to answer the lord's letter of enquiry about his former tutor, Glenthorn eventually enlightens him as to his new circumstances, and is for two reasons surprised and pleased by the nobleman's response. Firstly, Lord Y explains that he is already aware of Glenthorn's 'real character', having 'learnt it from [Mr Cecil Devereux,] a particular friend of mine, of whose judgement and abilities I have the highest opinion' (1: 287). This gentleman, 'repeated an assertion, that was supported with much energy by the charming Lady Geraldine, that Lord Glenthorn had *abilities to be any thing he pleased*' (1: 287). I will be returning to the significance of Cecil Devereux and, even more particularly, of Lady Geraldine below, but for now I merely want to note that Edgeworth's emphasis here supports her ostensible didactic contention regarding the essential malleability of the native Irish race. Although it is true that neither Mr Devereux nor Lady Geraldine are aware of Glenthorn's true condition when they discuss him with Lord Y, an important point of Edgeworth's narrative is that they not only admire the integrity of his character, but also perceive that this character can be transformed. Upon discovering that Glenthorn is, in fact, a penniless native Irish man, Lord Y is still entirely confident that it will prove possible for him to transform the former earl and to efface the lineaments of his original, native station.

Crucially, Lord Y provides Glenthorn with the means and the motive for submitting to this ontological process; he introduces him to Cecilia Delamere, 'the heir at law' to the Glenthorn estate, and convinces him that, if he reforms himself, he could hope to make her his wife (1: 289). In choosing a husband, Cecilia's 'disposition and excellent understanding will ... direct her preference

to the essential good qualities, and not to the accidental advantages, of the candidates for her favour', the nobleman emphasizes, and this means that she will
favourably receive any efforts that Glenthorn makes to transform his 'self' and
obliterate forever the insignificance of his original station in life (1: 293). '[Y]ou
have now the most powerful of motives, and in proportion to your exertions
will be your success', he tells Glenthorn, 'In our country, you know, the highest offices of the state are open to talents and perseverance; a man of abilities
and application cannot fail to secure independence, and obtain distinction' (1:
293). Patently rehearsing a theme that we have already seen is central to tales
like 'Lame Jervas', the effect that this advice has upon Glenthorn is underlined
in Edgeworth's narrative. Insisting that Lord Y's observations 'made a great and
ineffaceable impression' upon his mind, Glenthorn pointedly declares that he
'date[s] the commencement of [his] new existence' from this moment (1: 294).
'Fired with ambition … to distinguish myself among men, and to win the
favour of [Cecilia Delamere], … all the faculties of my soul were awakened …
The enchantment of indolence was dissolved, and the demon of ennui was cast
out for ever' (1: 294).

In tracing the evolution of Glenthorn's 'new existence', Edgeworth shows
her hero this time voluntarily plunging himself into a state of nothingness with
the clear intention of transforming himself entirely. Observing that he has 'no
more wonderful incidents to relate, no more changes at nurse, no more sudden
turns of fortune', Glenthorn insists that he henceforth pursued a steady course
in order to effect the final transformation of his self and his affairs (1: 294). 'I
am now become a plodding man of business', he notes, 'poring over law-books
from morning till night, and leading a most monotonous life' (1: 294).
Persevering 'resolutely' in his legal studies, Glenthorn's friendship with Lord Y
also impresses upon him what he could have accomplished while he occupied
his aristocratic station and, when he is taken by the nobleman to visit his estates
and those of his friends, Glenthorn becomes 'convinced that much may be done
by the judicious care and assistance of landlords for their tenantry' (1: 294–6).
'I saw this with mixed sensations of pleasure and of pain', he remarks, 'for I
reflected how little I had accomplished, and how ill I had done even that little,
whilst the means of doing good to numbers had been in my power' (1: 296).

Although his regrets are many, Glenthorn's regular correspondence with
Mr M'Leod convinces him that his efforts are proving far more successful that
those of the true earl. Learning from M'Leod that Glenthorn Castle has become
'a scene of riotous living', Glenthorn imparts to his reader his perception that
the former Christy O'Donoghoe's difficulties are primarily caused by the affectation of his wife, for her (fatal) desire is to replicate 'her' version of her family's
original status. Filling the castle 'with tribes of her vagabond relations', Lady

Glenthorn chooses 'to be descended from one of the kings of Ireland', and invites those who 'acknowledge her high descent' to live in 'the barbaric magnificence of Glenthorn Castle' (1: 297). 'Every instance that she could hear of the former Lady Glenthorn's extravagance or of mine', Glenthorn observes, 'she determined to exceed' (1: 297). Manifestly condemning both her hero's former existence and the native Irish identity that Ellinor would have had him adopt when he was still an earl, Edgeworth impresses upon the reader her own and her father's perception that it is necessary to remain ontologically alert when dealing with the (predatory) native Irish race. As well as decking herself out 'in the most absurd manner', Lady Glenthorn, the tale therefore notes, often 'indulged in the pleasures of the banquet, till, no longer able to support the regal diadem, she was carried by some of the meanest of her subjects to her bed' (1: 298). Although comical, Edgeworth's narrative intimates that this Lady Glenthorn's affection finally has disastrous implications: 'The thefts committed during these interregnums were amazing in their amount, and the jewels of the crown were to be replaced as fast as they were stolen' (1: 298).

By tracing the entwined fates of Glenthorn and his foster-brother in her narrative, Edgeworth brings to their logic conclusion the didactic assertions that have framed and impelled her tale. Unlike Glenthorn, who eventually triumphs in his desire to '[make] a lawyer of himself', Christy O'Donoghoe never comes to terms with his new-found status, and eventually loses forever the estates of the family he (unwillingly) represents (1: 298). Derided by those about him 'as a mean-spirited *cratur*', and mocked because he has 'no notion of living like a prince', Christy thus finds himself 'scarcely considered as the master of [his] house' and languishes away for the want of gainful employment (1: 298). '[I]sn't it … a great hardship upon a man like me to have nothing to do, or not to be let do any thing', he observes to M'Leod, 'If it had not been for my son Johnny's sake, I never would have quit the forge; and now all will be spent in *coshering*, and Johnny, at the last, will never be a penny the better, but the worse for my consinting to be lorded' (1: 298). In other words, Edgeworth's emphasis here is that Christy's inability to overcome his ontological confusion renders him incapable of holding on to what he should always have possessed, whereas Glenthorn's essential malleability means that he is eventually able to reverse his misfortunes and to occupy his former status legitimately. Through his marriage to Cecilia Delamere, he aligns himself with the 'heir at law' to his former possessions, which ultimately enables him to once more (re)occupy all of his former (e)states (1: 289).

Glenthorn's union with Cecilia is hugely important on an allegorical level, for it clearly symbolizes the greater union that Edgeworth believes should exist between the Irish and the English race. In order to overcome his future mother-in-law's objections, we saw earlier, Glenthorn significantly agrees to 'take and bear the name and arms' of his future bride (1: 306). While ostensibly illustrating nothing more than the complacency with which Glenthorn acquiesces to the transformation of his identity in order to facilitate his marriage, this act at the same time illuminates the more subversive connotations of Edgeworth's narrative. By taking Cecilia's name, after all, Glenthorn (indirectly) brings his native mother's plans to fruition: that is, he 'murders' his self in order to '(re)take' the true earl's life.

In due course, Glenthorn receives a letter from his grieving foster brother, and this tells him that the O'Donoghoes have destroyed themselves as a result of their inability to come to terms with their true situation. 'The castle's burnt all down to the ground', Christy writes, 'and my Johnny's dead, and I wish I was dead in his place' (1: 308). For her part, Edgeworth could not make the significance of the circumstances surrounding Johnny's death clearer for her reader; Christy observes, 'The occasion of his death was owing to drink, which he fell into from getting too much money, and nothing to do – and a snuff of a candle. When going to bed last night, a little in liquor, what does he do but takes the candle, and sticks it up against the head of his bed, as he used oftentimes to do, without detriment, in the cabin where he was reared, against the mud wall' (1: 308). The fact that Johnny forgets whom and where he now is leads directly to the death of this future earl of Glenthorn: he dies precisely because he adheres to the lineaments of his former status. Observing that the candle set fire to a curtain and then Johnny's bed, the heartbroken Christy consequently tells Glenthorn, 'before he waked at all, it appears the unfortunit *cratur* was smothered' (1: 308). Although he managed to save himself and his wife, Christy recalls that none of their relations or servants 'thought ... to save any thing at all, but just what they could for themselves' (1: 308). Observing that 'there's nothing remaining of the castle but the stones', Christy as a result 'beg[s]' his foster brother, 'being married ... to Miss Delamere, that is the *hare* at law, [to] take possession of all immediately, for I am as good as dead, and will give no hindrance' (1: 308). Explicitly, Christy here offers Glenthorn his material and his ontological 'holdings'; he intimates that he will vacate all of his (e)states if his foster brother comes back.

By having Christy plead with her reformed hero to 'come to reign over us again', Edgeworth appears to immediately satisfy the familial and colonial imperatives that frame not only this tale, but all of her Irish writing (1: 308). Would-be rulers of Ireland must replicate Glenthorn's example and assume the lineaments of an Edgeworthian identity, she implies, this will inevitably efface questions of legitimacy in Ireland and facilitate the nation's reform. In order to facilitate this argument, though, Edgeworth is obliged to once more draw upon the amnesia motif of romance, and to intimate that all of Ireland's inhabitants will quickly learn to forget the difficulties of their past. The members of the Protestant Ascendancy will cheerfully embrace the lineaments of their reformed (Edgeworthian) identities, according to Edgeworth, and, dazzled by its evident superiority, the native Irish will forget that they were ever anything more than the willing subjects of this class. When Glenthorn initially informs his foster brother that he is, in truth, 'of a *ra-al* good *ould* family born', Christy therefore at first crucially mistakes his meaning (1: 274). Believing that is referring to the O'Donoghoe family's Milesian identity, he declares that he neither thinks upon, nor mourns, the passing of this life: '"Och!" said he, laughing and scratching his head, "your honour's jesting me about them kings of Ireland, that they say the O'Donoghoes was once: but that's what I never think *on*, that's all idle talk for the like of me, for sure that's a long time ago, and what use going back to it? One might as well be going back to Adam, that was the father of all, but which makes no differ now"' (1: 274). Similarly, when Christy writes to beg Glenthorn to return to Ireland, he insists not only that he will be no 'hindrance', but also that he will 'go back to [his] forge, and, by the help of God, forget at [his] work what has passed' (1: 308). This emphasis in *Ennui* manifestly rehearses the didactic implications of the preface to *Castle Rackrent*: it intimates that, in the light of the post-Union dawn, the native Irish are cheerfully casting off their former (unreformed) state.

Despite this particular argument in the narrative, however, *Glenthorn's* reactions following his discovery that he is not the rightful earl engage with, and destabilize, the didactic imperatives that impel Edgeworth's story, for he rejects the suggestion that he could continue to live with the new earl and his family and manifests a significant reluctance to live as a 'subject' upon his former estates. 'If your honour could live on here, and share with us', Christy observes, 'But I see your honour's displeased at my naming *that*' (1: 277). Similarly, when he traces the difficulties and regrets that he encounters in coming to terms with his 'new' situation, Glenthorn expresses his desire to once more enjoy the privileges and, pointedly, the power of his former status. '[R]eview[ing] the whole of my past life', he remarks, 'I considered ... how little advantage I had derived from my education, and from all my opportunities of acquiring knowledge ... I wished that I could live my life over again; and I felt that, were it in my power, I should live in a manner very different from that in which I had fooled away existence' (1: 283).

In point of fact, of course, Glenthorn here reviews an 'existence' that was never really his own; to put this another way, he explicitly mourns and desires to (re)live the earl of Glenthorn's life. The fact that he eventually satisfies this ambition raises a very significant question for the reader of Glenthorn's

'Memoirs': namely, how truthful is his literary representation of his life? Although the explicit emphasis of his 'memoirs' is that he 'endure[d]' the 'pains' of reform in order to win Cecilia Delamere's 'applause', his musings following the first 'twelvemonth' of his marriage intimate that his may be an act of singularly duplicitous narration (1: 303, 307). Significantly noting that it was neither Cecilia nor Lord Y, but, rather, Mr Devereux and Lady Geraldine who 'first awakened my dormant intellects, made me know that I had a heart, and that I was capable of forming a character for myself', Glenthorn further admits, 'The loss of my estate continued the course of my education, *forced me to exert my own powers*, and to rely upon myself' (1: 307) (my emphasis). Immediately raising the question of the expediency of Glenthorn's relationship with Cecilia, this also helps to account for the peculiar tension that informs his depiction of Lady Geraldine in his narrative. If Cecilia is his projected reader, it is much more understandable that Glenthorn should seek to efface the extent to which he was both attracted and influenced by Lady Geraldine; for Cecilia's sake, he must insist that it was *she* who first truly captivated him and inspired his reform.

In this context, then, Glenthorn maintains that he was caught off guard by the 'singularities' of Lady Geraldine's 'character', and also that he was prompted to act despite himself by this 'representative of an ancient house' (1: 212). As he would have it, he was unwillingly intoxicated by Lady Geraldine's peculiar powers and this unfortunately played into the hands of their matchmaking relations and friends. Strolling together one day through the grounds of Ormsby Villa where they were staying, Glenthorn recalls, he and Lady Geraldine were locked by others into 'the temple of Minerva' in the villa's grounds (1: 237). Conscious that such 'locking-up' usually ends 'in matrimony', Lady Geraldine assured the startled Glenthorn she had no suspicion of his having played any part in the 'vulgar manoeuvre' (1: 238). Although he has previously declared his determination not to be ensnared by Lady Geraldine, Glenthorn remembers that he immediately forgot all of his 'prudential arrangements', and suddenly found himself 'at her ladyship's feet, and making very serious love' (1: 238). With one eye on Cecilia, his projected reader, however, he protests that he was not responsible for this behaviour; it all transpired 'before [he] knew where [he] was' (1: 238).

Despite similar protestations throughout the 'memoirs', though, Glenthorn's narrative seriously implies not only that he was seriously attracted to Lady Geraldine, but also that this attraction was to a large part due to her ability to 'touch' his Irish heart. Although he does not admit this directly, Glenthorn intimates that he was attracted to Lady Geraldine because she so eloquently represented Ireland and the Irish way of life. Recalling their first meeting, for instance, Glenthorn remembers how the manifest originality of Lady Geraldine's character encouraged him to consider her 'with more attention than I had ever bestowed

on any other woman. The words *striking – fascinating – bewitching,* occurred to me
as I looked at her and heard her speak' (1: 211). '[P]ositively determined not to
like her, [as he] dreaded so much the idea of a second Hymen',[65] he nonetheless
admits that 'fresh singularities' in Lady Geraldine's character continued to strike
him (1: 211–2). The fact that Lady Geraldine continually succeeded in prompt-
ing him to act despite himself alarmed Glenthorn; as he puts it, 'A slight degree
of fear of Lady Geraldine's powers kept my attention alert' (1: 211).

'Confident of her talents, conscious of her charms, and secure of her station, Lady Geraldine', according to Glenthorn, 'gave free scope to her high spirits, her fancy, and her turn for ridicule. She looked, spoke, and acted, like a
person privileged to think, say, and do, what she pleased' (1: 212). What 'pleased'
Lady Geraldine, of course, was to expose the affectation of others; in particular, to reveal the foibles of those who would denigrate their own country.
'[A]mongst the company of Ormsby Villa', Glenthorn thus recalls, there were
'a Mrs Norton and Lady Hauton' (1: 226). Although 'persons of no consequence and of no marked character in [England]', they made 'a prodigious *sensation* when they came over to Ireland, and turned the heads of half Dublin by
the extravagance of their dress, the impertinence of their airs, and the audac-
ity of their conduct' (1: 226–7). By coming to Ireland, Edgeworth implies, in
other words, Mrs Norton and Lady Hauton succeed in (re)defining their selves
at the expense of others; they profit by the gullibility of those who are predis-
posed to believe that the Irish are a necessarily inferior race. Unlike the rest of
the company, Lady Geraldine sees through Mrs Norton and Lady Hauton's
affectation, and she pleads with her fellow countrywomen not to 'abase' themselves by seeking a 'pattern' of these English ladies (1: 229, 227). 'O! my dear
countrywomen', she declares to the assembled company, 'let us never stoop to
admire and imitate these second-hand airs and graces, follies and vices. Let us
dare to be ourselves!' (1: 229). This in the first instance immediately illustrates
a theme that is central to all of Edgeworth's writing; in *The absentee,* for example, it is the affected Lady Clonbrony's deprecation of Ireland and of all things
Irish that prompts the elderly Lady Oranmore to an eloquent defence of her
country.[66] Lady Geraldine's exclamation also has a further significance in that
it again draws attention to the fact that Glenthorn has a peculiarly receptive
(native Irish) 'heart' (1: 229). Noting that his eyes were 'fixed upon [Lady
Geraldine's] animated countenance' while she was speaking, Glenthorn as a
result remembers not only that he 'continued gazing even after her voice ceased',

---

65 Glenthorn's first marriage was a disaster. His choice of wife was dictated by the dire state of his finances and
he consequently treated Lady Glenthorn 'as an incumbrance, that [he] was obliged to take along with [his] fortune' (1: 168). Lady Glenthorn ultimately eloped with Captain Crawley, Glenthorn's agent, and the marriage ended
in divorce.   66 *Novels and selected works,* 5: 48.

but also that the lady's declaration 'wakened dormant feelings in [his] heart' (1: 229). Like Ellinor before her, in other words, Lady Geraldine helped to make Glenthorn 'sensible' that he had a distinctly Irish 'soul', and that he was '*superior* to the puppets with whom [he] had been classed' (1: 229) (my emphasis).

Notwithstanding this emphasis in the tale, though, Edgeworth is clearly unable to countenance the prospect of a union between this lady and her hero in her narrative, for Lady Geraldine's name not only 'links her to the Fitzgeralds or Geraldines, for centuries the dominant aristocratic family in the Irish Midlands, where the Edgeworths lived', but also acts as 'a reminder of the highest-ranking United Irishman, Lord Edward Fitzgerald, who died in prison after his capture in the 1798 rebellion'.[67] To facilitate her ambition to produce an image of Ireland where such uncomfortable reminders of the nation's (rebellious) past are effaced, or disguised, Edgeworth consequently sends Lady Geraldine off to India with Cecil Devereux, and this clears the way for Glenthorn and Cecilia's eventual marriage. In effecting this union in her narrative, Edgeworth therefore ostensibly satisfies the colonial imperatives that impel all of her writing, and she implies that, in order to secure socio-political stability in Ireland, the nation's rulers must resist the (sometimes alluring) remnants of the past and submit to a process of Edgeworthian reform. While appearing to facilitate the didactic imperatives that impel the tale, the conclusion of *Ennui* nonetheless challenges the very efficacy of this vision, and it reveals Edgeworth's peculiar awareness of the seductive power, and duplicity, of the native Irish race. Thus it is that, although Glenthorn emphasizes that his 'passion for the amiable and charming Cecilia was … motive sufficient to urge [him] to persevering intellectual labour' following Lady Geraldine and Cecil Devereux's departure to India and the loss of his estates, he himself appears to doubt the permanence of his transformation (1: 307). Immediately before he receives the letter wherein Christy begs him to return to Ireland, for example, Glenthorn wonders what the outcome would be if he were plunged once more into his former life: 'Whether, if I were again a rich man, I should have sufficient voluntary exertion to take a due portion of mental and bodily exercise, I dare not pretend to determine, nor do I wish to be put to the trial' (1: 307). Similarly, when he notes that he and his wife will return to Ireland when the Glenthorn castle is finished 'rebuilding', Glenthorn significantly only 'flatter[s]' himself that he 'shall not relapse into indolence' upon his return (1: 308). In truth, the recognition that Glenthorn has already proven himself to be peculiarly susceptible to ontological temptation cannot be effaced from his narrative, and this disturbs the ostensible didactic conclusion of Edgeworth's tale.

---

67 Butler, introduction, Castle Rackrent *and* Ennui, 43.

A similar tensions disrupts the didactic message of *The absentee*, which, like *Ennui* and *Ormond*, revolves around the hero's return to his Irish home. Newly come down from his college at Cambridge, Lord Colambre rejoins his parents in London, and at once perceives that confusion of identity is responsible for his family's prolonged absence from their Irish estates. Impelled by her desire to convince the circles in which she moves that she is truly '*Henglish*, born in *Hoxfordshire* ', Colambre's mother, Lady Clonbrony, insists upon remaining in London, and 'works ... hard, and pays ... high' as a result of her affectation.[68] Not noticing 'that the renegado cowardice with which she denied, abjured, and reviled her own country, gained [her] nothing but ridicule and contempt', Lady Clonbrony is also blind to the fact that her husband is being turned into a '[n]othing, [or] [a] nobody' as a result of her '*Londonomania*' (5: 8, 6, 153). Divorced from the time, place, and circumstances that truly define him, Lord Clonbrony is being slowly effaced by London life: 'Whilst Lady Clonbrony, in consequence of her residence in London, had become more of a fine lady, Lord Clonbrony, since he left Ireland, had become less of a gentleman ... [He] was somebody in Ireland, ... a great person in Dublin, [but] found himself nobody in England, a mere cipher in London' (5: 20).

Colambre grows increasingly alarmed by his discoveries, particularly when he witnesses the effects of an affectation similar to that of his mother's on the family and fortune of Mr Berryl, his Cambridge friend. Following the death of his father, the new Lord Berryl is horrified to discover that he has been left nothing more than the outward trappings of his aristocratic status and, 'without any income', must choose between ignoring his father's 'just debts' or letting 'his mother and sisters starve' (5: 44). Pointedly, the tale draws the moral:

> All this evil had arisen from Lady Berryl's passion for living in London and at watering places. She had made her husband an ABSENTEE ... from his home, his affairs, his duties, and his estate. The sea, the Irish Channel, did not, indeed, flow between him and his estate; but it was of little importance whether the separation was effected by land or water – the consequences, the negligence, the extravagance, were the same. (5: 44)

Although we shall see below that his return to Ireland is crucially impelled by his complicated relationship with Grace Nugent, his mother's ward, Colambre's journey 'home' is in the first place informed by his sense of ontological crisis or alienation. All too conscious of the difficulties of his father, he must discover for himself whether he too 'shall ... be an absentee' (5: 9).

---

68 *Novels and selected works*, 5: 5–6. Further references to this tale are cited parenthetically in the text.

Clearly representing one of Edgeworth's more detailed (re)workings in her fiction of her father's 1782 return to Ireland, Colambre's return 'home' in *The absentee* is likewise compelled by his conviction that a precise correlation necessarily exists between his own and his nation's identity. Thus he observes to his mother, he returns to Ireland in order 'to become acquainted with it – because it is the country in which my father's property lies, and from which we draw our subsistence' (5: 59). To put this another way, he returns because he is beginning to believe, like Edgeworth's father before him, that 'if it [is] in the power of any man to serve the country which [gives] him bread, he ought to sacrifice every inferior consideration, and ... reside where he [can] be most useful.'[69] For Colambre, as for Edgeworth's father, the man and the nation are inextricably connected; each needs the other in order to survive.

Upon arriving in Dublin, Colambre is fortunate to make the acquaintance of Sir James Brooke, ' a very gentlemanlike, sensible-looking' English officer whose long experience of Ireland ideally places him to give the young traveller a crucial insight into Irish life (5: 64). Sir James has it 'in his power ... to save [the young lord] from the common error of travellers – the deducing [of] general conclusions from a few particular cases, or arguing from exceptions, as if they were rules', and so persuades Colambre to reject his parents' '[mis]representations of [Dublin] society' and to assess 'the reality' for himself (5: 65). Failing to observe 'any of that confusion of ranks or predominance of vulgarity, of which his mother had complained', the bewildered Colambre shares with Sir James a story his mother had told him about once being angrily rebuked by 'a grocer's wife' for accidentally treading upon her train in Dublin Castle (5: 66). Sir James allows that the story may be true, but emphasizes that, if so, it is representative of a very particular moment in Irish history: specifically, of that instant when the passing of the Act of Union temporarily disordered Irish affairs. As such, the story should be viewed as 'one of the extraordinary cases which ought not pass into a general rule, – that it was a slight instance of that influence of temporary causes, from which no conclusion, as to national manners, should be drawn' (5: 66). Following the enactment of the Union, Sir James tells Colambre, 'most of the nobility and many of the principal families among the Irish commoners, either hurried in high hopes to London, or retired disgusted and in despair to their houses in the country. Immediately, in Dublin, commerce rose into the vacated seats of rank; wealth rose into the place of birth' (5: 66). Echoing the sentiments of the preface to *Castle Rackrent* and of the *Essay on Irish Bulls*, he insists that the eventual results of the Act of Union justified its immediate effects. '[N]ow it's all over', as he puts it, 'we may acknowl-

69 *Memoirs*, 1: 360.

edge, that, perhaps, even those things which we felt most disagreeable at the time were productive of eventual benefit' (5: 66–7). Those members of the Irish aristocracy who fled Dublin 'immediately upon the first incursions of the vulgarians' in due course returned, and there is now 'a society in Dublin composed of a most agreeable and salutary mixture of birth and education, gentility and knowledge, manner and matter; and … pervading the whole new life and energy, … [and the] perception that higher distinction can now be obtained in almost all company, by genius and merit, than by airs and address' (5: 66–7).

Armed with the benefit of Sir James' observations, Colambre commences his journey and spends some time in the home of the sister of Nicholas Garraghty, one of Lord Clonbrony's agents. In so doing, he comes to an important realization: that affectation is not confined to those of high birth and that his mother's inappropriate aspirations are precisely reflected by those of Mrs Raffarty and her friends:

> It was the same desire to appear what they were not, the same vain ambition to vie with superior rank and fortune, or fashion, which actuated Lady Clonbrony and Mrs Raffarty; and whilst this ridiculous grocer's wife made herself the sport of some of her guests, Lord Colambre sighed, from the reflection that what she was to them his mother was to persons in a higher rank of fashion (5: 72).[70]

Disgusted by what he sees of Dublin's mercantilist class, Colambre begins to lose sight of Sir James' warning that a traveller should never judge by exceptions as if they were rules, and this renders him peculiarly vulnerable when he encounters Lady Dashfort and her daughter. '[C]ounterfeits' both, these 'dangerous ladies' represent a very real threat to Colambre, for they seek to impose an inauthentic view of reality upon him and to thereby frustrate his desire to become properly (re)acquainted with Ireland and the native Irish race (5: 78, 76). Contradicting Colambre's insistence that he is quite safe from their influence as his 'heart is engaged', Sir James warns his friend that this precise circumstance would render it peculiarly 'Lady Dashfort's sport, and Lady Isabel's joy' to ensnare him (5: 75). '[T]he fairer, the more amiable, the more beloved' Colambre's mistress, he notes, 'the greater the triumph, the greater the delight in giving pain' (5: 75). While believing himself immune to the Dashforts' power, Colambre instead falls inexorably under their spell, with Lady Dashfort in par-

---

70 As McCormack puts it, Colambre's sojourn at Mrs Raffarty's villa brings him to 'a halt; it forces him to consider his surroundings and his domestic background, to *relate* his Irish and English experience' (*Ascendancy and tradition*, 129).

ticular using all of her arts to persuade the young lord that she can be both 'entertaining' and 'agreeable' (5: 79–80). For her part, Lady Isabel compliments her mother's endeavours by affecting a 'dignity, grace, and modesty' that convinces Colambre 'that it was impossible all that he had seen could be acting. "No woman, no young woman, could have such art"' (5: 76–7).

In making the acquaintance of the Dashforts, Colambre's powers of deduction are thus sorely tried, and his initial inability to see through their 'drama' has potentially disastrous implications.[71] Lady Dashfort's 'settled purpose [is] to make the Irish and Ireland ridiculous and contemptible to Lord Colambre … To confirm him an absentee was her object, previously to her ultimate plan of marrying him to her daughter' (5: 83). Lady Isabel is poor, and so Lady Dashfort wants 'to *get* an Irish peer for her', but neither mother nor daughter intend that this should mean that Isabel would be 'banished to Ireland' (5: 83). While professing herself a friend to Ireland, Lady Dashfort therefore deliberately introduces him to an example of the worst type of resident Irish landlord in the person of Lord Killpatrick, and she succeeds in weakening Colambre's 'enthusiasm' for his native country by trailing him in and out of the miserable hovels upon the Killpatrick estate (5: 86).

Potentially much more dangerous for Colambre, however, is the fact that the Dashforts also mount an insidious assault upon the character of Grace Nugent, the young woman whom he loves. '[R]eceived' into the Clonbrony family when she was left an orphan, Grace has succeeded in securing Colambre's affection precisely because of her lack of affectation (5: 35). She is, as the tale puts it, 'quite above all double dealing' and exactly 'that which she seem[s] to be' (5: 36). Although increasingly convinced of his love for Grace, Colambre believes a union with her to be impossible; Lady Clonbrony believes that a marriage between cousins raises neither a family's 'interest' nor 'consequence', and so Colambre's sense of loyalty to his mother prevents him from contemplating such a match (5: 36). Similarly, Colambre recognizes that Grace herself is 'so well apprised, and so thoroughly convinced' of Lady Clonbrony's opinion 'that she never for one moment allowed herself to think of [him] as a lover. Duty, honour, and gratitude – gratitude, the strong feeling and principle of her mind – forbade it' (5: 36). As a consequence of all of this, Colambre's return to Ireland is therefore impelled not only by his desire to decide for himself whether he will emulate his father's absentee example, but also by the complicated nature of his relationship with Grace. Aware that she is intent on marrying him to

71 The fact that the Dashforts are essentially putting on a production for Colambre is made peculiarly apparent by one of Lady Dashfort's observations to her daughter. 'To do you justice', she remarks, 'you play Lydia Languish vastly well … but Lydia, by herself, would soon tire; somebody must keep up the spirit and bustle, and carry on the plot of the piece; and I am that somebody … Is not that our hero's voice which I hear on the stairs?' (5: 80).

Miss Broadhurst, an English heiress, Colambre is compelled to admit to his mother that his 'affections are engaged to another person', but insists he will not act without his parents' consent (5: 57). In the meantime, he declares, he will take himself to Ireland and reside upon his father's Irish estates.

Lady Dashfort quickly discerns Colambre's affection for Grace and, in tracing her own genealogy for the young lord, consequently expresses a false desire to pass over the 'little blot' in her family's 'scutcheon ... that prudent match of great uncle John's ... [whereby he married] into *that* family [the St. Omars], where, you know, all the men were not *sans peur*, and none of the women *sans reproche*' (5: 86). Insisting that the maiden name of Grace's mother was not Reynolds, as Colambre believes, but St Omar, Lady Dashfort succeeds in implying that Miss St Omar was never married, and also in linking Grace to a Catholic, Jacobite past. This is the case because, as McCormack points out, the name Nugent in itself implies 'an Irish, aristocratic, Jacobite background',[72] while that of St Omar recalls the town of St Omer in Northern France, the site of a Jesuit College.[73] Colambre already has expressed his 'dread of marrying any woman whose mother had conducted herself ill', and so is devastated by the apparent implications of Grace's lineage (5: 88). His terrors are further amplified by Lady Clonbrony's answer to her son's letter of enquiry, wherein she reveals that Grace's 'mother's maiden name was *St Omar*; and there was a *faux pas*, certainly', but, knowing that nothing could be 'more disadvantageous to Grace than to have [this story] revived', the Clonbronys have 'kept it secret' (5: 96). At this moment, and as Lady Dashfort has intended, all of Colambre's 'hopes, [and] plans of future happiness' appear to be 'shaken to their very foundation'; feeling as he does, he cannot even consider taking such a wife (5: 88).

It is for this reason that the presence of Count O'Halloran in *The absentee* is so important, for this 'old man who spends his days hunting the traditional game of the island and his nights poring over its great names and monuments represents an ideal past ... [and] an Ireland which can and does give Colambre strength and direction'.[74] Thus, it is the Count who weakens the Dashforts' influence over Colambre, by causing Lady Dashfort to reveal that she is entirely unmoved by the report of an insult that an English officer of her acquaintance has paid to the elderly Lady Oranmore and her daughters. Having passed off his mistress as his wife to Lady Oranmore, this officer has gone so far as to allow the unsuspecting lady to 'send her carriage for this woman ... [so] that she ... dined at [the] Oranmore [home]' (5: 97). By insisting that she will pre-

72 McCormack, *Ascendancy and tradition*, 142. 73 As McCormack and Walker observe in their endnotes to *The absentee*, 'the sustained attack on the good name of Grace's ancestry is concentrated here ... By the late eighteenth century, the name [St. Omer] had become synonymous with a profession of Catholicism, in Ireland as well as in England' (303–4). 74 Flanagan, *Irish novelists*, 89–90.

tend to be 'shocked! shocked to death!' at this piece of effrontery, Lady Dashfort makes 'a great mistake'; Colambre's 'eyes [begin] to open to Lady Dashfort's character; and he [is], from this moment, freed from her power' (5: 98). Very shortly after this incident, Colambre similarly realizes the duplicitous nature of Lady Isabel, when he accidentally overhears her conversation with Elizabeth, 'one of the young ladies of the [Killpatrick] house' (5: 98). Admitting that she has only 'flirted' with a certain Lord de Cressy in order 'to plague his wife', Isabel reveals that her detestation of this lady is such 'that, to purchase the plea-sure of making her feel the pangs of jealousy for one hour, look, I would this moment lay down this finger and let it be cut off' (5: 98). 'The face, the whole figure of Lady Isabel, at this moment, appeared to Lord Colambre suddenly metamorphosed; instead of the soft, gentle, amiable female, all sweet charity and tender sympathy, formed to love and to be loved, he beheld one possessed and convulsed by an evil spirit – her beauty, if beauty it could be called, the beauty of a fiend' (5: 98).

Patently functioning as 'recognition scenes' in the narrative, these episodes illustrate why Edgeworth's depiction of the Dashforts in *The absentee* is so impor-tant.[75] In the first instance, while the heroes and heroines of romance typically exist to symbolize a contrast between two worlds, so, too, it must be remem-bered, do the *villains*. Clearly representing the 'demonic' realm in *The absentee*, the Dashforts' desires are implicitly satanic; their ambition is to drag Colambre into an 'underworld' existence by preventing him from getting a proper view of the Irish nation and race. Plainly supporting Frye's argument that the 'standard escape device of romance is that of escape through a shift of identity',[76] Colambre therefore begins his ascent from the lower world represented by the Dashforts and, indeed, by his father's 'bad' agent, Nicholas Garraghty, only once he sees through the formers' machinations. 'Lord Colambre ... announced this night that it was necessary he should immediately pursue his tour in Ireland ... [W]hen he was gone, Lady Dashfort exclaimed, "That man has escaped from me"' (5: 99).

Colambre resolves 'to make himself amends for the time he [has] lost [with the Dashforts], by seeing with his own eyes, and judging with his own under-standing, of the country and its inhabitants, during the remainder of the time he was to stay in Ireland', and, significantly, elects to travel '*incognito*' through his father's estates (5: 100–1). By voluntarily suspending his identity, and by moving between the two parts of his father's patrimony, he in due course receives a valu-able existential lesson: he learns, that is, what type of landlord he and Lord Clonbrony should become. Upon the Colambre estate, he is first of all

75 Frye, *Secular scripture*, 136.   76 Ibid.

impressed by the exemplary Mr Burke, who practices the same model of land-lord/tenant relations as Edgeworth's father upon his part of Lord Clonbrony's holdings. As an Irish innkeeper observes, Mr Burke is an ideal landlord because he 'encourage[s] the improving tenant', '[resides] always in the country', and is scrupulously fair when demanding rent or negotiating a lease (5: 103). The Clonbrony part of his father's estates, Colambre discovers, are on the other hand mismanaged by the symbolically named '[O]ld Nick' Garraghty and his brother, 'St Dennis' (5: 109):

> Dennis, the first bishop of Paris, was beheaded in the 3rd century; in legend, he walked some distance after he was decapitated, carrying his head in his hands. 'Old Nick' is a familiar, euphemistic name for Satan. Given the contemporary war with France, and the revolutionary tur-moil of the previous two and a half decades, France's patron saint and the devil might well be brothers, just as they stand for the evil admin-istration (and likely collapse) of Irish landlordism.[77]

Together, Colambre comes to realize, Old Nick Garraghty and his brother have reduced the Clonbrony part of his father's holdings to 'the picture ... of that to which an Irish estate and Irish tenantry may be degraded in the absence of those whose duty and interest it is to reside in Ireland, ... [and who] abandon their tenantry to oppression, and their property to ruin' (5: 125).

Returning to England just in time to prevent Nicholas Garraghty from defrauding his father,[78] Colambre shares with his family the lessons of his fate-ful journey, impressing upon his mother in particular his discovery that affec-tation has national as well as personal consequences. The Clonbronys have indeed managed to force their way into the 'frozen circles' of London society, he tells her, but only by sacrificing 'a great part' of their timber in order to pay for one winter's 'entertainments' (5: 154). 'But let the trees go: I think more of your tenants – of those left under the tyranny of a bad agent, at the expence of every comfort, every hope they enjoyed! – tenants, who were thriving and prosperous; who used to smile upon you, and to bless you [and Lord Clonbrony] both!' (5: 154). Colambre likewise draws Lady Clonbrony's attention to the adverse effects that her '*Londonomania*' has had upon his father. Lord Clonbrony has been 'forced away from [his] home' and 'set down, late in life, in the midst of strangers, to him cold and reserved', Colambre emphasizes, '[I]s he not more to be pitied than blamed for ... the degradation which has ensued?' (5: 154).

77 McCormack and Walker, endnotes, *The absentee*, 309. 78 When Colambre reveals his identity, Nick Garraghty hastens to London with some leases through which he hopes to defraud his employer for one last time (5: 139).

Stressing that Lady Clonbrony's efforts have won her nothing but ridicule from those whom she most desires to impress, Edgeworth once again invokes the amnesia motif of romance to diffuse the socio-political difficulties threatening the Irish nation. Colambre pleads with his mother to 'restore' her husband to his proper condition, inferring that, if she 'remembers' her duties to the Clonbronys' tenants, it will be easy for the family to efface the terrible mistakes of their past (5: 154). The native Irish are 'an unsophisticated people ... [with] grateful hearts', he stresses, and these long remain 'warm with the remembrance of [the] kindness' of past times (5: 155). Patently intended to diffuse the several anxieties of Edgeworth's Protestant Ascendancy readers, Colambre's insistence is that the Clonbronys may be assured of the loyalty of their tenants despite years of ill treatment and neglect. His emphasis is that the Clonbronys' tenants are 'still blessing [his mother] for favours long since conferred', and have effectively forgotten everything except her kindness and their desire 'to see [her] once more' (5: 155). Countering Lady Clonbrony's assertion that she 'thought all in Ireland must have forgotten me, it is now so long since I was at home', Colambre is emphatic: 'You are not forgotten in Ireland by any rank, I can answer for that' (5: 155).

Having used romance in order to impress both her hero and her reader with the undesirable nature of the absentee existence, Edgeworth further employs the genre's conventions to clear up the shadow hanging over Grace Nugent's 'past.' Although more than ever convinced of his love for Grace, Colambre cannot bring himself to marry her so long as he believes that her mother was not *sans reproche*. Rather than join his family on their return to Ireland, he therefore resolves to join the army and travel. Crucially, though, Colambre's plans are transformed by the unexpected appearance of Count O'Halloran in London. Like Thady in *Castle Rackrent*, or Ellinor in *Ennui*, he, too, has marvellous powers of recollection, and his memories finally prove that Grace is in fact an entirely suitable prospective bride for Colambre. Recalling his 'particular regard' for Captain Reynolds, 'a young English officer who had been at the same time with him in the Austrian service', Count O'Halloran assures his astonished friend that this gentleman not only 'privately married ... Miss St Omar', but also that there was definitely documentary proof of the match (5: 173). In the type of set-piece so beloved of romances, Colambre and Sir James Brooke subsequently recover the marriage certificate of Grace's mother and father, which has been languishing for years tied up in 'a bundle of old newspapers at the bottom of a trunk' (5: 176). In this way, Grace is revealed to be both 'legitimate' and the heiress of the vast estate of the English 'Ralph Reynolds'; in other words, she is discovered to be the type of young lady who would make an eminently suitable marriage partner for any young lord (5: 195, 176).

An essential point about this revelation in *The absentee*, however, is that it
demonstrates that Grace's 'ties to Ireland' are 'based less in biology than in "early
association"', a fact that helps to explain, perhaps, why Edgeworth's narrative
so quickly dismisses the prospect of Colambre and Miss Broadhurst's 'projected' marriage (5: 55).[79] Unlike Grace, Miss Broadhurst is not particularly
attached to Ireland and so, in Edgeworth's terms, she is not in a position to
properly promote the future harmony of Anglo-Irish relations. In choosing a
bride, Edgeworth maintains, Colambre must look to the state of his future
wife's national affections, rather than to that of her bank balance; to put this
another way, he must satisfy himself that his choice of bride is a true 'friend'
to Ireland in her heart (5: 59). With Grace by his side, Colambre will be as a
result ideally placed to help shape Ireland's future, for neither he nor the future
Lady Clonbrony will ever 'forget' their sense of 'duty and patriotism' to that
nation following their marriage (5: 59, 9).

By concluding *The absentee* with a 'Letter' purportedly written by a native
Irish man to his brother in London, however, Edgeworth introduces some
incredibly subversive resonances into her tale (5: 199). Firstly, and most obviously, Larry Brady's description of the Clonbronys' homecoming reveals the
aspirational nature of the narrative, expertly demonstrating the reasons why
Edgeworth draws so heavily upon romance conventions to convince her readers that all of Ireland's absentee landlords will be joyfully welcomed 'home' by
the native Irish race. Reflecting the contention that the 'closer romance comes
to a world of original identity, the more clearly something of the symbolism
of the garden of Eden reappears, with the social setting reduced to the love of
individual men and women within an order of nature which has been reconciled to humanity',[80] Larry describes a scene where the Clonbronys are welcomed back to Ireland by nature as well as their tenants:

> we all got to the great gate of the park before sunset, and as fine an
> evening as ever you see; with the sun shining on the tops of the trees,
> … the leaves changed, but not dropped, though so late in the season.
> I believe the leaves knew what they were about, and kept on, on pur-
> pose to welcome them; and the birds were singing, and I stopped
> whistling, that they might hear them; but sorrow bit could they hear
> when they got to the park gate, for there was such a crowd, and such a
> shout, as you never see – and they had the horses off every carriage
> entirely, and drew 'em home, with blessings, through the park. (5: 201)

---

79 Corbett, *Allegories of union*, 74.   80 Frye, *Secular scripture*, 149.

If all of this clearly demonstrates the colonial anxiety that impels Edgeworth's narrative, so, too, does the fact that Colambre's symbolic marriage with Grace is never actually accomplished within the story. Instead, Larry relates to his brother the 'dream' that he has had of this union, insisting that Grace Reynolds 'will be sometime, and may be sooner than is expected, my lady Viscountess Colambre' (5: 203). Larry's insistence that he only 'dreamt' of Colambre's marriage to Grace effectively suspends the vision of harmonious landlord/tenant relations towards which Edgeworth works in her narrative; to all intents and purposes, it comes to exist only in the native Irish man's dream-like state (5: 203). This in the first place demonstrates Edgeworth's awareness that the paradigm that she is unfolding is both aspirational and conditional upon the complicity of the native Irish, but it also intimates her perception that, in order to govern successfully, the Ascendancy and the English will have to acknowledge and respect the peculiar power of their Irish dependents. Although from here it is but a short step to the processes of 'identification' and union that Edgeworth promotes throughout her writing, her protracted treatment of her protagonists' marriage in *The absentee* illuminates her awareness that, for the English at least, these may exact too high of an ontological price. By delaying Colambre and Grace's marriage, after all, Edgeworth also delays the consummation of their union; in romance terms, she further 'postpone[s] [Grace's] first sexual act.' In so doing, Edgeworth protects her heroine from 'the annihilation of … identity' that follows the loss of virginity,[81] and ensures that Grace preserves her virgin (English) state. This 'refusal to conclude with wedding bells', as McCormack puts it, 'avoids easy sentiment and acknowledges the persisting difficulties in bringing Catholic and Protestant, Jacobite and Williamite, together',[82] but it also demonstrates Edgeworth's perception that the English may not be prepared to take the final step that is necessary in order to promote a truly successful (national) 'marriage.' In order for such a union to be accomplished, both partners must be willing to compromise and, despite their protestations to the contrary, Edgeworth intimates, the English are still not ready to willingly embrace the lineaments of Irish life.

Edgeworth develops these several themes in *Ormond*, her last 'great' Irish tale. This novel was written during the final illness of her father and, as family memoirs and letters make clear, its production was, for Edgeworth, a highly charged affair.[83] Knowing that this tale would be literally the last that she would put into his hands, she manifestly intended it to function as tribute to her father's vision, one that would finally impress upon her readers the incontrovertible

81 Ibid. 72–3 and 86.   82 McCormack, *Ascendancy and tradition*, 165.   83 Frances Edgeworth recalls Edgeworth 'sitting up at night and struggling with her grief as she wrote Ormond' (*A memoir of Maria Edgeworth*, 2: 1).

efficacy of his paradigm of Anglo-Irish relations.[84] Ormond, an ill-educated, English foundling, consequently only achieves moral and ontological maturity once he replicates the example of Edgeworth's father, and the romance journey that is described in the tale therefore serves as Edgeworth's last great fictional vindication of his life.

Left 'at nurse in an Irish cabin', the young Ormond is taken into the home of the apostate Sir Ulick O'Shane; twin events, the tale implies, which combine to affect his development adversely.[85] '[N]ever the same man' since he '*conformed*', Sir Ulick engages in constant acts of cynical self-creation, and is, thus, an entirely unsuitable guardian, for either Ormond or the Irish race (8: 29).[86] Maintaining 'that there was no use in giving Harry Ormond the education of an estated gentleman, when he was not likely to have an estate', Sir Ulick allows the boy to grow up 'with all the faults that were incident to his natural violence of passions, and that might necessarily be expected from his neglected and deficient education' (8: 11). More than this, he also exposes Ormond to 'ontological contamination' by allowing him to spend huge tracts of his childhood upon Cornelius O'Shane's determinedly Irish estates. Ormond is treated as the 'prince presumptive' of the Black Islands, and is clearly in danger of being overwhelmed by 'King Corny' and his dependents (8: 35, 29). These 'proclaim' him as their future ruler *because* they expect him live out their expectations of his future life (8: 30). 'When he was invested with [a] petty principality', Edgeworth therefore observes,

> it was expected of him to give a dinner and a dance to the island: so he gave a dinner and a dance, and every body said he was a fine fellow, and had the spirit of a prince. 'King Corny, God bless him! couldn't go astray in his choice of a favourite – long life to him and Prince Harry! and no doubt there'd be fine hunting, and shooting, and coursing continually. Well, was not it a happy thing for the islands, when Harry Ormond first set foot on them? From a boy 'twas *asy* to see what a man he'd be. Long may he live to *reign* over us!' (8:49)

Upon the Black Islands, an inappropriate 'love of popularity seize[s]' Ormond, blinding him to the fact that '[t]o be popular among the unknown, unheard-of

---

84 Trumpener makes a similar point, observing: 'Edgeworth's letters make clear [that] the writing of *Ormond*, and especially the death of King Corny, is bound up, on many levels, with the final illness of her own father ... *Ormond* ... is in several senses a testimonial to a dying patriarch' (*Bardic nationalism*, 64). 85 *Novels and selected works*, 5: 11. Further references to this tale are cited parenthetically in the text. 86 The national implications of Sir Ulick's inconstancy are highlighted for Ormond when a young lady recites some comic lines about his guardian at a party. 'Pay [Sir Ulick] by the job', she declares, and 'you have his vote' (8: 146).

inhabitants' of the islands could not 'be an object to any man of common sense' (8: 50). Nonetheless, 'the fact was as is here stated; and let those who hear it with a disdainful smile, recollect that whether in Paris, London, or the Black Islands, the mob are, in all essential points, pretty nearly the same' (8: 50).

This last point is crucial, of course, for it expertly illustrates a contention that is central to this tale and all of Edgeworth's writing. As she traces Ormond's wanderings between Castle Hermitage, the Black Islands, and Paris, Edgeworth simultaneously impresses upon her readers her conviction that an individual's ontological recovery is dependent upon the essential integrity of his character rather than upon his location; any place, she insists, can either impede or facil-itate his reform. When he was a carefree child with no responsibilities, Edgeworth intimates, Ormond did, indeed, find an idyllic world upon the Black Islands. 'The hunting and shooting, and the life of lawless freedom he led on the Islands, had been delightful', and he did not then perceive the danger of *unreservedly* believing King Corny to be 'the richest, the greatest, the happiest of men' (8: 36). As he grows up, though, Ormond's relationship to Corny changes, so much so that even he begins to perceive that there may be demons lurking upon this native 'king's' estates. Following his accidental wounding of Moriarty Carroll,[87] for example, he becomes increasingly aware of his need to 'improve' himself and, when he is banished to the Black Islands by Sir Ulick, begins 'to question the utility and real grandeur of some of those things which had struck his childish imagination' (8: 27, 37). Doubting 'whether it were worthy of a king or a gentleman to be his own shoemaker, hatter, and tailor', Ormond comes to realize that Corny should exercise a greater self-consciousness in dealing with his subjects; specifically, that he should conduct himself as befits his station (8: 37). Although it is not explicitly stated in the tale, Ormond's sentiments here also represent an oblique criticism of Corny as a ruler. As Adam Smith points out in *The wealth of nations* (1776):

> It is the great multiplication of the productions of all the different arts, in consequence of the division of labour, which occasions, in a well-governed society, that universal opulence which extends itself to the lowest ranks of the people. Every workman has a great quantity of his own work to dispose of ... and every other workman being in exactly the same situation, he is enabled to exchange a great quantity of his own goods for a great quantity, or, what comes to the same thing, for the price of a great quantity of theirs. He supplies them abundantly with what they have occasion for, and they accommodate him as amply

87 This occurs as a result of a night of drinking at King Corny's (8: 16).

> with what he has occasion for, and a general plenty diffuses itself
> through all the different ranks of the society.[88]

Edgeworth obviously draws upon Smith's arguments in her depiction of Corny
in *Ormond*, intimating that, by acting as his own shoemaker, hatter, and tailor,
he is effectively clinging to a version of his 'self' that will prove ultimately detrimental to his island race.

Ormond is likewise enlightened as to the true nature of Castle Hermitage,
when the revelation that he has inherited 'a very considerable property' prompts
Sir Ulick to recall his ward to his estate (8: 126). After his long period of retire-
ment upon the Black Islands, Castle Hermitage at first appears an 'earthly
Paradise' to Ormond, until, that is, he begins to perceive that each of its inhabitants variously affects an inauthentic form (8: 131). 'During the course of the
first three weeks', he is thus 'three times in imminent danger of falling in love',
but frees himself from the power of the Misses Darrell and Miss Lardner once
he sees through their affectation (8: 132). Of much more consequence for
Ormond, however, are the concerted, but subtle efforts that Sir Ulick makes
to secure a complete ascendancy over his young ward's life. Introducing him 'to
some of those who had distinguished themselves in political life', Sir Ulick is
delighted when he perceives that Ormond is catching 'their spirit' and that 'the
noble ambition' to 'distinguish' himself in the world is 'rising in his mind' (8:
137). Sir Ulick's intention is to debase this ambition 'to servile purposes', and
so an essential point of Edgeworth's tale is that Ormond will have to free himself of his guardian's influence before he can reach moral maturity (8: 137).

This process takes a long time, and Ormond only truly escapes Sir Ulick's
clutches once he satisfies his ambition to live 'independently and happily, with
some charming, amiable woman' upon 'a comfortable house and estate' (8: 136).
Significantly, this aspiration is crucially informed by his reading, and it is his
choice of books, together with the exemplary Lady Annaly's observation that
'far the greatest part of our happiness or misery in life depends upon ourselves',
that eventually convinces Ormond that he can transform his existence and lead
a useful and happy life (8: 27). Immersing himself initially in *The history of Tom
Jones* (1749), Ormond is at first (inappropriately) 'charmed by the character' of
Henry Fielding's hero, and very nearly reaps what Edgeworth intimates are the
inevitably bad rewards of trying to live out this fictional character's life (8: 51).
'[W]ith his head full' of the novel, he is 'prone to run into danger … and rashly
ready to hurry on [Peggy Sheridan,] an innocent girl to her destruction' (8: 52).
Although prevented from seducing Peggy by the discovery that she is the sweet-

---

88 Adam Smith, *An inquiry into … the wealth of nations* (1997), 1: 115.

heart of Moriarty Carroll, the narrative emphasizes that this is a solitary example of good behaviour and that 'no other scrap of good can be found of which to make any thing in his favour for several months to come' (8: 54). Whether it was because of the deleterious effects of *Tom Jones*, or of King Corny's example, or of the boredom that set in upon the Black islands, it remarks, he 'took to "vagrant courses," in which the muse forbears to follow him' (8: 54).

Upon receipt of a box of books from Lady Annaly, though, Ormond fortunately discovers *Sir Charles Grandison* (1753), which 'completely counteracted in his mind the effects of his late study' (8: 56). '[I]nspired' with what is significantly denoted as 'virtuous emulation', Ormond resolves 'to be a *gentleman* in the best and highest sense of the word'; that is, one who is not only 'eminently *useful*, respected and beloved, as [a] brother, friend, master of a family, guardian, and head of a large estate, [but also] loved, passionately loved, by ... the highest and most accomplished of the [fairer] sex' (8: 56).

Clearly rehearsing themes that we have seen are central to all of Edgeworth's writing, this species of reading predisposes Ormond to appreciate Dr Cambray's careful guidance and, as a consequence, to perceive the national significance of Sir Herbert Annaly's paradigm for landlord/tenant reform.[89] Central to *Ormond* is the point that, like Edgeworth's father, Lady Annaly's son 'govern[s] neither by threats, punishments, abuse, nor tyranny; nor yet ... by promises nor bribery, *favour* and *protection*, like Sir Ulick' (8: 161). Treating his tenants, instead, 'as reasonable beings, and as his fellow-creatures, whom he wished to improve, that he might make them and himself happy', Sir Herbert identifies his interests with those of his tenants and, 'By the sacrifice of his own immediate interest, and by great personal exertion, strict justice, and a generous and well secured system of reward ... produced a considerable change for the better in the morals and habits of the people' (8: 161–2).

The fact that Sir Herbert's efforts are explicitly informed by the 'domestic happiness' that he enjoys with his mother and sister at Annaly is similarly crucial to Edgeworth's narrative (8: 159). As is the case with the heroes of *Ennui* and *The absentee*, Ormond discovers that he must endeavour to recreate this domestic happiness in his home, and must, therefore, exercise extreme discretion in choosing his future wife. In this context, Edgeworth's narrative emphasizes that King Corny's daughter is profoundly wrong for Ormond, firstly because she has been 'engaged' by her father to 'White Connal, of Glynn – from her birth', and secondly because her early education has been mismanaged (8: 36). As a result of her determination that she and her niece should one day

---

89 Dr Cambray is the 'very agreeable, respectable, amiable' Church of Ireland clergyman who is given the living at Castle Hermitage contrary to Sir Ulick O'Shane's wishes (8: 109).

reside in Paris, '*Mademoiselle*' O'Faley has effectively rendered Dora a changeling; that is, she has effaced the innocent young Irish girl who once existed and put a French coquette in her place (8: 59).[90] Although he has long nursed an (ill-advised) affection for Dora,[91] it is therefore significant that even Ormond is capable of perceiving that she is 'much changed for the worse' when she returns with her aunt to the Black Islands, and that she was 'a hundred times more agreeable when she was a child' (8: 71).

Following White Connal's untimely death in a riding accident, Dora's fundamental lack of character manifests itself in the ease with which she is persuaded to accept the hand of his 'twin brother', Black Connal, in marriage (8: 85). Like Mademoiselle O'Faley, this gentleman has been tremendously affected by his love for France, and he overpowers Dora by playing upon her inability to distinguish between real and inauthentic behaviour. Never joining her in conversation, he treats Dora with ostentatious and 'scrupulous deference', 'shrinking into himself with the utmost care' whenever she passes, but continuing his conversation with Mademoiselle O'Faley (8: 92). Not surprisingly, this behaviour bewilders Dora, who remarks: 'It really is very extraordinary, …he seems as if he was spell-bound – obliged by his notions of politeness to let me pass incognita' (8: 92). Appealed to by her niece for guidance, Mademoiselle O'Faley places a very French interpretation upon Monsieur de Connal's actions. 'The young ladies in Paris [pass] for nothing', she declares, 'scarcely ever appearing in society till they are married … [I]n fact, the young lady is the little round what you call cipher, but has no value in société at all, till the figure of de husband come to give it the value' (8: 93). Dora retorts, 'I have no notion of being a cipher … I am not a French young lady', but the fact that she is in imminent danger of becoming such a lady is central to Edgeworth's story (8: 93). As a result of the foolish affectation of Mademoiselle O'Faley on the one hand, and the machinations of Monsieur de Connal on the other, Dora is on the point of being irrevocably 'metamorphosed' from an 'Irish country girl … into a French woman of fashion' (8: 194). To put this another way, she is on the verge of being estranged from her true self and of being plunged into an underworld life.

Perceiving that 'the improvement' in her behaviour towards him 'might be transient as passion', Ormond therefore loses Dora to Monsieur de Connal with little regret; 'She was not that superior kind of woman which his imagination had painted, or which his judgement could approve in a wife' (8: 85). Increasingly convinced that he has found this ideal in Florence Annaly, Ormond

90 The 'daughter of an officer of the Irish Brigade and of a French lady of good family', Mademoiselle O'Faley is dismissive of King Corny's way of life upon the Black Islands (8: 60). 91 When his head 'was full of' *Tom Jones*, 'Dora … [was] his idea of Sophy Western'; once *Sir Charles Grandison* replaced Fielding's novel, 'Dora, with equal facility, turned into his new idea of a heroine' (8: 59).

comes to appreciate this lady's authenticity in particular, and this is a crucial point in Edgeworth's narrative. Florence is like Grace Nugent in *The absentee* in that it is emphasized that her 'features were all in natural repose' and she never suffered her face to assume an inauthentic expression (8: 151). With such a woman by his side, Edgeworth intimates, Ormond can confidently look forward to a happy marriage.

Before Ormond can accomplish his union with Florence, however, he has to undergo one more trial: namely, he has to visit the de Connals in Paris and prove that he can withstand the dangers of *ancien régime* France. Mistakenly believing that Florence has rejected his written proposal of marriage, Ormond joins Dora and her husband, and, at first, he is too confident of his ability to resist the temptations of their (demonic) environs. Initially 'absolutely dazzled by the brilliancy of Dora's beauty', he makes the mistake of beginning to relax once he perceives that 'the coquette of the Black Islands' has simply been 'transformed into the coquette of the hotel de Connal. The transformation was curious, was admirable; Ormond thought he could admire without danger, and, in due time, perhaps gallant with the best of them, without feeling – without scruple' (8: 193–4). Carefully managed by Monsieur de Connal, whose intention is to control the young man's fortune by making him the lover of his wife, Ormond finds himself increasingly 'charmed' by French society (8: 197). Constantly in Dora's company, he begins to dread 'lest his principles should not withstand' the growing attraction he feels for her: 'Every thing seemed to smooth [his] slippery path ... the indifference of [Dora's] husband – the imprudence of her aunt ... the general customs of French society – the peculiar profligacy of the society in which he happened to be thrown' (8: 201–3).

This latter distinction is vital, of course, for, just when he is on the point of being overwhelmed by the demonic world of Paris, Ormond makes the acquaintance of the Abbé Morellet,[92] who introduces him to a different, idyllic France. Appropriately, Ormond first makes the acquaintance of the abbé in front of a picture, a circumstance that once again demonstrates how Edgeworth's didactic imperatives are peculiarly facilitated by her skilful use of romance conventions. Frye points out that pictures, tapestries, and statues are staples of romance, usually appearing near the beginning of narratives to indicate the threshold of a romance world. 'A central image of descent', he writes, is 'that of being involved with pictures or tapestries or statues or mirrors in a way that suggest[s] the exchange of original identity for its shadow or reflection'.[93] In drawing upon this device in *Ormond*, Edgeworth crucially situates her hero's (pictorial) encounter

92 Edgeworth made the acquaintance of this distinguished man of letters during her family's visit to Paris in 1802. See Butler, *Maria Edgeworth*, 189.   93 Frye, *Secular scripture*, 109 and 155.

with the Abbé Morellet near the end of her story, and Ormond's genuine reaction to the painting distinguishes him in relation to the affectation of those who surround him and, implicitly, symbolizes the beginning of his final ascent to an upper-world life. The narrative thus emphasizes Ormond's amazement at the affected 'transports' of those viewing the picture: 'It was real! and it was not real feeling! Of one thing he was clear – that this superfluity of feeling or exaggeration of expression completely silenced him, and made him cold indeed: like one unskilled or dumb he seemed to stand' (8: 205). For Edgeworth, this moment is important for two reasons: it demonstrates not only Ormond's essential (English) integrity, but also, by extension, the inferiority of France. Pointedly, then, the tale describes what Ormond witnesses as 'a display of French sensibility, that eagerness to feel and to excite a *sensation*; that desire to *produce an effect*, to have a scene; that half real, half theatric enthusiasm, by which the French character is peculiarly distinguished from the English' (8: 205). In response to Mademoiselle O'Faley's observation that he must 'contrive to find [this sensibility] quick at Paris, or after all you will seem but an Englishman', Ormond therefore not only remarks, 'I must be content to seem and to be what I am', but also does so 'in a tone of playful but determined resignation' (8: 205).

As a result of winning the 'good opinion and goodwill' of the Abbé Morellet, Ormond begins to remember his true 'self', and this facilitates his final escape from France's demonic regions (8: 206). Apart from introducing him to 'the literary men at Paris', the abbé also introduces him to the 'no longer dissipated' Marmontel,[94] who is on the point of taking Mademoiselle Montigny, one of the abbé's nieces, as his wife (8: 208). '[A]greeably surprised and touched at the unexpected sight of an amiable, united, happy family, when he had expected only a meeting of literati [,] ... [t]he sight of this domestic happiness [reminds Ormond] of the Annalys', bringing 'the image of Florence to his mind' (8: 209). Coming upon Ormond at 'just at the right moment', this image 'contrasted with all the dissipation he had seen', and recalls him to what the narrative very significantly denotes as 'his better self' (8: 209).

Notwithstanding this moment of insight, Ormond does not completely recover his 'self' with the abbé and his friends, and an essential point of Edgeworth's tale is that he must be exposed to the healing powers of the Irish nation and race once again before this can be accomplished. On the point of seducing Dora, Ormond is thus stopped by the sight of a ring with a twist of

94 A celebrated French writer, Jean François Marmontel's radicalism invited controversy: 'His political novel, *Bélisaire* (1767), in which he defended individual liberty, was the cause of a pamphlet war between the religious establishment who condemned its impiety and philosophes like Voltaire who jumped to its defence. He emerged triumphantly from the quarrel to be named royal historiographer of France ... [and in] 1783 he became secretary of the Académie Française': J. Black and R. Porter (eds), *A dictionary of eighteenth-century history* (2001), 446–7.

King Corny's hair upon her hand. 'The full recollection of that fond father, that generous benefactor, that confiding friend, rushed upon his heart', and the ring effectively reminds Ormond of his true situation, impressing upon him the proper nature of his relationship to the daughter of his benefactor and friend (8: 214). 'And is this the return I make', he observes to Dora, 'Oh, if [King Corny] could see us at this instant!' (8: 214). Fleeing from the stricken Dora, Ormond arranges to return to the de Connal household the next day, 'with the firm intention of adhering to the honourable line of conduct he had traced out for himself' in his heart (8: 214). Crossing the Pont-Neuf, though, he literally runs into Moriarty Carroll, and it is the dramatic reappearance of this native Irish man that peculiarly facilitates the working out of Edgeworth's story. Firstly, and most obviously, it is Moriarty who alerts Ormond to the fact that he is in financial danger, telling him there is 'great fear of the breaking of Sir Ulick's bank' (8: 215). Ormond has signed a power of attorney for his guardian the previous day, and so immediately realizes that Sir Ulick's intention is to try to save himself by selling '£30,000 out of [his ward's] Four per Cents' (8: 211). Secondly, Moriarty to all intents and purposes acts as Ormond's ontological saviour by causing his precipitous departure from France. Despite his best intentions, Ormond may not have proved finally capable of resisting the power of Paris; the city, after all, has already had a profound effect upon his outward appearance. When Moriarty collides with Ormond on the Pont-Neuf, therefore, the Irish man is at first unable to recognize his young master; he is, instead, amazed to discover that 'it's the man himself – master Harry! – though I didn't know him through the French disguise' (8: 214).

Having drawn upon the shipwreck device in order to explain Moriarty Carroll's unexpected appearance in Paris,[95] Edgeworth ultimately utilizes the convention of the missing letter in order to facilitate Ormond and Florence Annaly's union at the end of her tale. Returning to Ireland, Ormond discovers there was an answer to his written proposal of marriage, but that the servant had the 'misfortune to lose [it], and ... thought no more about it till, please your honour, after you was gone, it was found' (8: 230). Pursuing Lady Annaly and her daughter to where they are residing in Devon, Ormond acquaints them with all that has passed, and his account of himself emphasizes his perception that he has undergone a severe trial that has tested his resolution and caused him to discover that the 'paint[ings]' of the 'imagination' seldom resemble real life (8: 233). 'The last few months, though they might seem but a splendid or feverish dream in his existence', Ormond insists, 'had in reality been ... of essen-

---

95 Under sentence of transportation for a crime of which he is innocent, Moriarty 'got on board of an American ship ... and this ship being knocked against the rocks ... came safe ashore in [France] on one of the *sticks* of the vessel' (8: 215).

tial service in confirming his principles, settling his character, and deciding for ever his taste and judgement, after full opportunity of comparison, in favour of his own country – and especially of his own countrywomen' (8: 233). Naturally delighted with these observations, Florence accepts Ormond's renewed proposal of marriage, and it is agreed that the couple 'should return to Ireland, to Annaly; and that their kind friend, Dr. Cambray, should be the person to complete [their] union' (8: 234). On a didactic level, Ormond's marriage to the exemplary Florence is symbolic of the degree to which he has been reformed; it indicates that he has at last made his 'self' worthy of such a wife.

Despite this emphasis, there are distinctly subversive implications to be traced in Edgeworth's narrative. Firstly, following Sir Ulick's death, Ormond is petitioned by his son, now Sir Marcus O'Shane, to buy Castle Hermitage, but instead accepts Monsieur de Connal's offer to sell him the Black Islands. 'Castle Hermitage was the finest estate, and by far the best bargain', the tale observes, but 'While Sir Ulick O'Shane's son and natural representative was living, banished by debts from his native country, Ormond could not bear to take possession' (8: 234). This assertion indirectly raises the questions of legitimacy that inform all of Edgeworth's Irish work, particularly given the fact that Ormond is ultimately the son of a British army officer who has distinguished himself in his nation's service. When he considers going into the army himself, Ormond thus agrees with King Corny's observation that he 'could not be of the Irish Brigade', insisting he would 'infinitely prefer ... the service of [his] own country' (8: 106). 'I know nothing of my father, but I have always heard him spoken of as a good officer; I hope I shall not disgrace his name. The English service for me, sir, if you please' (8: 106).

Clearly significant, the true import of Ormond's English origins can only be understood once we recognize that Captain Ormond's career had a distinctly colonial trajectory. Following his posting to Ireland, he moved on to India, thereby directly facilitating that military process through which England endeavoured to impose its view of reality across the face of the earth. The fact that Ormond refuses to take possession of Castle Hermitage while Sir Marcus is still alive may therefore be read on an allegorical level: unlike his English father, it implies, Ormond will concern himself with the rights of Ireland's native inhabitants. Considered 'as the lawful representative of their King Corny' by the Black Islanders (8: 234), Ormond's return to the islands in this context signifies not only the return of 'legitimate rule in Ireland', but also Edgeworth's perception that this will only be accomplished once the nation's ruling class adopts 'a traditional, simpler way of life, closer to the common people'.[96]

---

96 Hollingworth, *Maria Edgeworth's Irish writing*, 196.

In terms of my reading, I would suggest that Ormond's decision to return
to the Black Islands further demonstrates that he is ultimately captivated by King
Corny's dominions; as Sheelah Dunshaughlin of the islands would put it, he has
roamed all over '*the continent*' only to discover that his heart will remain forever
captivated by these native lands (8: 120). Although the explicit emphasis of
Edgeworth's tale is that Ormond returns to the islands because he wishes to do
'a great deal of good ... by farther civilising the people', it also significantly
observes that he intends to accomplish this '*by carrying on* [King Corny's] improvements' (8: 234) (my emphasis). In a literal sense, then, the conclusion of
Edgeworth's narrative anticipates the perpetuation of King Corny's style of
monarchy; it intimates that, as the Black Islanders have all along desired, it is not
they, but Ormond who will be transformed. From here springs the particular
importance of the memorial to King Corny that is cut into one of the Black
Islands' bogs by Moriarty Carroll. Blazing forth 'in large letters of about a yard
long[,] the words – "LONG LIVE KING CORNY"' are forgotten by Moriarty until
he and Ormond happen upon them just before the latter leaves the islands after
the Corny's death (8: 120). Sown 'with broom-seed in the spring', they are now a
symbolic 'green' and striking to the eye (8: 120). Effectively 'transfigur[ing] the
very landscape of the Black Islands, transforming boggy terrain into a site of
national memory', these letters also anticipate the final destination of Ormond's
journey.[97] They imply that, as Corny's heir, Ormond cannot evade his destiny;
however far he may travel from the islands, he will have to come back. More
importantly, this tribute to the native Irish king also anticipates the form that
Ormond will take as the islands' ruler, for, as Trumpener would have it, 'Bog
drainage synecdochically represents the project of Enlightenment land reform'
typically carried on by Anglo-Irish landlords such as Edgeworth's father, or Sir
Herbert Annaly. As such, Edgeworth implies that Ormond will never truly be
'like' either of these landlords because he will not be able to bring his self to
create 'arable, profitable soil' out of this bogland,[98] and, thus, efface what Moriarty
calls the last 'trace' of the late king's life (8: 120). In this context, Ormond will
succeed in 'carrying on' King Corny's 'improvements', because, as ruler of the
islands, he, too, will put sentiment before economics.

We have already observed that Edgeworth's writing of *Ormond* was curiously bound up with her awareness of the imminent death of her own father,
and so it is crucial to recognize that, in mourning the passing of the fictional
King Corny, Edgeworth also implicitly lamented the passing of her father's life.
This is particularly true because, while at first glance there appear to be few

---

97 Trumpener, *Bardic nationalism*, 64–5. 98 Ibid. 42. Edgeworth's father conducted experiments in bog reclamation throughout his life and, as Butler notes in her biography of the author, 'accepted the role of adviser to the
new government survey of the Irish bogs' in 1809 (*Maria Edgeworth*, 211).

similarities between Edgeworth's father and this whimsical, native Irish king, each man to all intents and purposes rejected the reality in which he found himself, and then '*for* himself, and *by* himself, hewed out his own way to his own objects, and then rested, satisfied – "Lord of himself, and all his (*little*) world"' (8: 38) (Edgeworth's emphasis). Once we recognize that an analogy can be drawn between the imaginative vision of King Corny and Edgeworth's father, I would suggest that we are one step closer to understanding why *Ormond* represents Edgeworth's last-ever substantial piece of Irish fiction. In the first place, we have already seen that Edgeworth's writing was primarily inspired by her compulsion to celebrate her father's achievements and theories. Once he passed away, her 'ideal' reader was gone,[99] and so it was inevitable that this compulsion was greatly weakened, if not effaced. Secondly, following his death, Edgeworth clearly felt more able to criticize her father, and this is nowhere more clearly demonstrated, perhaps, than in her volume of his *Memoirs*, where she sums up her assessment of his life. Although completed and published within three short years of his passing, the text makes a startling and an unexpected admission: specifically, it openly acknowledges that, for 'many years of his life', he laboured 'under one important mistake.' Convinced that if people could be made to see that virtue would make them happy and vice miserable, Edgeworth observes, her father believed that this would necessarily lead them to follow virtue and avoid vice. In other words, she intimates that he constructed his educational theories around his belief that humans were ultimately rational creatures. 'Hence, both as to national and domestic education, he dwelt principally upon the cultivation of the understanding, meaning chiefly the reasoning faculty as applied to the conduct. But to see the best, and to follow it, are not, alas! necessary consequences of each other. Resolution is often wanting, where conviction is perfect.' By conflating 'national and domestic education' here, Edgeworth illustrates her perception that neither the individual nor the nation can be entirely governed by reason, and this, of course, engages with and destabilizes the didactic theories that ostensibly impel her work. It acknowledges that, in order to govern either an individual or a nation wisely, allowances must be made for the effects of that individual's or nation's passions and emotional life. As she puts it: 'under the influence of any passion, the perception of pain and pleasure alters as much as the perceptions of a person in a fever vary from those of the same man in sound health. The whole scale of individual happiness, as well as of general good and evil, virtue and vice, is often distributed at the very rising

99 The enjoyment that Edgeworth took in her father's reading of her work is eloquently illustrated at one particular moment in 'her' volume of his *Memoirs*. He would encourage her to '*Sketch*' promising material, she recalls, and, if he thought her efforts were going well, 'the pleasure in his eyes, the approving sound of his voice, even without the praise he so warmly bestowed, were sufficient and delightful excitements to "go on and finish"' (2: 344–5).

of the passion, and totally overthrown in the hurricane of the soul.' At such 'perilous, and critical moments', Edgeworth perceives, 'the conviction of the understanding is, if not reversed, suspended', and so, at such moments, an appeal to the better judgement of such an individual or nation is clearly of little use.[1]

When we try to account for Edgeworth's failure to publish on Irish matters during the 1820s, 30s, and 40s, it is tempting to pursue one of two courses: namely, to suggest that this silence can be explained either by the way in which her personal life unfolded following her father's death,[2] or by the fact that she found herself overawed by the increasingly volatile nature of Ireland's political affairs during these years. Critics who adopt the latter course typically quote from her famous letter to her brother, Michael Pakenham Edgeworth, in India, wherein she compares the similarities of their respective (colonial) situations and comments upon the impossibility of 'draw[ing] Ireland as she now is in a book of fiction – realities are too strong, party passions too violent to bear to see, or care to look at their faces in the looking-glass'.[3] While Edgeworth plainly became ever more disillusioned by Irish politics as the years went by, her writing demonstrates that she did not have had to wait until the advent of Daniel O'Connell's Repeal movement, for example, in order to be convinced 'that the ends she sought were a chimera'.[4] Rather, her use of romance throughout her work finally reveals her perception that the image of Ireland she laboured to produce in her works would ultimately prove to be an impossible, aspirational vision, and that it would not be possible to reproduce her father's (romantic) vision of that nation in real life. Once her father passed away in 1817, it is therefore not surprising that Edgeworth ceased to publish on Irish affairs: now that he was gone, she could (silently) admit that, if the possibility of creating such an Ireland had ever existed, it had long since passed.

1 *Memoirs*, 2: 401–2.   2 Edgeworth devoted the years immediately following her father's demise to the completion of his *Memoirs*, and it can and has been argued that the adverse reception that this work received upon publication hugely informed her decision to henceforward concentrate primarily upon writing for children. In a 'situation where a reference to her was likely to be accompanied by abuse of [her father]', Butler observes, Edgeworth maintained that the great glory of writing children's books was that they were thought scarcely 'worth mentioning' by critics (*Maria Edgeworth*, 412–13). Secondly, in the years after 1817, Edgeworth clearly embarked upon a new and exciting phase in her life. Between 1820 and 1823, she made several trips to England and the continent, for instance, and moved confidently in society without her father. Similarly, after 1825, she took on the responsibility for running the Edgeworthstown estates and, contrary to her father's dire predictions upon his deathbed, she displayed a remarkable strength of character in this regard, proving that it was *she*, and not her brother, Lovell, who was 'wise and economic' (Butler and Butler, *The black book*, 210).   3 Michael Pakenham Edgeworth (1812–81) had a distinguished career in the East India Company and, when Edgeworth wrote to this letter to him on 19 February 1834, he was serving in the Bengal Civil Service. In the letter, Edgeworth expresses her gratitude to her brother for his observations on the state of his part of India, noting: 'Many of the observations on India apply to Ireland … Some of the disputes that you have to settle at Cucherry, and some of the viewings that you record of boundaries, &c., about which there are quarrels, so put me in mind of what I am called upon to do here continually in a little way': Maria Edgeworth to Michael Pakenham Edgeworth, 19 Feb. 1834, quoted in F. Edgeworth, *A memoir of Maria Edgeworth*, 3: 87–8. See also the entry on Michael Pakenham Edgeworth in J.F. Riddick, *Who was who in British India* (1998), 113.   4 Hurst, *Maria Edgeworth and the public scene*, 33.

Epilogue

In 1961, Sir Francis Tuker published *The yellow scarf: the story of the life of Thuggee Sleeman or Major-General Sir William Henry Sleeman, K.C.B. 1788–1856 of the Bengal army and the Indian political service*. As a military officer and an employee of the East India Company, Sleeman had the type of colonial career of which Maria Edgeworth would have been proud, being best remembered, perhaps, for breaking the power of the murderous Thuggees and restoring the rule of law to upper India.[1] In tracing Sleeman's adventures, Tuker draws widely upon the publications and papers of this 'noble adventurer, [or] … righteous pioneer'[2] and, importantly, one extract peculiarly reveals the profound respect that Sleeman had for Edgeworth's writing. Recalling his one-time commanding officer, a Colonel Gregory, Sleeman observes,

> He was an old man when I first became acquainted with him. I put into his hands, when in camp, Miss Edgeworth's novels, in the hope of being able to induce him to read by degrees and I have frequently seen the tears stealing down over his furrowed cheeks as he sat pondering over her pages in the corner of his tent. A braver soldier never lived than old Gregory, and he distinguished himself greatly in the command of his regiment, under Lord Lake, at the battle of Laswaree and siege of Bhurtpore. It was impossible ever to persuade him that the characters and incidents of these novels were the mere creation of fancy; he felt them to be true, he wished them to be true, and he would have them to be true. We were not very anxious to undeceive him, as the illusion gave him pleasure and did him good. Bolingbroke says, after an ancient author, 'History is philosophy teaching by example.' With equal truth we say that fiction, like that of Maria Edgeworth, is philosophy teaching by emotion. It certainly taught old Gregory to be a better man,

---

1 For the details of Sleeman's career in India, see the entry for Sir William Henry Sleeman in the *DNB*, or in *Who was who in British India*, 333. Patrick Brantlinger's introduction to the 1998 edition of Philip Meadows Taylor's *Confessions of a Thug* (1839) provides a useful insight into the Thuggee (vii–xvii).   2 Memmi, *The colonizer and the colonized*, 69.

> to leave much of the little evil he had been in the habit of doing, and
> to do much of the good he had been accustomed to leave undone![3]

This passage is clearly significant for several reasons, but it in the first place
demonstrates the incredibly powerful emotional and imaginative responses that
Edgeworth's works were capable of eliciting from their nineteenth-century readers. Sleeman's point, after all, is not simply that Edgeworth's writing 'taught old
Gregory to be a better man', but, rather, that it did so by ensuring that he was
first of all entertained. As Sleeman would have it, Edgeworth was an edifying
author *because* she was an enthralling one, and her ability both to educate and
engage her reader emotionally represented her particular talent.

Sleeman's opinion of Edgeworth's work, of course, is in marked distinction
to that held by most late-twentieth- and early-twenty-first-century readers and
critics. In the first place, many of Edgeworth's works are little known outside
of academic circles, and *Castle Rackrent* is typically perceived by the general reader
as the only truly noteworthy example of her writing. In the second place, many
of Edgeworth's critics still tend to focus primarily upon her didacticism and, in
so doing, pay too little attention to the imaginative force of her work. If this
sad state of affairs is to be remedied, one thing is particularly needful: namely,
more must be done to emphasize both Edgeworth's recognition of the power
of make-believe in her writing, and the ways in which this aspect of her work
influenced later generations of writers, readers, and critics. By doing this, we
will further illuminate an important aspect of Maria Edgeworth's writing, and
come closer to understanding what the novel as we know it today owes to a
woman who spent most of her life in a small Irish town.

---

3 F. Tuker, *The yellow scarf* (1961), 26–7. I am grateful to my brother, Dr David Murphy, for bringing this reference
to my attention.

Bibliography

PRIMARY TEXTS

Edgeworth, Maria, *Belinda*, ed. Éilean Ní Chuilleanáin, Everyman edn (London 1993).

——, *Comic dramas, in three acts* (London 1817).

——, *Continuation of Early lessons*, 3rd edn (2 vols, London 1816).

——, *Early lessons*, new edn (2 vols, London 1815).

——, *Frank: a sequel to Frank in Early lessons*, 2nd edn (3 vols, London 1822).

——, *Harry and Lucy concluded: being the last part of Early lessons*, 5th edn (4 vols, London 1853).

——, *Letters for literary ladies, to which is added an essay on the noble science of self-justification*, ed. Claire Connolly, Everyman edn (London 1993).

——, *The modern Griselda: a tale*, 2nd edn (London 1805).

——, *Moral tales for young people*, 2nd edition (3 vols, London 1802).

——, *The novels and selected works of Maria Edgeworth*, general editors Marilyn Butler and Mitzi Myers, Pickering Masters series (8 vols to date, London 1999–).

——, *The parent's assistant; or, Stories for children*, 1845 edn (3 vols, London 1845).

——, *Popular tales* (3 vols, London 1804).

——, *Rosamond: a sequel to Early lessons*, 2nd edn (2 vols, London 1821).

——, *Tales of fashionable life*, First series (3 vols, London 1809).

——, *Tales of fashionable life*, Second series (3 vols, London 1812–13).

——, and Richard Lovell Edgeworth, *Essay on Irish bulls*, 2nd edn (London 1803).

——, *Practical education* (2 vols, London 1798).

Edgeworth, Richard, *A letter to the right hon. the earl of Charlemont, on the tellograph and on the defence of Ireland*, not published (Dublin 1797).

——, *Essays on professional education*, 2nd edn (London 1812).

——, and Maria Edgeworth, *Memoirs of Richard Lovell Edgeworth, esq. Begun by himself and concluded by his daughter, Maria Edgeworth* (2 vols, London 1820).

SECONDARY TEXTS

Adam Matthew Publications. 'Part 1: Edgeworth papers from the Bodleian
    Library, Oxford' in *Women, education and literature: the papers of Maria Edgeworth,
    1768–1849*, microfilm edn (Marlborough, Wilts. 1994).

——, 'Part 2: Edgeworth papers from the National Library of Ireland' in *Women,
    education and literature: the papers of Maria Edgeworth, 1768–1849*, microfilm edn
    (Marlborough, Wilts. 1994).

Adams, Percy G., *Travel literature and the evolution of the novel* (Lexington 1983).

Aikin, Dr John and Mrs Barbauld, *Evenings at home; or, The juvenile budget opened*, new
    edn (London n.d.).

Altieri, Joanne, 'Style and purpose in Maria Edgeworth's fiction' in *Nineteenth-
    Century Fiction* 23 (1968), 265–78.

Armstrong, Nancy, *Desire and domestic fiction: a political history of the novel*, University
    Press paperback edn (Oxford 1989).

Atkinson, Colin B., and Jo Atkinson, 'Maria Edgeworth, *Belinda*, and women's
    rights' in *Eire-Ireland* 19:4 (Winter,1984), 94–118.

Austen, Jane, *Mansfield Park*, ed. Tony Tanner, Penguin Classics edn (London
    1966).

——, *Northanger Abbey*, ed. Anne Henry Ehrenpreis, Penguin Classics edn (London
    1972).

Baird John D. and Charles Ryskamp (eds), *The poems of William Cowper* (Oxford
    1980).

Barbauld, Anna Laetitia, *Hymns in prose for children*, new edn (London n.d.).

Barrell, John, *English literature in history: an equal, wide survey* (London 1983).

Bate, W.J. (ed.), *Samuel Johnson: selected essays from the Rambler; Adventurer; and Idler*
    (New Haven and London 1968).

Beer, Gillian, *The critical idiom: the romance* (London 1970).

Behn, Aphra, *Oroonoko, The rover and other works*, ed. Janet Todd, Penguin Classics
    edn (London 1992).

Belanger, Jacqueline, 'Educating the reading public: British critical reception of
    the Irish fiction of Maria Edgeworth and Lady Morgan, 1800–1830', unpub-
    lished PhD thesis, University of Kent at Canterbury, 1999.

——, 'Educating the reading public: British critical reception of Maria
    Edgeworth's early Irish writing' in *Irish University Review* 28:2 (autumn/
    winter,1998), 240–55.

Black, Jeremy and Roy Porter, *A dictionary of eighteenth-century history*, Classic Penguin
    edn (London 2001).

Brantlinger, Patrick, Introduction, *Confessions of a Thug*, by Philip Meadows Taylor,
    Oxford World's Classics edn (Oxford 1998).

Brookes, Gerry H.,'The didacticism of Edgeworth's *Castle Rackrent*' in *Studies in English Literature*, 17 (1977), 593–605.

Brewer, John, *The pleasures of the imagination: English culture in the eighteenth century* (London 1997).

Buckley, Mary, 'Attitudes to nationality in four nineteenth century novelists: 1. Maria Edgeworth' in *Journal of the Cork Historical and Archaeological Society*, 78 (1973), 27–34.

Burgess, Miranda J., *British fiction and the production of social order, 1740–1830* (Cambridge 2000).

Burke, Edmund, *Reflections on the Revolution in France, and on the proceedings in certain societies in London relative to that event in a letter intended to have been sent to a gentleman in Paris*, ed. Conor Cruise O'Brien, Penguin Classics edn (London 1968).

Burney, Fanny, *Evelina*, ed. Edward A. Bloom with the assistance of Lillian D. Bloom, Oxford World's Classics edn (Oxford 1982).

Butler, H.J. and H.E., *The black book of Edgeworthstown and other Edgeworth memories, 1585–1817* (London 1927).

Butler, Marilyn, General Introduction, *The novels and selected works of Maria Edgeworth*, 1: vii–lxxx.

——, Introduction, Castle Rackrent *and* Ennui, by Maria Edgeworth, Penguin Classics edn (London 1992).

——, *Jane Austen and the war of ideas* (Oxford 1975).

——, *Maria Edgeworth: a literary biography* (Oxford 1972).

——, *Romantics, rebels and reactionaries: English literature and its background, 1796–1830* (Oxford 1981).

——, 'The uniqueness of Cynthia Kirkpatrick: Elizabeth Gaskell's *Wives and daughters* and Maria Edgeworth's *Helen*' in *Review of English Studies* 23 (1972), 278–90.

Cleary, Jean Coates, Introduction, *Memoirs of Miss Sidney Bidulph*, vii–xxxiii.

Cohen, Paula Marantz, *The daughter's dilemma: family process and the nineteenth-century novel* (Ann Arbor 1991).

Colby, Vineta, *Yesterday's woman: domestic realism in the English novel* (Princeton 1974).

Congreve, William, *Incognita, or Love and duty reconciled* (London 2003).

Connolly, Claire, Introduction, *Letters for literary ladies*, xvi–xxvi.

——, 'Reading responsibility in Castle Rackrent' in Colin Graham and Richard Kirkland (eds), *Ireland and cultural theory: the mechanics of authenticity* (London 1999).

——, 'Representing Ireland' in Rainer Schöwerling, Harmut Steinecke and Günter Tiggesbäumker (eds), *Literatur und Erfahrungswandel, 1789–1830* (n.p. 1996).

——, 'Uncanny Castle Rackrent' in Bruce Stewart (ed.), *That other world: the supernatural and the fantastic in Irish literature and its contexts* (vol. 1, Gerrards Cross 1998).

Connolly, S.J., *Religion, law, and power: the making of Protestant Ireland, 1660–1760* (Oxford 1992).

Corbett, Mary Jean, *Allegories of union in Irish and English writing, 1790–1870* (Cambridge 2000).

——, 'Public affections and familial politics: Burke, Edgeworth, and the "common naturalization" of Great Britain' in *ELH* (Winter, 1994), 877–97.

Croker, John Wilson, unsigned review of the 1812 series of *Tales of fashionable life* in *Quarterly Review*, 2nd edn (vol. 7, London 1814), 329–342.

Cronin, John, *Anglo-Irish novel: volume one, the nineteenth century* (Belfast 1980).

Davidoff, Leonore, and Catherine Hall, *Family fortunes: men and women of the English middle class, 1780–1850* (London 1987).

De Cervantes Saavedra, Miguel, *Don Quixote de la Mancha*, ed. E.C. Riley, tr. Charles Jarvis, Oxford World's Classics edn (Oxford and New York 1998).

Deane, Seamus, *Strange country: modernity and nationhood in Irish writing since 1790*, Clarendon paperback edn (Oxford and New York 1998).

Defoe, Daniel, *The life and adventures of Robinson Crusoe*, ed. Angus Ross, Penguin Classics edn (London 1965).

Dictionary of national biography.

Doody, Margaret Anne, Introduction, *The female Quixote*, xi–xxxii.

——, *The true story of the novel*, Harper Collins edn (London 1997).

Duncan, Ian, *Modern romance and transformations of the novel: the Gothic, Scott, Dickens* (Cambridge 1992).

Dunne, Tom, '"A gentleman's estate should be a moral school": Edgeworthstown in fact and fiction, 1760–1840' in Raymond Gillespie and Gerard Moran (eds), *Longford: essays in county history* (Dublin 1991).

——, *Maria Edgeworth and the colonial mind* (Cork 1984).

Dunleavy, Janet Egleson. 'Maria Edgeworth and the novel of manners' in Bege K. Bowers and Barbara Brothers (eds), *Reading and writing women's lives: a study of the novel of manners* (Ann Arbor 1990).

Eagleton, Mary (ed.), *Feminist literary theory: a reader* (Oxford 1986).

——, *Feminist literary theory: a reader*, 2nd edn (Oxford 1996).

Eagleton, Terry, *Heathcliff and the Great Hunger: studies in Irish culture* (London and New York 1995).

Edgeworth, Frances, *A memoir of Maria Edgeworth, with a selection from her letters*, not published (3 vols, London 1867).

Edgeworth, Maria. Longford: Saint Mel's college: catalogue of the library of the Edgeworth family, c.1831, not published (1 vol., Microfilm in the National Library of Ireland).

Edwards, Bryan, *An historical survey of the French colony in the island of St. Domingo: comprehending a short account of its ancient government, political state, population, productions,* and exports; a narrative of the calamities which have desolated the country ever since the year 1789, with some reflections on their causes and probable consequences; and a detail of the military transactions of the British army in that island to the end of 1794 (London 1797).

——, *The history, civil and commercial, of the British colonies in the West Indies* (2 vols, Dublin 1793).

Edwards, Duane, 'The narrator of *Castle Rackrent*' in *South Atlantic Quarterly* 71 (1972), 124–29.

Elam, Diane, *Romancing the postmodern* (London 1992).

Equiano, Olaudah, *The interesting narrative and other writings*, ed. Vincent Carretta, Penguin Classics edn (London 1995).

Ferguson, Moira, *Subject to others: British women writers and colonial slavery, 1670–1834* (New York and London 1992).

Ferris, Ina, *The achievement of literary authority: gender, history and the Waverley novels* (Ithaca 1991).

Fielding, Henry, *The history of Tom Jones, a foundling*, ed. R.P.C. Mutter, Penguin Classics edn (London 1966).

Fitzgerald, Laurie, 'Multiple genres and questions of gender in Maria Edgeworth's *Belinda*' in *Studies on Voltaire and the Eighteenth Century* 304 (1992), 821–3.

Flanagan, Thomas, *The Irish novelists: 1800–1850*, Greenwood Press edn (Westport, Conn. 1976).

Frye, Northrop, *The secular scripture: a study of the structure of romance* (Cambridge, Mass. and London 1976.

Gallagher, Catherine, *Nobody's story: the vanishing acts of women writers in the marketplace, 1670–1820* (Oxford 1994).

Gallop, Jane, *Feminism and psychoanalysis: the daughter's seduction* (London 1982).

Gee, Maggie, Introduction, *Helen*, by Maria Edgeworth, Pandora Press edn (London 1987).

Gelpi, Barbara Charlesworth, *Shelley's goddess: maternity, language, subjectivity* (New York 1992).

Gilbert, Sandra M., and Susan Gubar, *The madwoman in the attic: the woman writer and the nineteenth century literary imagination* (New Haven 1979).

Goldsmith, Elizabeth C. (ed.), *Writing the female voice: essays on epistolary literature* (Boston and London 1989).

Godwin, William, 'Of history and romance', Appendix IV to *Things as they are; or, the adventures of Caleb Williams*, ed. Maurice Hindle, Penguin Classics edn (London 1988).

von Goethe, Johann Wolfgang, *The sorrows of young Werther*, ed. and tr. Michael Hulse, Penguin Classics edn (London 1989).

Gonda, Caroline, *Reading daughters' fictions, 1709–1834: novels and society from Manley to Edgeworth* (Cambridge 1996).

Hare, Augustus J.C. (ed.), *The life and letters of Maria Edgeworth* (2 vols, London 1894).

Hawthorne, Mark D, *Doubt and dogma in Maria Edgeworth* (Gainesville 1967).

——, 'Maria Edgeworth's unpleasant lesson: the shaping of character' in *Studies* 64 (1975), 167–77.

Hays, Mary, *Memoirs of Emma Courtney*, ed. Eleanor Ty, Oxford World's Classics edn (Oxford 1996).

Hollingworth, Brian, *Maria Edgeworth's Irish writing: language, history, politics* (Houndmills and London 1997).

Hurst, Michael, *Maria Edgeworth and the public scene: intellect, fine feeling and landlordism in the age of reform* (London 1969).

Inchbald, Elizabeth, *A simple story*, ed. Pamela Clemit, Penguin Classics edn (London 1996).

James, Henry, Author's Preface, *The American*, Everyman edn (London 1997).

Jameson, Fredric, *The political unconscious: narrative as a socially symbolic act*, Methuen University Paperback edn (London 1983).

Jeffrey, Francis, unsigned review of *Harrington, a tale; and Ormond, a tale* in *Edinburgh Review* (vol. 28, Edinburgh and London 1817), 390–418.

——, unsigned review of the 1809 series of *Tales of fashionable life* in *Edinburgh Review* (vol. 14, Edinburgh and London 1809), 375–88.

Johnson, Samuel, *A dictionary of the English language: in which the words are deduced from their originals, and illustrated in their different significations by examples, from the best writers. To which are prefixed a history of the language, and an English grammar*, Times Books edn (London 1983).

Jones, Darryl, '"Distorted nature in a fever": *Enniu*, Irish Gothic and the 1798 rising' in Chris Fauske and Heidi Kaufman (eds), *An uncomfortable authority: Maria Edgeworth and her contexts* (Newark, forthcoming 2004).

Kauffman, Linda S., *Discourses of desire: gender, genre and epistolary fictions* (New York 1986).

Kelly, Gary, 'Amelie Opie, Lady Caroline Lamb, and Maria Edgeworth: official and unofficial ideology' in *A Review of International English Literature* (October 1981), 3–24.

——, 'Class, gender, nation, and empire: money and merit in the writing of the Edgeworths' in *The Wordsworth Circle* (Spring, 1994), 89–93.

——, *Women, writing, and revolution, 1790–1827* (Oxford and New York 1993).

Kiberd, Declan, *Inventing Ireland: the literature of the modern nation*, Vintage edn (London 1996).

Kowaleski-Wallace, Beth, 'Home economics: domestic ideology in Maria Edgeworth's *Belinda*' in *The Eighteenth Century: Theory and Interpretation* (Fall, 1988), 242–262.

——, 'Milton's daughters: the education of eighteenth century women writers' in *Feminist Studies* (Summer, 1986), 275–293.

——, *Their father's daughters: Hannah More, Maria Edgeworth, and patriarchal complicity* (New York and Oxford 1991).

Lane, Maggie, *Literary daughters* (London 1989).

Langbauer, Laurie, 'Romance revised: Charlotte Lennox's *The female Quixote*' in *Novel* 18 (1984), 29–49.

——, *Women and romance: the consolations of gender in the English novel* (Cornell 1990).

Lawless, Emily, *Maria Edgeworth*, English Men of Letters Series (London 1904).

Leerssen, Joep, *Remembrance and imagination: patterns in the historical and literary representation of Ireland in the nineteenth century* (Cork 1996).

——, and A.H. van der Weel, and Bart Westerweel (eds), *Forging in the smithy: national identity and representation in Anglo-Irish literary history* (vol. 1, Amsterdam and Atlanta, Georgia 1995).

Lennox, Charlotte, *The female Quixote*, ed. Margaret Dalziel (Oxford 1989).

Locke, John, *Some thoughts concerning education* in *Works of John Locke*, Routledge/Thoemmes Press reprint of 1794 edn (vol. 8, London 1997).

Lubbers, Klaus, 'Author and audience in the early nineteenth century' in Peter Connolly (ed.), *Literature and the changing Ireland* (Gerrards Cross 1982).

MacDonald, Edgar E., *The American Edgeworths: a biographical sketch of Richard Edgeworth (1764–1796) with letters and documents pertaining to the legacy of his three sons*, not published (Richmond, Virginia, 1970).

——, *The education of the heart: the correspondence of Rachel Mordecai Lazarus and Maria Edgeworth* (Chapel Hill 1977).

MacFadyen, Heather, 'Lady Delacour's library: Maria Edgeworth's *Belinda* and fashionable reading' in *Nineteenth Century Literature* (March 1994), 423–39.

McCormack, W.J., *Ascendancy and tradition in Anglo-Irish literary history from 1789–1939* (Oxford 1985).

——, 'Setting and ideology: with reference to the fiction of Maria Edgeworth; a collection of interpretations' in Otto Rauchbauer (ed.), *Ancestral voices: the big house in Anglo-Irish literature* (Hildesheim 1992).

——, and Kim Walker (eds), *The absentee*, by Maria Edgeworth, Oxford World's Classics edn (Oxford 1988).

McDowell, R.B., *Ireland in the age of imperialism and revolution, 1760–1801* (Oxford 1979).

McKeon, Michael, *The origins of the English novel, 1600–1740* (Baltimore 1987).

Maguire, W.A., 'Castle Nugent and Castle Rackrent: fact and fiction in Maria Edgeworth' in *Eighteenth Century Ireland* 11 (1996), 146–159.

Mellor, Anne K, 'A novel of their own: Romantic women's fiction 1790–1830' in John Richetti et al. (eds), *The Columbia history of the British novel* (New York 1994).

——, '"Am I not a woman, and a sister?"': slavery, Romanticism, and gender' in Alan Richardson and Sonia Hofkosh (eds), *Romanticism, race, and imperial culture, 1780–1834* (Bloomington and Indianapolis 1996).

——, *Romanticism and gender* (New York and London 1993).

Memmi, Albert, *The colonizer and the colonized*, tr. Howard Greenfield, Earthscan publications edn (London 1990).

Michals, Teresa, 'Commerce and character in Maria Edgeworth' in *Nineteenth Century Literature* (June, 1994), 1–20.

Miller, Julia Ann, 'Acts of union: family violence and national courtship in Maria Edgeworth's *The absentee* and Sydney Owenson's *The wild Irish girl*' in Kathryn Kirkpatrick (ed.), *Border crossings: Irish women writers and national identities* (Tuscaloosa and London 2000).

Moore, Sean, 'Maria Edgeworth's Irish novels: *The absentee* and the manufacture of Anglo-Irish hybridity', unpublished MA thesis, Georgetown University, 1995.

More, Hannah, *Coelebs in search of a wife*, Thoemmes Press edn (Bristol 1995).

——, *Strictures on the modern system of female education, with a view of the principles and conduct prevalent among women of rank and fortune*, reprint of 3rd edn of 1799 (Oxford and New York 1995).

Moynahan, Julian, *Anglo-Irish: the literary imagination in a hyphenated culture* (Princeton and Chicester 1995).

Murray, Patrick, 'Maria Edgeworth and her father: the literary partnership' in *Eire-Ireland* 6.3 (1971), 39–50.

——, *Maria Edgeworth: a study of the novelist* (Cork 1971).

Myers, Mitzi, 'De-romanticizing the subject: Maria Edgeworth's "The bracelets", mythologies of origin, and the daughter's coming to writing' in Paula R. Feldman and Theresa M. Kelly (eds), *Romantic women writers: voices and counter-voices* (Hanover and London 1995).

——, 'The dilemmas of gender as double-voiced narrative: or, Maria Edgeworth mothers the *Bildungsroman*' in Robert W. Uphaus (ed.), *The idea of the novel in the eighteenth century* (East Lansing 1988).

——, 'Impeccable governesses, rational dames, and moral mothers: Mary Wollstonecraft and the female tradition in georgian children's books' in *Children's Literature* 14 (1986), 31–59.

——, 'Quixotes, orphans, and subjectivity: Maria Edgeworth's Georgian heroism and the (en)gendering of young adult fiction' in *The Lion and the Unicorn* (June 1989), 21–40.

——, 'Romancing the moral tale: Maria Edgeworth and the problematics of pedagogy' in James Holt McGavran, Jr. (ed.), *Romanticism and children's literature* (Athens, Georgia and London 1991).

——, 'Socialising Rosamond: educational ideology and fictional form' in *Children's Literature Association Quarterly* (Summer, 1989), 52–8.

Newby, P.H., *Maria Edgeworth* (London 1950).

Newcomer, James, *Maria Edgeworth* (Lewisburg 1973).

——, *Maria Edgeworth: the novelist, 1767–1849: a bicentennial study* (Fort Worth 1967).

Ní Chuilleanáin, Éilean, 'Women as writers: Dánta Grá to Maria Edgeworth' in Éilean Ní Chuilleanáin (ed.), *Irish women: image and achievement* (Dublin 1985).

Ó Gallchoir, Clíona, 'Maria Edgeworth's revolutionary morality and the limits of realism' in *Colby Quarterly* 36:2 (2000), 87–97.

Opie, Amelia, *Adeline Mowbray, or the mother and daughter*, eds Shelley King and John B. Pierce, Oxford World's Classics edn (Oxford 1999).

Owens, Coilin (ed.), *Family chronicles: Maria Edgeworth's Castle Rackrent* (Dublin 1987).

Owenson, Sydney, *The wild Irish girl: a national tale*, ed. Kathryn Kirkpatrick, Oxford World's Classics edn (Oxford 1999).

Owens-Weekes, Ann, *Irish women writers: an uncharted tradition* (Lexington 1990).

Perera, Suvendrini, *Reaches of empire: the English novel from Edgeworth to Dickens* (New York 1991).

Plumb, J.H., 'The new world of children in eighteenth-century England' in *Past & Present* 67 (1975), 64–93.

Poovey, Mary, *The proper lady and the woman writer: ideology and style in the works of Mary Wollstonecraft, Mary Shelley and Jane Austen* (Chicago 1984).

A report of the debate in the House of Commons of Ireland, on Tuesday and Wednesday the 22nd and 23rd of January, 1799, on the subject of an union (Dublin 1799).

Radford, Jean (ed.), *The progress of romance: the politics of popular fiction* (London 1986).

Reeve, Clara, *The old English baron*, ed. James Trainer, Oxford University Press edn (Oxford 1977).

——, *The progress of romance through times, countries, and manners; and the history of Charoba, queen of Aegypt*, Facsimile Text Society edn (New York 1930).

Richardson, Alan, *Literature, education, and Romanticism: reading as social practice, 1780–1832* (Cambridge 1994).

——, and Sonia Hofkosh, Introduction in Alan Richardson and Sonia Hofkosh (eds), *Romanticism, race, and imperial culture, 1780–1834* (Bloomington and Indianapolis 1996).

Riddick, John F., *Who was who in British India* (Westport, Conn. and London 1998).

Rose, Jacqueline, *The case of Peter Pan, or, the impossibility of children's fiction*, revised edn (Houndsmills and London 1992).

Rousseau, Jean-Jacques, *Émile*, ed. P.D. Jimack, tr. Barbara Foxley, Everyman edn (London and Rutland, Vermont 1993).

——, *La nouvelle Héloïse*, tr. Judith H. McDowell, abridged edn (University Park, Pennsylvania 1968).

Said, Edward W., *Culture and imperialism* (London 1993).

Sartre, Jean Paul, Introduction, *The colonizer and the colonized*, by Albert Memmi, tr. Lawrence Hoey, 19–27.

Scott, Walter, *Waverley; or, 'Tis sixty years since*, ed. Andrew Hook, Penguin Classics edn (London 1972).

Shaffer, Julie, 'Not subordinate: empowering women in the marriage plot. The novels of Frances Burney, Maria Edgeworth, and Jane Austen' in Arthur F. Marotti et al. (eds), *Reading with a difference: gender, race and cultural identity* (Detroit 1993).

Sheridan, Frances, *Memoirs of Miss Sidney Bidulph*, ed. Patricia Köster and Jean Coates Cleary, Oxford World's Classics edn (Oxford 1995).

Showalter, Elaine, *A literature of their own: from Charlotte Brontë to Doris Lessing*, revised edn (London 1978).

Smith, Adam, *An inquiry into the nature and causes of the wealth of nations*, ed. Andrew Skinner, revised Penguin Classics edn (London 1997).

Smollett, Tobias, *The adventures of Roderick Random*, ed. Paul-Gabriel Boucé, Oxford World's Classics edn (Oxford 1979).

——, *The life and adventures of Sir Launcelot Greaves*, ed. Peter Wagner, Penguin Classics edn (London 1988).

Spacks, Patricia Meyer, *Desire and truth: functions of plot in eighteenth century English novels* (Chicago 1990).

Spencer, Jane, *The rise of the woman novelist: from Aphra Behn to Jane Austen* (Oxford 1986).

Spender, Dale, *Mothers of the novel: 100 good women writers before Jane Austen* (London 1986).

Stephen, Henry, unsigned review of the 1809 series of *Tales of fashionable life* in *Quarterly Review*, 4th edn (vol. 2, London 1818), 146–54.

Stone, Lawrence, *The family, sex and marriage in England, 1500–1800*, abridged edn (London 1979).

Tobin, Mary Elisabeth Fowkes, '"The power of example": Harry Ormond reads Tom Jones' in *Reader* (spring, 1988), 37–52.

Todd, Janet (ed.), *Dictionary of British women writers* (London 1989).

——, *Sensibility: an introduction* (London and New York 1986).

Tracy, Robert, 'Maria Edgeworth and Lady Morgan: legality versus legitimacy' in *Nineteenth Century Literature* (June, 1985), 1–22.

Trumpener, Katie, *Bardic nationalism: the Romantic novel and the British empire* (Princeton and Chicester 1997).

Tuker, Francis, *The yellow scarf: the story of the life of Thuggee Sleeman or Major-General Sir William Henry Sleeman, K.C.B. 1788–1856 of the Bengal army and the Indian political service*, White Lion edn (London, Sydney, and Toronto 1961).

Turner, Cheryl, *Living by the pen: women writers in the eighteenth century* (London 1992).

Unthank, Tessa B., 'Little but good' in *Michigan Quarterly Review* 11 (1972), 119–21.

Vesser, Aram H. (ed.), *The new historicism* (New York and London 1989).

Walpole, Horace, *The castle of Otranto: a Gothic story*, ed. Michael Gamer, Penguin Classics edn (London 2001).

Watson, Nicola, *Revolution and the form of the British novel, 1790–1825: intercepted letters, interrupted seductions* (Oxford 1994).

Watt, Ian, *The rise of the novel: studies in Defoe, Richardson and Fielding*, Hogarth edn (London 1987).

Wollstonecraft, Mary, *A vindication of the rights of woman*, ed. Miriam Brody, Penguin Classics edn (London 1975).

Williams, Ioan (ed.), *Novel and romance, 1700–1800: a documentary record* (London 1970).

Wilson, Anne, *Traditional romance and tale: how stories mean* (Ipswich and Totowa, NJ, 1976).

Zimmern, Helen, *Maria Edgeworth*, Eminent Women series (London 1883).

Zwinger, Lynda Marie, *Daughters, fathers, and the novel: the sentimental romance of heterosexuality* (Madison, Wn and London 1991).

Index